MSC Michela, a mainline container mother vessel, at Vallarpadam ICTT

NOTES FROM WILLINGDON ISLAND

NOTES FROM WILLINGDON ISLAND

THE PAST, THE PRESENT, AND THE FUTURE OF COCHIN PORT AND ITS HINTERLAND

N. RAMACHANDRAN
IPS (RETD)

Konark Publishers Pvt. Ltd
206, First Floor,
Peacock Lane, Shahpur Jat,
New Delhi - 110 049
+91-11-4105 5065
india@konarkpublishers.com, us@konarkpublishers.com
www.konarkpublishers.com

The photographs used in this book are from the personal collection of the author, unless otherwise stated.

ISBN: 978-81-987405-6-4

Edited by Dipali Singh
Jacket design by Sourish Mitra
Typeset by Saanvi Graphics, Noida
Printed and bound in India by Thomson Press India Ltd.

वागर्थाविव संपृक्तौ वागर्थप्रतिपत्तये।
जगतः पितरौ वन्दे पार्वतीपरमेश्वरौ॥

Vāgarthāviva saṃpṛktau vāgartha-pratipattaye |
Jagataḥ pitarau vande Pārvatīparameśvarau ||
—Raghuvamsham 1.1.

To My Mother and Father,
who taught me the deeply spiritual and secular meaning of this prayer
and
Girija, Unni, Hari, Lakshmi & Ameya
who continue to embody its meaning

“

History is more than just a record of past events;
it is a study of change and transformation.
It helps us understand the present and anticipate the future.

”

Yuval Noah Harari

KOCHI OR COCHIN?

Cochin is the anglicised name for the city and port of Kochi, India. A few years ago, the name Kochi was reinstated to reflect its historical roots. However, the port continues to be officially known as "Cochin Port" to maintain continuity in international maritime navigation, shipping, logistics, and regulatory systems.

Retaining the name "Cochin Port" preserves its historic maritime identity and prevents confusion with other international port cities, such as Kochi in Japan. Throughout this book, the term "Cochin" is used to refer to both the port and the port city, for the sake of consistency, and ease of reference.

CONTENTS

FOREWORD

Notes from Willingdon Island: The Past, the Present, and the Future of Cochin Port and Its Hinterland by N. Ramachandran is a masterful exploration of Kerala's maritime legacy and its untapped potential for economic resurgence. With his invaluable experience as a former Chairman of Cochin Port Trust, Ramachandran offers readers a first-hand account of transformative leadership — blending memoir, institutional history, and public policy insights into a compelling narrative.

At a time when Vizhinjam Port's inauguration has sparked debates about the relevance of Vallarpadam ICTT, Ramachandran presents a bold counternarrative, advocating for a complementary vision of India's port infrastructure. His argument is clear: Kerala needs both Vallarpadam and Vizhinjam, along with many more ports, to meet the demands of a rapidly growing economy. Drawing stark comparisons between India's and China's port performance, he underscores the urgency of expanding India's maritime capabilities to unlock its blue economy potential.

What sets this book apart is its insider perspective on the extraordinary transformation of Cochin Port—from a unionized legacy institution to a digitally-enabled hub of modern logistics. Ramachandran recounts how his team overcame bureaucratic inertia and entrenched labour practices, implementing reforms that made Cochin India's first e-Port. His candid reflections on labour rationalisation, digital transparency, and institutional discipline offer valuable lessons for Kerala's wider political economy, particularly in confronting outdated practices like *Nokku kooli.*

The book's final chapter, "Reflections from Willingdon Island", is a provocative call to action for Kerala's policymakers and citizens. Ramachandran critiques the state's economic stagnation, urging diversification into sectors like shipbuilding, blue tourism, and LNG utilisation. His roadmap for Kerala's future is scathing and hopeful, animated by personal experience and written with candour, wit, and a deep concern for the state's development.

As I have often argued, the greatest obstacle to Kerala's economic resurgence is inertia—the tendency to prioritise short-term political considerations over long-term structural growth. Our willingness to surrender to bureaucratic over-regulation, along with our resigned acceptance of negative, damaging political practices and entrenched habits, are other banes that have impeded our development. What Kerala needs are not piecemeal adjustments but a comprehensive maritime policy that:

- Encourages investment by removing bureaucratic hurdles and implementing investor protection laws.
- Modernises labour policies, ensuring that trade unions evolve into responsible stakeholders rather than obstacles to progress. We must outlaw such outdated, regressive and frankly destructive practices as *hartals* and *Nokku kooli*.
- Promotes sectoral innovation by integrating Kerala's strengths in education and technology with new avenues in shipbuilding, logistics, and marine research.

Kerala has never lacked human capital, intellectual depth, or natural advantages. Nor has it lacked ideas, initiative or inclination. What has been missing is the political resolve to translate potential into performance. Ramachandran's vision for resurgence is not merely about ports; it is about rethinking Kerala's economic trajectory altogether. His book is a wake-up call to leaders, policymakers, and citizens alike—urging Kerala to shed its hesitations, embrace pragmatic reform, and position itself as a global maritime powerhouse.

For anyone invested in Kerala's progress—whether in maritime development, public sector reform, or ethical governance—this book is an essential read. Ramachandran's insights are not just a testament to his leadership but also a blueprint for Kerala's revival, presenting a vision that is as ambitious as it is achievable.

19 April 2025

Dr Shashi Tharoor
Member of Parliament, Thiruvananthapuram

ENDORSEMENTS

Notes from Willingdon Island by N. Ramachandran is a timely and insightful addition to India's maritime discourse. Drawing on his tenure as Chairman of Cochin Port, the author delivers a compelling first-person narrative of transformation—covering digitalisation, major infrastructure projects such as the Vallarpadam ICTT and LNG terminal, labour reforms, and strategic policymaking.

The book vividly recounts how Cochin Port's landmark labour reforms (2006–2008) were driven forward with the active and progressive support of the then Chief Minister Shri V.S. Achuthanandan, Labour Minister Shri P.K. Gurudasan, and Industries Minister Shri Elamaram Kareem, which brought about a positive transformation at the port.

With Vizhinjam Port now operational, Ramachandran makes a persuasive case for a complementary port strategy, reaffirming the relevance of both Vizhinjam and Vallarpadam as pillars of India's maritime future.

Seamlessly blending memoir, institutional history, and a bold policy vision, the book urges Kerala's leadership to embrace economic diversification and reform. With clarity and conviction, it also calls for a national push to scale up India's port infrastructure, shipbuilding capacity, and the broader economic potential of the sea in diverse forms. This is essential reading for those interested in public sector leadership, institutional reform, and India's maritime ambitions.

It goes without saying that one need not necessarily agree with the entire content of a particular work of this nature. Even when you recognise the overall worth of the very significant analysis contained in this, there is room for divergent views on certain formulations. However, that seldom diminishes the overall quality or importance of this study.

M.A. Baby
General Secretary
Communist Party of India (Marxist)

Ramachandran's book presents a striking comparison between the LNG terminals at Dahej in Gujarat and Cochin in Kerala. Both projects were conceived simultaneously by the Government of India, each with an approved initial capacity of 5 million tonnes per annum. While the Dahej terminal has steadily grown and is now nearing a capacity of 22.5 million tonnes, the Cochin terminal, 12 years after its commissioning, continues to operate at just 1.25 million tonnes, a mere quarter of its capacity.

Dahej has played a transformative role in Gujarat's industrial development and has facilitated both industrial and domestic gas distribution across northern India. In contrast, in spite of the availability of clean energy, Kerala has failed to effectively utilise the Cochin terminal—built at a huge national cost—even for basic domestic city gas distribution.

The book calls for serious introspection by Kerala's policymakers—not only on this squandered opportunity but on decades of missed chances— the consequences of which are now tangible and visible in the state's current precarious economic situation. This, in turn, emphasises the urgent need for a bold, long-term vision that integrates infrastructure, investment, employment, and economic strategy.

Ramachandran outlines a broad roadmap for Kerala's economic diversification and expansion, with a strong focus on harnessing its untapped potential in the blue economy and sustainable marine tourism.

Rajeev Chandrasekhar
Former Union Minister of State for Electronics & IT,
State President, Bharatiya Janata Party, Kerala

Notes from Willingdon Island by N. Ramachandran is far more than a history of a port—it unveils a bold and forward-looking vision for Kerala's development, delineating a Pre- and Post-Vizhinjam context. This compelling blueprint reorients Kerala's growth trajectory from a focus on inland milestones to harnessing its immense coastal potential, opening doors to global opportunities. Dismissing naysayers with clarity and conviction, the book demonstrates how Vizhinjam not only complements Vallarpadam but also revitalises ports across the nation, reigniting India's long-neglected maritime trade prospects.

With clear-eyed analysis and extensive hands-on experience, Ramachandran offers practical prescriptions for Kerala's future development and long-term progress. He masterfully weaves together the state's human capital and geopolitical advantages into a vivid, lived narrative.

Essential reading for those invested in Kerala's ascent into the 22nd century, this book is a clarion call to the planners of *Nava Keralam* to embrace its insights. To expect anything less from Ramachandran would be a mistake—this is a must-read for anyone interested in India's public policy and development discourse.

Dr John Brittas
Member of Parliament (Rajya Sabha)

Having spent many years in Kerala, I have always been inspired by the resilience, ingenuity, and spirit of the state—a land where tradition and progress go hand in hand. My professional journey in Kerala's development deeply shapes how I see its potential. It is with this perspective that I read N. Ramachandran's *Notes from Willingdon Island*, a volume that captures the rich history and complex present of Kerala's maritime gateway—the heart of Cochin Port.

More than a chronicle of infrastructure milestones such as India's first International Container Transshipment Terminal at Vallarpadam and the Cochin LNG Terminal, this book confronts the pressing challenges Kerala faces today. It explores critical issues like safeguarding workers' rights, managing waste pollution, and tackling land constraints—questions that are vital for the region's sustainable future.

What resonated most with me is the way this volume goes beyond technical development; it critically examines the underlying factors that have held Kerala back and offers a thoughtful, strategic outlook towards unlocking its untapped potential. As someone who has observed Kerala's growth journey first-hand, I believe this book provides invaluable insights into diverse sectors like the Blue Economy and blue tourism, highlighting how leadership, consensus-building, and political responsibility are indispensable in charting a new course.

From the corridors of Willingdon Island's storied past to the promise of its future, this book offers a compelling and comprehensive exploration of Kerala's immense possibilities—and the challenges that must be overcome with vision, unity, and resilience. It is a must-read for all stakeholders committed to shaping Kerala's tomorrow.

Amitabh Kant
India's G-20 Sherpa
Former CEO of NITI Aayog

This book will be of great value, not only to those interested in the history of Cochin Port but also to those seeking to understand the challenges Kerala must address in the future. It is, therefore, an important contribution to the existing body of literature, alongside works by Robert Bristow and D. Babu Paul. This book is comprehensive and extremely well-written. Rather than focusing solely on the port, the author places it in the larger context of the state and the nation. Real-life incidents are woven throughout, making the book highly readable and engaging.

K.M. Chandrasekhar
Former Union Cabinet Secretary

Notes from Willingdon Island by N. Ramachandran deserves a place alongside classics such as Francis Day's *Land of the Permauls of Cochin*, Robert Bristow's *Cochin Saga*, and Babu Paul's *The Queen's Story – Five Centuries of Cochin Port*, all of which document the remarkable evolution of a port that made history with the arrival of Cabral in 1500.

The book's early chapters, chronicling the author's efforts as Chairman of Cochin Port to tackle entrenched malpractice, unfold with the pace and intrigue of a crime thriller. Later, Ramachandran raises a compelling question: what lies ahead for the Vallarpadam ICTT—commissioned just over a decade ago—once Vizhinjam Port, with its immense potential, becomes fully operational? It is a question that should provoke serious reflection among Kerala's intelligentsia.

P.K. Hormis Tharakan
Former Secretary (R),
Former Director General of Police, Kerala

Notes from Willingdon Island is a valuable resource for common readers who are unaware of the complexities of managing a vast, unionised enterprise like a port. It provides a step-by-step guidebook to implementing transformative projects and overcoming resistance, making it a useful case study for business schools. The book demonstrates how a government enterprise, entrenched in anachronistic business practices, could be revived and brought to a high degree of excellence by a non-business professional through imagination, initiative, firmness and continuous dialogue with stakeholders.

Vappala Balachandran
Former Special Secretary, Cabinet Secretariat,
Author and columnist

ACKNOWLEDGEMENTS

The inspiration to write this book came from some of my mentors and colleagues. Writing it over a decade after leaving Cochin has been a journey of rediscovery and reflection, made possible by the invaluable support, encouragement and guidance of my former colleagues, well-wishers, and friends.

After relinquishing my role as the Chairman of Cochin Port in February 2011, I returned to my policing career, initially serving in the rank of Director General of Police (DGP) in Assam, and later as the DGP and Head of the Meghalaya Police during a time when half the state was grappling with militancy and violence. Following my retirement, I assumed the role of the President of the Indian Police Foundation, a law enforcement think tank that I had established. These demanding roles left little time for writing memoirs. By the time I finally began writing, many of the details had faded from memory, and I had to rely on my colleagues to help reconstruct specific events. I remain deeply grateful to each one of them for their support.

I am especially indebted to J. Karthikeyan, K.G. Nath, and Unnikrishnan Nair, who meticulously reviewed the first manuscript and provided insights into particular facts and events. My former colleagues—Deputy Chairmen Captain Subhash Kumar, and G. Krishnakumar, Deputy Conservator Captain Paul N. Joseph, Harbour Master Captain Joseph J. Alapatt, and Additional Traffic Manager Vipin R. Menoth—also provided valuable insights.

During my tenure at Cochin Port, I received tremendous support from all my colleagues, many of whom were consulted during the writing of this book. These included Secretary Cyril George; Chief Mechanical Engineers Niteen M. Borwanker, A.K. Gadkari, and M.S. Renjith; Chief Medical Officer (CMO) Dr P.V. Joy; Chief Vigilance Officers Mervin Alexander and Manoj Chandran; Central Industrial Security Force (CISF) Senior Commandant D. Shyamala; Additional Traffic Manager Jimmy George; VP Petronet LNG Limited (PLL) Pushp Khetrapal; and India Gateway Terminal Private Limited (IGTPL) Chiefs Suresh Joseph and Krishna Das. Superintending Engineers Susamma Xavier and E. Rema, who were part of the dynamic team, helped me recall the nitty-gritty of some of the projects. Jijo Thomas, the then Public Relations Officer (PRO), was the one-point contact and go-to person for every aspect!

The number of officers and staff who contributed to this effort is far too many and it is difficult to name each one of them individually. In the course of writing this book, I had the privilege of consulting several of my predecessors and successors as Chairpersons of Cochin Port, such as C. Babu Rajeev, Jacob Thomas, Paul Antony, M. Beena, and B. Kasiviswanathan. Their insights and support proved invaluable to this endeavour.

During my tenure as chairman, I was ably assisted by several secretaries at different points of time, beginning with Mary Kutty, S.V. Harshan, Sabu John, and N.X. Joseph. Each one of them was not only professionally efficient but also trustworthy and capable. They were supported by a dedicated team in the Chairman's Secretariat. I must place on record my deep appreciation for the hard work done by Nishi Nair in providing secretarial assistance for this work.

I am deeply grateful to the members of the Port Trust Board, whose support and guidance were instrumental in achieving many of the results mentioned here. I fondly recall the support and guidance of L. Radhakrishnan (IAS), Ajay Kumar (IAS), and Sanjeev Kaushik (IAS), who served on the Board representing the Kerala government at different points of time.

I also appreciate the assistance of P.C. Dhiman (IAS), P.K. Srivastava (IAS), Vishal Gagan (IAS), and Poiyaamozhi (Director, Engineering), representing the Ministry of Shipping; Customs Commissioners Donald Ingty (IRS), Syed Mohammed (IRS), and Rema Mathew (IRS); Special Economic Zone (SEZ) Commissioner C.J. Mathew (IRS); Titus P. Koshy (IRTS), K.S. Prasad (IRTS), and P. Raveendran (IRTS), representing the Indian Railways; B.K. Menon and N. Nandakumar, representing the Bharat Petroleum Corporation Limited (BPCL) Kochi Refinery; Commodores A.T. Lukose, S.K. Jha, and M.R. Ajay Kumar, representing the Indian Navy; DIG B.K. Loshali and ADG V.D. Chafekar, representing the Indian Coast Guard; and K.P. John, Principal Officer of the Mercantile Marine Department.

Industry and trade were represented on the port's Board at different times by many distinguished persons, including Abraham J. Tharakan, President of the Seafood Exporters Association of India; C.S. Kartha, representing the Cochin Chamber of Commerce; K. Mathew George from Aspinwal, C.P. Xavier, president of the Cochin Customs House Agents Association, V.R. Prasad, MD of TMML, Cherthala and others.

On the labour front, P.M. Mohammed Haneef, Working President of the Cochin Port Staff Association, and C.D. Nandakumar of the Cochin Port Employees' Organisation served as the labour trustees during these tumultuous times. Several Board members headed specific subcommittees to find solutions or offer critical recommendations on some of the complex and knotty issues, and I am grateful to each one of them. Senior state government officials, including T. Balakrishnan, V.J. Kurien, Tom Jose, P.H. Kurien, and Dr V. Venu provided exceptional support.

The Indian Ports Association (IPA), under the Ministry of Ports, Shipping and Waterways, is a forum for major ports to exchange ideas, shape policy, and drive developmental initiatives. The Chairperson is chosen from among the port Chairmen, reflecting its shared leadership. During my tenure at Cochin Port, IPA was capably administered by R.K. Jain and A. Janardhan Rao, who contributed significantly to port modernisation. I remain deeply thankful to IPA and its leadership for their valuable support.

It is a matter of honour that former Cabinet Secretary K.M. Chandrasekhar, former Secretary (R) P.K. Hormis Tharakan, and former Special Secretary (Cabinet Secretariat) Vappala Balachandran reviewed the manuscript and gave their critical comments. I am deeply grateful to Ambassador T.P. Sreenivasan and K. Kunhikrishnan, former Additional Director General, Doordarshan, for their guidance. At the last minute, I sent the manuscript to my IPS batchmate K. Ramanujam, former DGP of Tamil Nadu, with instructions to both censor and censure. He did a good job of both! Once again, my friend Sunil Varan Arya (IRTS) went through the drafts with great care and attention to detail, offering several corrections and suggestions.

I am deeply grateful to V. Sajeev Kumar and C. Sasi Kartha for helping with key resources.

Above all, I am deeply indebted to former National Security Advisor M.K. Narayanan and former Principal Secretary to the Prime Minister T.K.A. Nair, for their constant support and guidance. Their backing was instrumental in enabling the Cochin Port team to implement our ambitious projects, even as we navigated uncertainty and turbulence.

To all who have walked this path with me, I extend my sincerest gratitude. This book would not have been possible without their invaluable contributions.

Thiruvananthapuram **N. Ramachandran**
5 April 2025

PROLOGUE

The Story Begins Here

Appointing a police officer as the chairman of a major port was unusual. So, when I landed up as the Chairman of Cochin Port in October 2005, my presence naturally raised eyebrows. In the days that followed, my colleagues in the trade unions as well as political acquaintances would often taunt me with the metaphor of a bull let loose in a china shop—sometimes in jest, and sometimes out of sheer frustration. I would respond by saying that it takes a bull's recklessness to bring about the much-needed disruption, especially when the organisation's very survival was at stake.

In many ways, my approach to managing the port's daily operations and navigating the complexities of its waters was seen as unorthodox. My relationships with trade unions were equally unconventional—some were friendly but consistently volatile, while others were unfriendly but hopelessly predictable. From handling these uncertainties and the barrage of strikes and work stoppages to quelling aggressive industrial actions, from pushing for organisational reforms to overseeing the implementation of an array of mega infrastructure projects, my approach was often perceived as different—sometimes unpalatable, sometimes unacceptable—inviting a mix of curiosity, animosity, hostility and, in some cases, outright support.

This book recounts stories of those disruptions—some intentional, others unintended. It includes personal reflections on my journey as a police officer who unexpectedly found himself navigating the complexities of managing a major public sector port. These are human stories of people whose lives were intertwined with the port's daily operations and growth—from its staff and workers to senior management officers, union leaders, politicians, traders, business partners, consultants, government officials, and citizen stakeholders.

The book shares stories of how they collaborated to clean up the cobwebs and build the future, bringing about an unprecedented transformation of the organisation, its infrastructure, systems, and processes. This transformation decisively changed the face of the port and propelled the fortunes of the port city itself. These are stories of bonding, friendships, suspicions, distrust, and animosities. The narratives capture seemingly endless debates and consultations, intense negotiations, arguments, disagreements, disputes, quarrels, flash strikes, *hartal*s, *dharna*s, and work stoppages under different names, alongside real-life tales of teamwork, camaraderie, conflict, and resilience. The events described in the book took place in and around the port of Cochin during a critical period of its development and transformation in the early years of this millennium.

This is not to say that all good work happened exclusively during this time frame. Indeed, previous generations laid much of the foundational work that led to the progress we see today. Their perseverance will be carried forward by those who come after us, and the legacy will continue to evolve and shape the future. Every era builds upon the accomplishments of the past, merging silently with an ever-evolving future. The purpose of this narrative is to give a human face to some of the *dramatis personae* of a particular period, whose stories might be of interest to readers in a future era!

The book is more than just a chronicle of a port's daily life and operations; it is a testament to the power of human potential and the resilience of individuals in the face of adversity and challenge. The teamwork, determination, grit, and fortitude of those instrumental in the port's development and organisational change are evident throughout. It is also a tribute to the humble port workers, on whose toil and sweat the organisation has flourished over the years. Above all, the book celebrates life in

Cochin, where the ancient and the modern coexist, blending diverse cultures, religious faiths, pursuits, and beliefs that coalesce to form a harmonious and thriving community—a remarkable example of unity in diversity.

A Personal Journey

Many readers might wonder how in the world a policeman got appointed as the chairman of a major public sector port. It surprised and intrigued many. However, I must disappoint them, as there were no mysteries or intrigues involved! Typically, this role is reserved for officers of the Indian Administrative Service (IAS), who hold the rank of joint secretary in the Government of India. This time, however, the Shipping Ministry decided to open its doors to officers across all services who held a rank equivalent to Joint Secretary, including the Indian Police Service (IPS).

My personal tryst with Cochin Port began in February 2005, when a colleague from the Home Ministry called to inform me about an advertisement posted on the Shipping Ministry's website. The ad invited applications from officers empanelled as joint secretaries for the position of chairpersons at several major ports, including Cochin. The opportunity piqued my interest, especially since I had spent most of my service career far from home. I was tempted to apply, as it would give me a chance to serve in my home state. The idea was quirky, offbeat, and instantly appealing. However, I still harboured some reservations, as no IPS officer had ever held this position before. Nevertheless, since I met all the eligibility criteria, I submitted my application, fully aware that my chances of being selected were rather slim.

During this period, I was posted as the Inspector General (IG) of the Special Protection Group (SPG), the elite organisation responsible for the Indian Prime Minister's security. In fact, I had visited Cochin just a few days earlier to make preparations for Prime Minister Manmohan Singh's visit, during which he laid the foundation stone for the Vallarpadam International Container

Transhipment Terminal (ICTT). Little did I know at that time that just a few months later, I would find myself there as the chairman of the port. So, how did this happen? It was a combination of unexpected events and a series of instinctive decisions.

A few weeks after submitting my application, a senior officer in the Shipping Ministry called to congratulate me, informing me that my name was at the top of the shortlisted candidates for the Cochin position. He mentioned that the panel had been forwarded to the Ministry of Personnel's Establishment Office for the Appointments Committee of the Cabinet (ACC) to decide. Although I was "cautiously excited", to put it in bureaucratic parlance, I still was not fully hopeful. In fact, a few months after this conversation, I checked with a friend in the Ministry of Personnel, but he said there was no such file!

It is not uncommon for official files to get delayed or drift aimlessly in the corridors of power. Several months passed, and the chairmanship positions for other ports were filled, but there was still no news about Cochin. Eventually, I lost hope and decided not to pursue the matter further or make any more inquiries. I was personally acquainted with numerous political leaders and knew many key officials in the Government of India. However, I worked in an organisation that upheld high standards of professional and ethical conduct, where leveraging one's proximity with political functionaries for personal matters was a strict no-no.

Eight months later, as my deputation period with the SPG was nearing its end, I began preparing for my return to my IPS home cadre, Assam–Meghalaya. On one occasion, while travelling with a high-ranking official of the Prime Minister's Office (PMO), he asked about my future plans. I shared that I had been shortlisted for the Cochin Port Chairman's position but was now preparing to return to Assam, as there seemed to be no decision on the matter. The officer, a kind and affectionate figure, gently reprimanded me and told me not to "covet thy neighbour's job", a position that rightfully belonged to the IAS.

And then, just a week before I was to return to my cadre, a twist in the tale occurred during an informal conversation with my boss in the security hierarchy when the matter of the "missing" file was brought up. Two days later, my boss informed me that he had spoken to a senior official. Miraculously, the "missing" file reappeared in the Department of Personnel and swiftly went through the ACC process. Just one day before I was set to relinquish charge, my posting orders arrived.

Meanwhile, an important project my team had worked on was nearing completion. As a special gesture, the Prime Minister himself had consented to inaugurate the project in the lawns of 9, Race Course Road, and the date happened to coincide with my last day in the SPG. During tea and informal interactions, Prime Minister Dr Manmohan Singh took me aside and quietly asked, "Do you really want to go to Cochin?"

I was taken aback and asked him, "Sir, is there a problem?"

"My only concern," Dr Singh said after a long pause and a very concerned expression, "is that there are too many Malayalees in Cochin!"

An Unwelcome Welcome

On the day I arrived in Cochin to take over as Chairman, the Cochin edition of a national newspaper published a hard-hitting editorial, questioning the suitability of a police officer for the role. The editorial argued that the position should have gone to an IAS officer, in keeping with tradition. It insinuated that I must have leveraged my "connections" with influential politicians to secure the post, even suggesting the name of a top politician. The editorial further said that Chief Minister Oommen Chandy had written to the Prime Minister, inquiring why a Kerala cadre IAS officer was not chosen instead. Thus, my first day in Cochin began with a negative indictment. The insinuation of a "nexus" with politicians was particularly disheartening.

The newspaper's reporting reflected a lack of understanding of the appointment process under the Government of India. The ACC, chaired by the Prime Minister and including the Minister of Home Affairs, is the highest authority for approving senior government appointments. The ACC evaluates recommendations from selection committees based on merit, qualifications, eligibility, and suitability. Proposals usually undergo a rigorous process of scrutiny by the Establishment Office as well as the Civil Services Board, which is chaired by the Cabinet Secretary. While the process may entail delays, it ensures checks and balances in the system, although "bypass surgeries" do occasionally happen.

A friend who had read the editorial, humorously remarked that it was an ideal way to begin my new role. "Your supposed closeness to the most powerful politician of the day will serve you well," he said with a grin. "It instantly grants you power, and no one will dare needle you unnecessarily!"

This brings us to the existential question of the relationship between government officials and political leaders. This book seeks to explore this complexity, particularly in a politically sensitive state like Kerala. While democratically elected leaders have the legitimate right and authority to shape policy and direct governance, there is often a tendency among some to overreach, interfere, and attempt to micromanage for personal or political gain.

While I enjoyed excellent relationships with many political leaders in the state, there were instances of interference from certain quarters. Managing these situations required immense tact and resilience. At times, saying no—firmly but respectfully—was necessary to preserve the integrity of the work and maintain operational autonomy. Striking a balance between defending administrative independence and avoiding unnecessary conflict was essential, although it did occasionally strain relationships.

I witnessed this code of behaviour both in some exceptional superiors under whom I trained and in certain political leaders of that time, who set exemplary standards. They demonstrated how government officials and political leaders should define their relationships. Their message was clear: government officials are duty-bound to follow the law, remain steadfast in their principles, offer sound advice to political leadership, and firmly say "no" when necessary. However, it is troubling to see how easily some government officials yield to political pressure, disregarding their constitutional responsibilities.

I had the privilege of working with several outstanding politicians who respected our differences, particularly when I advised them to consider alternative courses of action. This often led to skirmishes or being overlooked for certain appointments. However, I cannot recall a single instance where I was persecuted, harassed, or severely reprimanded for standing firm on my decisions. In fact, being outspoken not only created some enemies but also earned me lasting professional relationships within both administrative and political echelons.

Nexuses are mutually beneficial or symbiotic partnerships. Thankfully, a large number of government officials continue to remain committed to the law and act with integrity. Similarly, we are fortunate to have some political leaders who consistently demonstrate high levels of honesty and character. Throughout my career, I have had the privilege of working with some upright and conscientious individuals, both in government and politics, who have set a positive example for my generation. However, one also encounters many others with contrasting traits, and an increasing number who prefers to sit on the fence, spanning the spectrum between integrity and opportunism.

It is often deeply disappointing to see senior government officials bending over backwards to please political superiors, engaging in blatantly illegal actions and disregarding the law. Yet, a few spicy stories involving a handful of individuals can sometimes lead to the unfair assumption that all officials and politicians are in cahoots.

In addition to recounting some past history, this book carries a simple message for future generations of government officials, echoing the wisdom passed down by many leaders who came before us: civil servants have a bounden duty to implement the political vision while steadfastly refusing to bow to illegal pressures. Even when confronted with political interference or personal risks, standing firm in our constitutional duties serves the greater public interest. While remaining steadfast may lead to being overlooked for certain top positions, it should never deter one's commitment to lawful conduct. The message is clear: persistent teamwork, coupled with a steadfast adherence to integrity and ethical service, can strengthen institutions and build the foundations for real change.

Government officials in India enjoy tremendous protection, including constitutional safeguards like Article 311, as long as their actions are lawful and they remain on the right path. When an officer asserts their lawful position and clearly explains why certain things should not be done, or why a particular course of action is incorrect, there is no reason for them to worry about job loss. While the government of the day has the authority to transfer individual officials at any time, no one can be removed arbitrarily from service. Even ousting someone from senior positions under the Central government has to go through a similar process of ACC approvals.

Obviously, salacious stories of officials bending in different directions, succumbing to pressure, failing to stand up to their responsibilities under the law, and compromising their integrity to please their masters—whether for personal gains or otherwise—cannot be entirely blamed on politicians.

Approaching the Land of Paradoxes

It was with some excitement and a pinch of trepidation that I approached my new job. Despite my lack of experience in port administration, I was eager to learn. Driven by a deep connection to my roots and a genuine desire to make a meaningful impact, I hoped to contribute to the port's growth and development. I understood that keeping an open mind would be key. Since I had left Kerala after college and never worked there before, my understanding of the state was somewhat unrealistic and possibly biased, shaped mainly by readings about the state's politics, its unique sociopolitical environment, and its uneven economic development in spite of its immense potential.

According to many economists and developmental scientists, Kerala stands out as a paradox in many ways. It is known for its long history of powerful social movements and a strong civil society, and has made commendable strides in human development with the highest literacy rates and remarkable levels of life expectancy. The state has successfully implemented comprehensive land reforms and has succeeded in uplifting the lives of thousands of peasants and downtrodden communities, thus restoring their dignity. Many of Kerala's social development indices, including its Human Development Index, are comparable to the standards set by the Organisation for Economic Cooperation and Development (OECD). The state has also established robust social welfare systems that have substantially improved the overall quality of life and welfare of its populace.

Kerala can take pride in being the least impoverished in the country, as evidenced by the Multidimensional Poverty Index (MPI) of the NITI Aayog, which reflects its commitment to inclusive growth. The state has not only managed to maintain impressive levels of societal peace and control over crime but has also earned recognition for its commitment to social justice. Kerala can also be regarded as a model for gender equality, in terms of the status and dignity that women enjoy, with a favourable sex ratio, universal female literacy, and strong representation of women in higher education. Yet, despite these advancements, patriarchy remains deeply entrenched. Traditional gender roles and cultural expectations continue to shape family and community life, limiting women's participation in economic and political spheres. And this is where the paradox begins.

Despite its high levels of social development and a surplus of educated and skilled people, Kerala remains one of the least industrialised states in the country, with limited economic diversification. This has led to massive levels of unemployment and underemployment, driving large segments of the youth and workforce to seek opportunities outside the state, both within India and abroad. This paradox of high levels of social development, coupled with a surplus of highly educated and skilled people without adequate opportunities, has remained a crucial challenge for the state's policymakers.

Interestingly, Kerala has become a prime destination for migrant workers from various parts of India. Known as "guest workers", these migrants make significant contributions to the state's workforce and economic activities, particularly in sectors such as construction, agriculture, hospitality, tourism, and domestic work. Their labour is essential in driving Kerala's economic growth. This paradoxical situation coexists with a unique scenario in which the state both exports and imports labour, highlighting the complex socioeconomic and labour dynamics of Kerala.

So, how does the Kerala paradox manifest in the lives and work of its people? We will explore some of its nuances as we delve deeper into this book.

Banter to Light Up the Room

What truly lifts our spirits is the light-hearted banter about life in Kerala and the humorous takes on its many complexities. Here, we vigorously debate the intricate affiliations and rifts between political creeds and personalities. We engage in seemingly endless TV debates, arguing over political ideologies, even if our politics itself maybe bereft of ideology. We passionately defend long-forgotten political beliefs, searching for their relevance in today's societal context. We fiercely champion the rights of workers—even where there is no work—and enthusiastically form trade unions long before the arrival of trade itself, continuing industrial action even long after the enterprise has ceased to exist. As devout nationalists and proud global citizens, we allow ourselves to be swayed by events both near and far. I vividly recall fervently participating in a student strike during my early college days, fuelled by anger over Che Guevara's execution, even though, at the time, I had little idea who Che Guevara was, or what he stood for!

And when God created a country in His own name, He also gifted its people with a powerful arsenal to keep themselves busy: an arsenal of collective action, protests, strikes, *hartal*s, rallies, demonstrations, and processions. In God's own country, we celebrate *hartal*s and *bandh*s (strikes) with the same zeal and festive spirit as we do Onam, Christmas, or Eid! One person's cause is everyone's cause, regardless of the ostensible reason, the colour of the flag, or party loyalties. Strikes are often conveniently scheduled for Fridays or Mondays, so as to brighten our weekends. Collective action is our lifeline. Yet, our first love will always remain football, played in other countries!

Setting Personal Goals and Priorities

Beyond the light-hearted banter, one cannot help but be in awe of the enigma that is Kerala and the immense potential it harbours. Cochin Port, widely acknowledged for its ability to drive Kerala's economic development, serves as both a catalyst and a positive force in the state's economic growth. At the same time, as a microcosm of Kerala's broader socioeconomic landscape, Cochin Port has faced many of the same challenges experienced by the state. While drawing direct comparisons may not always be entirely fitting, these challenges certainly demand urgent attention.

My top priority was to initiate a series of decisive actions to address some of these issues. I was deeply committed to proving that a peaceful and productive labour environment could be fostered at Cochin Port, all while managing day-to-day port operations and simultaneously overseeing the execution of planned mega infrastructure projects—from conceptualisation to completion—within my five-year deputation period.

Both tasks were formidable by existing Kerala standards. Accomplishing these goals required confronting tenacious resistance and navigating a sea of uncertainties, not least of which was the complete lack of funds at the disposal of the port to undertake such ambitious ventures. In the forthcoming chapters, I will recount stories about how the Cochin Port team grappled with these challenges, disrupting deeply entrenched practices, posing uncomfortable questions to ourselves, and venturing into politically risky territory to tackle some of the most existential challenges and threats.

Structure of this Book

It is with this background that this book has been written. It begins with a brief historical overview of Cochin Port, setting the context for the following chapters. Chapter 2 describes the labour situation, the series of debilitating strikes the port endured and the collective, determined efforts to build internal controls and usher in labour reforms. Chapter 3 details the immense tribulations and challenges our teams faced during the ambitious implementation of the Enterprise Resource Planning (ERP) project, a pioneering initiative in India's port sector. Both the labour reforms and the ERP system were truly transformative in reshaping the internal governance of the port. These initiatives will have a far-reaching impact on the port's operations in the years to come.

The next two chapters focus on the development and execution of major infrastructure projects, including the Vallarpadam International Container Transhipment Terminal (ICTT), the Cochin LNG Terminal Project, the road and rail connectivity, and the deepening and widening of navigation channels. These projects, along with several supplementary initiatives, have completely reshaped the port and left a significant imprint on the city itself.

The succeeding chapter celebrates life in Cochin, emphasising how the port touches the lives of the city's residents. The final chapter explores how Cochin Port's growth and Kerala's industrial and economic development are closely interconnected. It emphasises that the port's future expansion is dependent on a robust hinterland economy. Through 11 thought-provoking debate questions, the chapter outlines a roadmap for democratic discourse, encouraging discussions on Kerala's path to industrial and economic progress. The book concludes with reflections on the author's experiences over 64 tumultuous months at Cochin Port, and a future outlook for the port and its hinterland.

1

PAST FORWARD

Cochin Port's Journey Through Time

A seaport is not merely a place where ships come and go, where cargos are loaded and unloaded—it is a centre of human interaction and cultural fusion. Like other ancient port cities, Cochin, too, is a microcosm of the world, symbolising the interconnectedness of humanity and the enduring marvels of social and cultural exchange. Here, peoples, languages, cuisines, traditions, and faiths intermingle, creating a diverse cosmopolitan mosaic. Here, culinary traditions blend, folklore and stories take root, and places of worship from different faiths coexist. Any book on Cochin and its port must chronicle these indelible marks of the city's lasting relationship with the sea.

Cochin's history is intricately interwoven with ancient maritime commerce, sailing vessels, shipbuilding, and seaborne adventure, all of which have contributed to its economic prosperity and cultural diversity. To this date, the old city's waterfront teems with age-old docks, piers, and jetties that have welcomed vessels from distant shores, fostering trade, cultural exchange, and the convergence of diverse peoples. The city's maritime heritage is etched in its culture and architecture, where ancient lighthouses, Chinese fishing nets, museums, and maritime-themed landmarks stand as reminders of its seafaring legacy. Centuries-old maritime traditions and festivals continue to thrive, serving as living tributes to the city's enduring seafaring spirit. In this city, the sea is not just a backdrop but a defining element of its past, present, and future, shaping its character, resilience, and global citizenship. And beyond all these, over the years, this port has enormously driven the trade, economic growth, and prosperity of the region.

As we begin this book, it is necessary to embark on a cursory journey through the annals of Cochin Port's history, tracing its maritime evolution and cultural lineage across several phases of growth and transformation. The story takes us from its humble beginnings as an ancient roadstead to its transformation into a modern, technologically advanced, world-class seaport of the 21st century. The purpose of this chapter is not to present an authentic and comprehensive account of the port's rich history spanning centuries. In fact, Cochin Port's history has been masterfully chronicled by former port Chairman D. Babu Paul in his 1986 publication, *The Queen's Story: Five Centuries of Cochin Port. The Cochin Saga*, written by colonial-era harbour engineer Robert Bristow, is another fascinating historical account that chronicles the transformative journey of Cochin Port from ancient times, particularly during the early 20th century between the two world wars. Bristow's first-hand narrative weaves together the intricate details of the construction of the "new" Cochin Port, and the creation of the man-made Willingdon Island, utilising the dredge spoils while deepening the navigation channels. It recounts why and how Cochin Port evolved into a dynamic and modern maritime landmark on India's Malabar Coast. His book vividly captures the challenges, triumphs, and the pivotal moments that shaped the port's destiny, and how the strategic location of the port made it an enticing destination for traders and explorers alike. Bristow's work enriches our understanding of the port's historical significance, its transformative impact on the region, and the indomitable spirit of those who contributed to its conceptualisation and development.

While Bristow's book offers invaluable insights into the historical events leading to the migration of port activities from the "Old Port" substructures of Fort Cochin to the man-made Willingdon Island during the British era, my purpose here is to focus on the recent history of Cochin Port's transformation into a modern, world-class facility. The book covers the collective efforts of the port teams, the state and Central government departments, with the civil society overcoming challenges to build a new infrastructure, and completing various modernisation projects during the early 21st century.

To situate the context of this narrative and to truly appreciate the current story, I propose to begin with a swift journey back through time, briskly traversing some of the distinctive epochs that have defined the port's extraordinary journey of growth and evolution. While describing the port's developmental history in different phases, it is important to note here that progress and evolution is an ongoing and unceasing process, and various observers or stakeholders may have different perspectives about what constitutes a particular stage of development. Moreover, the stages of development do overlap or may occur in different sequences in the eyes of the beholder. What is being attempted is to glance through select events and developments that occurred during particular time periods for the sake of narrative convenience. Recounting specific events in the history of the port is expected to help the reader obtain an overall understanding of its developmental continuum.

Fuzzy Imaginations of the Past

Unfortunately, much of Cochin's age-old maritime past remains shrouded in mystery, and most of what passes for the port city's ancient history is akin to our efforts to recall blurry, childhood memories and imaginations. Authentic records of our ancient maritime history are scarce, and the lack of clear historical records from ancient times has left us with a fragmented and hazy understanding of the past. My own modest readings in ancient Kerala history, juxtaposed with pure imagination, often conjured vivid images of ancient sailing ships approaching our shores, laden with goods and crowded with explorers, traders, warlords, and soldiers. The enthralling storytelling of my father and some of my earliest school teachers, who brought to life tales of native princely rulers, their valiant soldiers, and the relentless invaders they faced, likely fuelled these imaginations. Tales of adventure, valour, and conquest, and accounts of maritime navigation through treacherous waters and unpredictable weather are recounted, alongside stories of the tough life aboard the ship, with sailors toiling long hours under the scorching sun, their hands calloused from hauling ropes and hoisting sails. Stories of disease, hunger, and the ever-present threat of dangers and violence that loomed over their maritime lives are recalled, as many ships never returned from their perilous journeys. Yet despite the risks, the allure of the sea, the promise of adventure, and the dream of discovering new lands continued to draw countless sailors to India's shores.

We rely on scattered relics as well as contested beliefs and narratives to piece together what may have transpired. These sources often mix myth and what may have been reality, leading to a blend of fantasy and belief that complicates our grasp of ancient events. Even as historians struggle to separate fact from myths and deduce the true happenings and influences of those distant times, the prevailing uncertainty profoundly distorts our interpretation of history, even though those events overwhelmingly shaped our experiences today and significantly impacted the subsequent history of India and the world.

While there is a dearth of comprehensive historical records of the earliest shipping expeditions to these regions, occasional copper plate inscriptions and archaeological and historical evidence provide some insights. Thus, historians and archaeologists have attempted to piece together Cochin's maritime history through an assortment of relics and references belonging to the earlier era. It is believed that the story of the ancient port city of Muziris and the development of the harbour of Cochin were linked through historical and natural events that shaped the region's future. Muziris (also known as Muchiri), situated a few nautical miles to the north of the present-day Cochin, is believed to have been a bustling maritime trade centre for over 2,000 years. And there are tales galore in the accounts left behind by seafaring merchants who ran lucrative trade networks, enticed by the lure of exotic spices and more. Evidently, Muziris served as a vital link, connecting India with the rest of the world, facilitating the exchange of goods, ideas, concepts, and cultures. Its strategic location close to the age-old international maritime routes situated at the crossroads of the Arabian Sea, the Red Sea corridor, and the Indian Ocean, always made it a coveted destination for traders, explorers, and conquerors alike. These exchanges not only boosted the local economy, but also facilitated cultural and technological exchanges between the trading partners of yesteryears.

The history of Cochin, and Kerala's Malabar Coast in general, is intertwined with stories surrounding its spice trade stretching back to the past. This region is known to have established early trading relationships with the Arabian Peninsula, China, Egypt, Rome, and later, Europe. The Kerala coast's fertile, rainfed lands were ideal for the cultivation of pepper and other spices, which were highly prized in Europe, Persia and Egypt of yore. The demand for pepper and other spices like cardamom, cinnamon, and cloves, positioned the Malabar Coast as a crucial hub for the ancient and medieval era global trade network.

Interestingly, the discovery of the monsoon winds marked a key advancement in early maritime navigation, greatly promoting shipping routes to India. The Greek–Egyptian sailor Hippalus is credited with the early understanding of the seasonal reversal of these winds in the Indian Ocean region and the Arabian Sea, around the first century AD. This knowledge allowed sailors to harness the predictable and strong southwest monsoon winds to sail from the Arabian Peninsula to the Malabar Coast during the summer months and return with the northeast monsoon in the winter. Alongside the monsoon winds, the discovery of the mud banks along the Malabar Coast, known as *chakara*s, further facilitated maritime activities. These mud banks are natural formations that develop near the coasts, enabled by the deposition of fine clay particles that create calm and navigable waters, allowing ships to anchor safely and facilitating the loading and unloading of goods even during the rough monsoon season. These veritable natural harbours aided in the emergence and prominence of these ports. Thus, the combination of monsoon wind navigation and the discovery of safe harbours created by mud banks played a crucial role in establishing and sustaining ancient Kerala's maritime trade links with the rest of the world. These discoveries revolutionised maritime trade, enabling quicker, safer, and more reliable sea voyages, thereby boosting the spice trade and cultural exchanges between India and other ancient civilisations.

Muziris: A Flourishing Port City

The ancient port city of Muziris, located near modern-day Kodungallur, was a thriving trade centre that lured merchants and voyagers from diverse corners of the ancient world. Archaeological evidence overwhelmingly indicates that Muziris was among the earliest ports in human history. It attracted Babylonians, Assyrians, Egyptians, Arabs, and Phoenicians, all converging on the Malabar Coast in pursuit of precious spices and other exotic wares. Muziris is believed to have been a thriving port since at least the first century AD, with some evidence suggesting it may have existed even earlier. A fascinating discovery linked to Ramesses II, one of Egypt's greatest pharaohs who ruled from 1279 to 1213 BCE, sheds light on Muziris' significance in early international trade. The examination of his mummy reportedly revealed fragments of pepper, a plant native to the Malabar Coast, tucked inside the pharaoh's nostrils. This finding suggests that black pepper was likely exported to Egypt through Muziris, highlighting the port's pivotal role in ancient global commerce.

Greek geographer Ptolemy mentioned Muziris in his work *Geographia* (circa 150 AD), providing geographical coordinates for the port. Roman and Greek merchants established trade links with Muziris primarily to procure valuable spices, particularly black pepper, and other exotic goods from the Indian subcontinent. Historians say that the *Periplus of the Erythraean Sea*, a first-century Greek maritime guide, offered valuable insights into navigation and maritime trade routes, ports, harbours, coastal landmarks, trade goods, and the indigenous peoples encountered along the maritime routes. Likely used by merchants and sailors engaged in trade between the Roman Empire, Egypt, the Arabian Peninsula, East Africa, India, and Southeast Asia, the *Periplus* described the extensive trade networks of the time, extending from Egypt and East Africa to the western coasts of India. It also mentioned Muziris and other harbours on the Malabar Coast, pointing to their significance in the bustling trade activities that existed in the ancient world.

The archaeological excavations at Pattanam, near Kodungallur, have yielded substantial evidence linking the site to the port of Muziris, a key hub in the Indo-Roman trade network during the first century AD. Discoveries of Roman coins, amphorae, pottery, and various artefacts indicate vibrant trade and cultural exchanges between local traders and Roman merchants, driven largely by the spice trade. Other findings, including remains of wooden structures and wharves, suggest Pattanam was an active port settlement, strategically located near the Periyar River. These excavations offer valuable insights into the early global trade and cultural interactions, making Pattanam a vital site for understanding the history of commerce in the region.

The Government of Kerala has launched the Muziris Heritage Project (MHP), a major conservation initiative aimed at understanding and preserving the relics recovered from the site of the ancient port of Muziris. This includes extensive archaeological excavations carried out by the Kerala State Department of Archaeology and the Archaeological Survey of India, which have uncovered a remarkable number of artefacts. The Pattanam Excavation Site Museum showcases these findings. Heritage trails, guided tours, and cultural programmes promote cultural tourism, while educational and research initiatives with the help of universities study Muziris' legacy. There have been efforts at infrastructure improvements to enable access to heritage sites, demonstrating the state government's commitment to preserving and promoting Muziris' historical and cultural significance. Incidentally, the hyphenation of Muziris and Pattanam has been contested. M.G.S. Narayanan, one of the most respected historians of Kerala, has noted—based on extensive research and archaeological findings—that Pattanam was most likely a key part of the ancient Muziris port complex, but probably not the entire city-port. Narayanan and other scholars suggest that Muziris was a larger urban and trading region, possibly including nearby areas such as Kodungallur and Azhikode. Thus, while Pattanam is closely associated with Muziris, the ancient port likely extended across a broader area along the Periyar River basin.

Even as the controversy surrounding the hyphenation of Muziris and Pattanam rages, Narayanan's influence helped mobilise scholarly and public interest in the Muziris Heritage Project. He also notes that Pattanam had trade relations with at least 34 countries at its peak. His key argument is that Muziris was not just a regional trading hub, but a global maritime centre as early as the 1st century BCE.

The controversy has been further fuelled by ideological and regional biases, intensifying scholarly disagreements. Unfortunately, this controversy has led to the halting of excavations at Pattanam, obstructing further research that could have confirmed or refuted the claims. In recent years, the Kochi–Muziris Biennale has played a significant role in celebrating and preserving the heritage and culture of Muziris, keeping the stories and knowledge of Muziris alive, ensuring they are passed on to future generations and integrated into contemporary cultural discourses. The prestigious Biennale has attracted thousands of domestic and international visitors and artists and has facilitated various art forms that reflect the diverse cultural influences of Muziris, including those from Roman, Greek, Egyptian, and Chinese civilisations, highlighting the historical significance of the region. It has encouraged collaborations and dialogues between artists, historians, and archaeologists, promoting deeper understanding and appreciation of Muziris' cultural legacy. Moreover, the Biennale's educational programmes and workshops engage the local community and visitors, fostering a sense of pride and awareness about their heritage. This blend of art, history, and community engagement ensures that the rich cultural heritage of Muziris continues to be celebrated and preserved.

Decline of Muziris and the Emergence of Cochin

The decline of the port of Muziris and the emergence of Cochin as a seaport is a fascinating story of historical transitions and natural phenomena. Muziris possibly began to decline following a catastrophic flood in 1341. This flood caused extensive siltation in the Periyar River, altering its course, and severely impacting the port's accessibility, leading to Muziris' eventual decline. The same flood event was, we surmise, a significant geological phenomenon that drastically altered the region's geography, resulting in the formation of Cochin's natural harbour at the confluence of the Vembanad Lake and the Arabian Sea. However, although there are mentions of the 1341 deluge in history books, the theory that the deluge transformed the region's geography, leading to Muziris' decline and Cochin's emergence, has also been disputed, for lack of sufficient evidence.

While ecological changes and shifting river geography may have rendered Muziris less suitable for large ships, it is evident that the ancient port did not disappear overnight. Instead, it appears to have undergone a gradual decline from the 5th century CE onwards, as emerging trade centres like Kodungallur (Mahodayapuram) and later Cochin (Kochi) gained prominence. The weakening of the Chera dynasty (which had supported Muziris) and subsequent political instability likely also contributed to the port's diminishing importance.

Beyond legends, not much is known about the precise origins of maritime activities in Cochin. These activities most likely began as a roadstead or a small natural harbour near the Cochin estuary. This geographical location would have made it a suitable place for maritime activities, given its proximity to both the inland waterways and the open sea. These developments might have led to the migration of trade from Muziris to Cochin, marking the beginning of its emergence as a leading harbour and trading hub on the Malabar Coast. Subsequent to these developments, there are clear accounts of mariners and merchants from diverse regions engaging with local traders and inhabitants, establishing the exchange point that would shape the port's destiny for centuries to come. Cochin's rise was marked by the increasing presence of merchants and mariners from various parts of the world, who established robust trade links with the local economy. The port's strategic location, combined with its natural advantages and the decline of Muziris, positioned Cochin as a critical node in the regional and global trade networks. The port evolved over centuries, adapting to the changing dynamics of maritime trade and continuing to play a vital role in the economic and cultural exchanges that defined the Malabar Coast. The rulers of Cochin were adept at fostering trade relationships with foreign merchants from Arabia, China, and Southeast Asia, further solidifying the port's place in global commerce. The port's prosperity attracted numerous foreign traders, establishing Cochin as a major hub for international trade.

Even as maritime trade expanded, many powerful kingdoms and dynasties vied for control over the port and its hinterland, engaging in intense struggles to assert dominion over the highly profitable trade routes in the region, leading to fierce competitions and triggering intense power rivalries. Throughout recorded history, the area witnessed the ascendancy and dominion of influential kingdoms. Arguably, they left behind their imprint on this region's history, their reigns marked by remarkable accomplishments and enduring legacies. The Chera dynasty was one of the earliest to exert its influence in the region, laying the foundation for Kerala's rich maritime traditions. The port's strategic significance also drew the attention of powerful dynasties like the Cholas and the Pandyas, who aimed to assert their dominance along the Malabar Coast. In the medieval period, the Zamorins of Calicut became prominent players in the region, extending their influence over Cochin. However, Cochin's rulers, often in conflict with the Zamorins, strove to maintain control over the port and its surrounding areas. These intense power struggles, defined by shifting alliances and rivalries, shaped the political landscape of the region for centuries.

The spice trade's lucrative nature led to the industrial-level mass production and systematic harvesting of pepper and other spices in Kerala. As trade flourished, European powers began to take a keen interest in monopolising the spice trade. The Portuguese were the first Europeans to establish a foothold in Kerala in the late 15th century, followed by the Dutch and the British. Each of these colonial powers sought to dominate the spice trade, often through force and strategic alliances. This European incursion disrupted the existing trade networks controlled by Arab merchants, who had long dominated the Indian Ocean trade routes. Conflicts between Arab traders and European powers were frequent, marked by naval battles and trade embargoes. The Mappilas, the Muslim community in Kerala with strong ties to Arab traders, faced persecution as European powers sought to eliminate their competition.

By the late 15th century, European influence had reached the region with the arrival of Portuguese explorer and trader Vasco da Gama. Cochin soon began to emerge as a vital hub for trade between Europe and Asia. The port's growing mercantile and strategic importance sparked intense competition among European powers, including the Portuguese, French, Dutch, and British, each vying for economic and political dominance. This gave rise to a series of power struggles between the Europeans and local rulers. Unfortunately, detailed records of these pre-colonial conflicts remain scarce. Between the 16th and 19th centuries, Cochin witnessed many such struggles, involving the princely rulers of the Cochin State, local merchants, and foreign invaders.

The arrival of Vasco da Gama on the southwestern coast of India in 1498 marked a historic turning point in global trade, as it established the first direct sea route from Europe to the spice-rich Malabar Coast. Although the Portuguese initially set up a trading post in Calicut, they soon forged a strategic alliance with the Kingdom of Cochin, which significantly shaped the region's political and economic history. With Cochin as a key partner, the Portuguese gained control over critical spice trade routes. However, European rivalries, conflicts with local powers, and growing competition—particularly from the Dutch and the British—eventually altered the dynamics of the spice trade, shaping the course of colonial history in India and leaving a lasting legacy on the region.

And then came the Dutch East India Company (VOC) which established its presence in Cochin in the early 17th century, primarily to gain control of the lucrative spice trade. They formed alliances with local rulers, including the Raja of Cochin. The Dutch influence in Cochin was marked by a series of skirmishes and conflicts with the Portuguese, who were already established in the area. The Dutch eventually gained control over some parts of Cochin, including Fort Kochi. Over the years, the port and its early infrastructure grew and prospered.

Recognising the port's strategic and commercial value, the Dutch invested in its infrastructure, drastically transforming the city's landscape through ambitious engineering and architectural projects. They constructed forts, religious institutions, and warehouses, many of which still stand today. Notable examples include the magnificent Mattancherry Palace (originally built by the Portuguese and later renovated by the Dutch), St. Francis Church, and the VOC Gate that commemorates the trade links between the Dutch and the Kingdom of Cochin.

Under Dutch influence, Fort Kochi and Mattanchery emerged as important centres of trade and commerce, their landscapes still preserving numerous pre-colonial and colonial structures that served as auction centres, trade offices, places of worship, and burial grounds. However, the Dutch dominance was relatively short-lived. Fierce competition with the British eventually led to the decline of Dutch influence. By the late 18th century, the Dutch were compelled to cede their territories to the British. Nonetheless, the Dutch influence on Cochin's history is significant, particularly through the legacy of Fort Kochi, which still bears traces of Dutch architecture and heritage.

All this while, the port city also served as the capital of the princely State of Cochin, ruled by the Cochin royal family for several centuries until India gained independence in 1947. These rulers had to often navigate a delicate balance between the competing European interests. Each of these relationships was characterised by a mix of cooperation and conflict, with the rulers leveraging their strategic position to maintain a degree of autonomy, in their quest to ensure the prosperity of their state.

To this day, Cochin's history continues to bear the indelible marks of the influences of diverse peoples, religions, races, and cultures. This legacy blends contributions from Europeans, Egyptians, Jews, Arabs, and the Chinese, apart from people from various other parts of India, alongside the uniquely rich culture of the native population. The city's unique cultural and architectural heritage is a reflection of this diverse past. From ancient synagogues, mosques, and churches to spice markets and colonial buildings, Cochin's landscape tells the story of centuries of trade, cultural exchange, and coexistence. The Jewish settlements in Cochin as well as earlier ones near the ancient port of Muziris are among the oldest in India, possibly dating back to the first century AD. There is considerable historical evidence, such as the "Copper Plates of Cochin" granted by the local Hindu ruler in the 10th century, which confirms the rights and privileges of the Jewish community in the region. Known as the Cochin Jews and Malabar Jews, these communities played a vital role in regional trade and significantly influenced local education and culture. This influence is still evident in Cochin's architecture, cuisine, and religious practices, including the Paradesi Synagogue, one of the oldest active synagogues in the Commonwealth. While the Jewish population has steadily dwindled over the years, their legacy remains a vital part of Cochin's multicultural heritage.

The "Old Port Era"

Over the centuries, the evolution of trade and human interaction went hand in hand with advancements in ship technology and navigation. As maritime trade routes expanded, the ports of earlier times underwent remarkable transformations to meet the evolving requirements of trade and ship technology. With the emergence of seafaring civilisations, small harbours evolved into bustling hubs that could accommodate larger vessels and facilitate long-distance trade. The development of new ship designs, navigation instruments, and sailing techniques allowed merchants and explorers to venture further into the unknown, opening up opportunities for global commerce. Ports adapted by constructing more extensive docks, warehouses, and facilities to handle the increasing flow of goods and passengers.

The British East India Company spearheaded the most visible transformations of Cochin Port during the 19th and early 20th centuries, ushering in a phase of remarkable development and progress. This era in the port's history, referred to as the "Old Port Era", spanning nearly a hundred years from 1836, bore witness to substantial advancements in the port's infrastructure. For the European traveller headed to the south of India, Cochin was the most preferred landing port, with its all-weather, safe, and reliable anchorages, conveniently located on the west coast. Recognising the commercial and strategic significance of Cochin Port, the British colonial government embarked on a journey of modernising and developing Cochin into a vital trade and commerce hub and a strategic base in the region. Their innovative and visionary efforts laid the foundations for Cochin's growth and prominence. These efforts were also strengthened by the linking of the port with other parts of India through a network of railways and roads.

The foundational journey of the modern-day Cochin Port began in 1836 with the creation of the first hydrographic chart of the harbour and its approach areas. This marked the earliest known scientific effort to understand the layout and potential of the region, paving the way for future developments. A port's nautical chart is a specialised one used by mariners and navigators for safe and efficient navigation in and around a port or coastal area. These charts provide detailed information about the seabed, water depths, underwater hazards, navigational aids like buoys and lighthouses, shoreline features, and other essential data necessary for plotting courses, avoiding dangers, and ensuring the safe passage of ships and boats in maritime environments.

This was followed by Captain Castor's appointment in 1859, signalling the recognition of the need for a dedicated port officer to oversee the functioning and management of the Cochin harbour. By this time, the local trade bodies like the chambers of commerce had begun to wield their influence in the port's development. Aspinwall's memorandum of 1870 had suggested the development of a sheltered harbour in Cochin. This visionary proposal laid the groundwork for the modernisation of the port. Responding to this, the governor sought the expertise of an experienced harbour engineer from England, and Sir Robert Bristow, a renowned civil engineer, accepted the opportunity.

The arrival of Sir Robert Bristow on 13 April 1920 marked a turning point in the port's history. His exceptional expertise and dedication would play the most crucial role in reshaping the harbour's destiny. In those days, Cochin Port berthed ships offshore, and the vessels remained vulnerable to the turbulent open seas. Cargo loading and unloading was done via lighters. However, Bristow's meticulous studies, observations, and experiments convinced him of the possibility of developing a safe inner harbour, envisioning ships entering the backwater channels.

The big challenge was the extensive sandbar blocking the Cochin backwaters' access to the sea, which was considered technically insurmountable. This densely packed sandbar prevented deep-draught vessels from entering. There were apprehensions that the removal of the sandbar might lead to potential environmental consequences of incalculable magnitude. Bristow, however, after exhaustive research, believed these challenges could be overcome. To address immediate issues like the foreshore erosion of the

Vypeen Island, he constructed rubble granite groynes parallel to the shore, creating automatic reclamations that protected it against monsoon seas.

The dredger *Lord Willingdon* arrived in Cochin in May 1926. It was estimated that the dredger would need to operate for at least 20 hours a day for the next two years. The undertaking demanded keen observation of the tidal and littoral phenomenon, meticulous planning, immense patience, and unwavering perseverance. Bristow, relying largely on his judgement, provided immediate technical solutions for the myriad challenges that arose. His meticulous and scientific efforts finally culminated in achieving the crucial milestone on 30 March 1928, when the sandbar at the mouth of the harbour was finally cut open, paving the way for maritime traffic inside the sheltered waters of the port.

This was followed by the visionary and historic creation of Willingdon Island, transforming a swampy wasteland into a thriving, commercially attractive island. Bristow not only designed and oversaw the construction of the island and its infrastructure, but he also planned and developed the island's layout, including the placement of warehouses, and residential areas. He topped it up with the construction of a rail-cum-road bridge connecting Willingdon Island to the mainland, a modern port terminal, and a railway station. The island was named after Lord Willingdon, who served as the governor of Madras from 1919 to 1924 and as the viceroy and governor-general of India from 1931 to 1936. To this day, the Port of Cochin operates from Willingdon Island, which also remains an important trade centre with a range of businesses operating from the island. For many decades, it has been a thriving hub of trade and commerce, with a bustling workforce and housing hundreds of ancillary businesses. Until recent years, it served as a vital travel and passenger hub, accommodating both the Cochin airport and the Harbour Railway terminus.

The first vessel *MT Padma* crossed the newly opened channel on 26 May 1928, marking the beginning of a new era for Cochin Port. Between 1930 and 1931, the port was officially opened for vessels with a draught of up to 30 feet, signifying its capacity to accommodate larger ships. It was on 1 August 1936 that the administration of the Cochin Harbour was formally taken over by the government of India, marking another significant milestone in its evolution. On 12 August 1936, the Maharaja of Cochin laid the foundation stone for what was called the Fourth Stage works, further developing and expanding the port's infrastructure.

Cochin Port owes much to Harbour Engineer Robert Bristow's visionary and innovative approach and transformative work that contributed to the port's growth and development. Apart from his contributions to Cochin Port, Bristow played a significant role in the development of other ports in India, including Bombay (Mumbai) and Madras (Chennai). His inputs in the field of port engineering and modernisation have made a lasting impact on India's maritime infrastructure. Robert Bristow served as the chief engineer of the Cochin Port Trust from 1920 to 1932. Today, Bristow's legacy lives on as Cochin Port continues to serve as a vital gateway for international trade, thanks in large part to his pioneering efforts. The modern Cochin Port stands as a lasting testament to the vision and determination of early pioneers who laid the groundwork for its development and success.

Unceasing Expansion, Upgradation, and Modernisation

Many of the infrastructure developments initiated by the British during their colonial rule continue to form the backbone of Cochin Port's infrastructure and operations to this day. Cochin Port owes much of its modernisation to the measures undertaken during the British colonial era, transforming it to become a major maritime gateway on India's western coast. In the years between 1935 and 2000, the port witnessed a remarkable period of infrastructure development and innovations that shaped it into the modern port as we see it today. This transformative journey began with the relocation of all port facilities, operations, and infrastructure from the Fort Cochin area to the then newly created Willingdon Island.

The consolidation of the artificial Willingdon Island, combined with the deepening of the Mattancherry and Ernakulam navigation channels, laid the foundation for the construction of the new jetties, warehouses, and administrative structures for the expansion of port services. During this period of growth and development, Cochin Port underwent unprecedented modernisation through the introduction of advanced cargo handling equipment, improved navigational aids, and better communication systems, allowing the port to handle larger ships and meet the increasing demands of international trade.

Several milestones were achieved during this time, including the construction of specialised jetties to cater to specific cargo types. On 2 June 1939, the port made history by welcoming *MV Braunfels*, the first ocean-going ship to dock at the new Mattancherry Wharf. This marked a significant achievement for the port and its continued growth as a major hub for international trade. The commissioning of the North Tanker Jetty on 31 December 1955, followed by the South Tanker Jetty, paved the way for the import and export of crude oil and petroleum products. On 6 February 1956, the port welcomed its first oil tanker, the *SS British Fortune*, which berthed alongside the newly completed South Tanker Jetty. In the years that followed, the port expanded further with the commissioning of the North Coal Berth on 11 November 1959. The commissioning of the new Ernakulam Wharf on 19 May 1964 marked a significant expansion of port activities to the Ernakulam channel side of Willingdon Island.

Strategic Importance of Cochin Port

Cochin Port holds strategic significance for both commercial and military purposes. During World War II, it served as a vital logistical hub for the Allied forces. The British Royal Navy made extensive use of the port for refuelling and resupplying ships operating in the Indian Ocean. To accommodate the heightened military activity, the port's facilities were expanded, including the construction of bunkers and storage infrastructure. These developments made

Cochin Port indispensable to maintaining the operational readiness of the Allied naval forces in the region.

Cochin Port's strategic importance was reaffirmed during the 1962 war with China. Although the primary conflict occurred in northern and northeastern India, the port played a critical role in sustaining supply chains and ensuring the Indian Navy's readiness across the southern and western seas. It facilitated the transportation of military equipment and supplies, highlighting its significance in national defence logistics. This role became even more prominent during the Indo-Pak Wars of 1965 and 1971, when Cochin Port served as a key logistical base for the Indian Navy. Supporting operations in both the Arabian Sea and the Bay of Bengal, the port's shipyard facilities were instrumental in the repair and maintenance of naval vessels, contributing directly to the Navy's operational effectiveness.

In contemporary times, Cochin Port continues to play a pivotal role in India's maritime strategy. Willingdon Island is home to the Southern Naval Command (SNC) of the Indian Navy, a critical naval base established in 1971. The SNC plays a crucial role in training, strategic operations, and maritime security in the region. It safeguards India's maritime interests in the southern region through regular patrols, joint exercises with international naval forces to enhance regional security and cooperation, and active involvement in humanitarian missions and disaster response efforts.

Declaration as a Major Port

In independent India, seaports under the Central government's direct control and jurisdiction are designated as "major ports" under the Major Port Authorities Act, 2021 (formerly under the Major Port Trusts Act, 1963). Under the new Act, these ports are now managed by Port Authorities, which replaced the earlier Port Trusts. The so-called "minor ports" or "non-major ports" on the other hand, are managed either by state governments or private port operators and are regulated by the respective state maritime boards. Traditionally, major ports were larger and more strategically important than non-major ports. However, in recent times, some non-major ports have surpassed major ones in terms of cargo throughput and strategic significance. Thus, the designation of major ports is losing its significance.

Cochin Port was directly administered by the British government since the early colonial days. In the year 1932, the maritime board of British India approved Cochin as a major port. It was formally declared as one of the major ports on 26 November 1935, under the Indian Ports Act, 1908. There were six other major ports under British India, namely Bombay (now Mumbai), Calcutta (now Kolkata), Madras (now Chennai), Karachi (now in Pakistan), Rangoon (now in Myanmar) and Chittagong (now in Bangladesh). Cochin joined them as the seventh major port. After independence, Cochin became one of the 12 major ports in the country on 29 February 1964, under the Major Port Trusts Act, 1963. This period heralded a quantum leap in its development history, adapting to the evolving demands of the domestic and global maritime sector. The Cochin Customs House, which in earlier years functioned from Fort Cochin, was shifted to Willingdon Island in 1956.

The synergetic relationship between a port's growth and the economic and industrial progress of its hinterland is well known. It creates a mutually beneficial cycle of growth and development. A prime example of such synergy is the development of Cochin Port alongside the establishment and growth of the Cochin Refineries Limited, now the BPCL Kochi Refinery. The refinery's need for a steady and reliable supply of crude oil drove the port's expansion, positioning it as a crucial gateway for importing crude oil and exporting petroleum products. Today, Cochin Port's largest cargo category comprises crude oil and petroleum products. In an earlier period, the growth of the Fertilisers and Chemicals Travancore Limited (FACT) and its transformation into a Central Public Sector Undertaking (PSU) in the 1960s also contributed to the port's growth. The port facilitated the import of fertiliser raw materials and transportation of finished products, mainly via coastal shipping, further advancing the growth of both FACT and the port. The collaboration also included the development of dedicated berths and specialised handling equipment for bulk fertiliser cargo, strengthening the supply chain for FACT and helping to meet regional fertiliser demands.

As the port's business scope expanded in the 1980s, strategic plans were initiated to construct dedicated berths for oil tankers and fertilisers, deepen navigation channels, and reclaim land for future development. The construction of the oil tanker and fertiliser berths necessitated deeper navigation channels and basins to accommodate larger ships. This required extensive dredging to deepen and widen the channels. Taking advantage of the dredged material, an ambitious land reclamation effort was undertaken, resulting in the creation of approximately 300 acres of land for future port development. This newly reclaimed area included the southern tip of Vallarpadam Island, Candle Island, and Ramanthuruth. The land reclamation and channel deepening efforts opened up possibilities for expansion on the northern side of the navigation channels. The new land formations would also train the flow of the water and help reduce siltation. The latter part of this period also saw major strides in building an extensive oil handling infrastructure within the port to meet the rising demands of the energy sector and facilitating larger sizes of oil tankers to berth and operate within the port. The establishment and commissioning of the Cochin Oil Terminal in 1984 marked a major turning point, as it facilitated the handling of large volumes of crude oil imports, leading to substantial savings in freight costs.

The establishment of the public sector Cochin Shipyard Limited (CSL) in 1972 fostered synergies with Cochin Port, with both entities complementing and supporting each other in many ways. The CSL has been building ships not only for India but has also been exporting them for the European, American, and Middle Eastern markets. Today, it is the largest shipbuilding and ship repair facility in India, having recently come into prominence after successfully building and commissioning India's prestigious aircraft carrier, *INS Vikrant*.

Advent of Containerisation

Containerisation marked a revolutionary shift in global cargo packaging, handling, and transportation practices. The port made history on 27 November 1973, when *MV President Tyler*, the first container vessel to visit any Indian port, docked at the Ernakulam Wharf. Cochin Port was quick to recognise the potential of the growing container-handling business and the possible business transformation it would bring to the world of maritime cargo. Over the years, Cochin Port has seen significant developments in container-handling facilities, thanks to the strategic vision of its successive chairpersons and their professional teams. Under the leadership of Chairmen Babu Paul, G. Krishnan, and C. Babu Rajeev, the port acknowledged the growing importance of containerisation, leveraging emerging opportunities in the maritime cargo industry. They proactively prepared for this shift by establishing an exclusive container terminal at the Ernakulam Wharf. It was during Chairman Babu Rajeev's tenure that Cochin Port took a major step forward, when in 1994–95, the Rajiv Gandhi Container Terminal (RGCT) was launched, marking a significant milestone in the port's capabilities. This facility was built and outfitted with specialised container-handling gantry cranes and other dedicated equipment. In the early 1990s, other milestones included the opening of the Container Freight Station (1992–93) and the integration of the Dock Labour Board with the Cochin Port Trust (1993–94). These forward-looking strategies made Cochin one of the pioneering Indian ports to provide container-handling services in the country.

The iconic Cochin Port Administrative Building, unveiled in 1996–97, is a remarkable architectural fusion, blending elements of colonial and traditional Kerala architectural styles. These elements of heritage and modernity are evident in the building's design, featuring ornate details reminiscent of colonial-era structures alongside traditional Kerala elements like sloping tiled roofs, wooden accents, and open spaces for natural ventilation. This architectural fusion not only reflects the port's cultural legacy but also signifies its forward-looking vision, making it a unique and visually captivating landmark on Willingdon Island. Abutting this new building are the charming colonial era port offices, bungalows of the chairman and other port officials, the colonial-era Customs Houses, and the present-day Taj Malabar Hotel which began as a port guest house for visiting British Officers during the colonial era. Preserving these architectural treasures is vital for safeguarding the region's rich history and cultural heritage.

Transitioning into the 21st Century

Towards the end of the 20th century, Cochin Port underwent a major transformation, involving modernisation and infrastructure expansion to meet the evolving trends in global shipping. Privatisation and public–private partnerships (PPPs) led to the establishment of multiple cargo terminals and advanced cargo-handling facilities. Cochin Port diversified its capabilities, leading to substantial growth, notably in container traffic. Simultaneously, the port enhanced its hinterland connectivity by constructing new road and rail networks and establishing Inland Container Depots (ICDs) and Container Freight Stations (CFSs) in the vicinity. These advancements significantly improved the port's efficiency and competitiveness, laying the foundation for its future development.

The dawn of the 21st century witnessed a profound transformation in Cochin Port's historical journey. An interesting feature of this change involved the relocation of significant parts of the port's cargo operations to new terminals developed in the Vallarpadam, Puthuvypeen, and Bolgatty Islands, all located on the northern aspect of the navigation channel, thereby substantially expanding its operational area. As the port entered the 21st century, it embarked on an ambitious journey of extensive infrastructure expansion, diversification of products and services, and a broader cargo profile. These initiatives were complemented by numerous modernisation projects, digitisation of systems, and substantial labour reform, all crucial to remain competitive and relevant in the continually evolving maritime industry. The introduction of many fundamental labour reforms, accompanied by some determined efforts to cleanse and streamline the system that the port undertook during this period, was an integral part of this transformation process.

Several external factors contributed to this, including the unprecedented expansion of international trade and commerce, rapid technological advancements, and government policies aimed to attract private investments into the port sector. These factors created new opportunities for the port to attract investment to increase its cargo-handling capacity and improve its infrastructure. Above all, the port needed to align itself with the changing developmental needs of the country, while also responding to the international globalisation trends. This necessitated the construction of modern facilities and the introduction of new technologies to improve efficiency and productivity. The newly introduced projects and technological changes that this book describes in some detail were designed to address these issues and prepare the port for the future.

The rapid technological advancements in the shipping industry also played a crucial role in shaping this stage of the development of Cochin Port. The emergence of containerisation, as well as the evolving dynamics of transshipment among other factors, necessitated the development of modern container-handling facilities, capable of dealing with larger volumes of cargo more efficiently. Advances in science and technology, which enabled the liquefaction of natural gas and its transportation to new parts of the globe in highly specialised vessels, opened up new horizons for liquefied natural gas (LNG) business. New vessel designs and larger, specialised ships also meant that the port needed to build specific technical terminals and deepen its channels and basins to accommodate larger ships.

Another factor that contributed to these drastic developments was the growing national appetite to build port infrastructure to keep pace with the country's economic and trade expansion. The Indian government recognised the need for modernising and upgrading the country's ports in tandem with global developments.

As a result, the government invested in the development of major ports across the country, which included policy measures to attract private investment into the port sector. We, at Cochin Port, decided to take full advantage of this policy, making sure that all infrastructure projects were implemented efficiently and within the scheduled timelines.

The "landlord ports" model had already gained traction in government policy. Under this framework, port authorities retain control over the overall administration, management, and regulatory oversight of major ports, while waterfront areas and other assets are leased to PPP concessionaires. These concessionaires are tasked with bringing in investments, introducing modern technology, and deploying advanced equipment to efficiently manage and operate new terminals. While the port administration continues to determine the Scale of Rates for port services and assets, PPP concessionaires are granted flexibility to set tariffs based on market conditions, under the guidance of regulatory authorities.

Although this formal transition into "Port Authorities" took place a few years later, this approach helped to bring in private investment and expertise to develop modern facilities and improve efficiency. It was the arrival of external investments that brought about the establishment of modern, state-of-the-art terminals on the north side of the navigation channels, leading to the relocation of a sizable part of the port's cargo handling operations to these new terminals. The advanced terminals enabled the handling of larger and more specialised vessels, which, in turn, dramatically altered the port's cargo profile. Representing a considerable deviation from earlier development stages, this heralded a new chapter in the port's evolution.

A slew of northern terminals were developed during this phase to meet the demands of diversification of cargo profiles, enabling the handling of larger volumes of cargo, such as crude oil, petroleum products, LNG, LPG, and container transshipment. These northern terminals included India's first ICTT at Vallarpadam, developed in partnership with the Dubai Ports World (DPW), as well as Single Point Mooring (SPM), the on-shore tank farms developed by the BPCL Kochi Refinery for the offshore docking and cargo operations of Very Large Crude Carriers (VLCCs). It encompassed the LNG terminal and its associated specialised cryogenic storage facilities and the LNG regasification plant, developed by Petronet LNG (PLL) Limited. Thus, containers and energy products have become the mainstay of Cochin Port's cargo today, gradually shifting from traditional cargo like coal and other breakbulk. The development of the northern terminals, along with the establishment of cargo evacuation systems via pipelines and direct road and rail connectivity from the north, significantly helped decongest Willingdon Island. Today, the island primarily handles bulk cargo such as fertilisers, timber, edible oils, and other traditional commodities, in addition to serving as a hub for cruise and passenger ships. A few cement packaging plants have also come up on the island. However, an unintended (and unfortunate) consequence of the northern expansion has been a marked decline in commercial and operational activity on Willingdon Island.

Streamlining Administration and Finance

During the latter half of the 20th century, India's major ports, including Cochin Port, faced considerable challenges in human resources management, reflecting broader systemic issues in the governance of large public sector organisations. Despite employing sizeable workforces, modern HR management principles and practices were largely absent. At Cochin Port, officer-level positions were filled exclusively through internal promotions until 1996. As a result, many officers lacked advanced qualifications, which limited their effectiveness in senior managerial roles. This gap in professional development hindered strategic planning, leadership, and operational efficiency. The situation necessitated the urgent need for the adoption of structured HR strategies and comprehensive training to equip leaders with the skills to manage large, complex organisations effectively.

The management of office records was entirely manual, and most transactions were conducted in cash. A separate cash section operated under the Central Accounts Department, staffed by an impressive number of cashiers and their supervisors. The methods and procedures for recording cash and bank transactions were archaic and did not adhere to sound principles of book-keeping. Computerisation was limited to payroll processing and a few isolated activities related to container terminal operations. Due to the maintenance of multiple manual records, the finalisation of monthly accounts was typically completed three months after the close of a given month. The organisation faced significant challenges during this period due to a lack of effective financial and administrative control. Recognising the need for professional management of administrative and financial functions, Chairman Babu Rajeev engaged with trade unions to introduce direct officer recruitment in the Administration and Finance Departments, which was vehemently opposed by trade unions. As a trade-off, some higher level positions were offered through the upgradation of existing lower level positions. This agreement paved the way for direct officer recruitment in 1996, resulting in the induction of qualified, young officers who would play a pivotal role in the organisation's professionalisation and development in the coming years. To their credit, trade unions understood the crucial need for infusion of fresh and qualified talent into the system and they cooperated whole-heartedly.

Another important initiative of Babu Rajeev was the strategic merger of the Cochin Port Dock Labour Board (DLB) and the absorption of its financial losses. The DLB, operating under the Dock Workers (Regulation of Employment) Act, 1948, was responsible for on-board cargo handling by supplying workers to ships for loading and unloading, while shore cargo-handling was managed by port labour. The DLB charged a levy per tonne of cargo for its services. On 6 June 1994, an agreement was signed to protect the existing benefits of employees. The port management then formed composite gangs for both on-board and shore cargo-handling, streamlining operations significantly. In 1998, the DLB Levy was merged under wharfage charges during the revision of the

Scale of Rates. Due to continuous financial losses, the DLB sought advances from the port, leading to its financial merger with the port on 31 March 2000. These initiatives, despite intense pressures from trade unions and extensive negotiations, resulted in substantial operational efficiency and cost-effectiveness. The strategic merger not only streamlined cargo-handling operations but also integrated the workforce, aligning them with the port's broader operational goals. This move was a critical step towards modernising the port's management practices and improving overall financial stability. This was another area where the port's trade unions worked closely with the management toward the desired outcome.

BPCL's Single Point Mooring (SPM)[1]

Sometime in the late 1990s, Cochin Port's main customer, the Kochi Refineries Limited (KRL), dropped a bomb shell when they announced plans to build their own SPM outside and away from the port, somewhere in Alappuzha district, to handle VLCCs. The then Chairman Jacob Thomas was quick to realise that the proposed diversion of KRL's cargo would pose a crushing threat to Cochin Port's survival, as crude oil accounted for 67 per cent of the port's annual cargo throughput. Very soon, trade unions too, joined the campaign to apply pressure on the management to engage in discussions with the KRL, demanding a commitment from them to install an SPM within Cochin Port waters. The unions threatened that if KRL went ahead with their plans to build their

1. Single Point Moorings (SPM) are modern and highly sophisticated offshore mooring systems designed for the transfer of liquid cargo such as crude oil and petroleum products. It enables the loading or unloading of liquid cargo between large tankers and onshore storage facilities via submarine pipelines. Typically anchored to the seabed, an SPM is used by Very Large Crude Carriers (VLCCs) and Ultra Large Crude Carriers (ULCCs)—vessels so massive that they often cannot dock at conventional ports. The system allows these tankers to remain securely moored in open waters while freely rotating with wind and current, ensuring safe, efficient, and uninterrupted cargo transfer.

own SPM for crude imports, they would not allow the export of finished petroleum products through Cochin Port. The situation was leading to a major crisis.

A team of port officers, comprising Deputy Chairman A. Janardan Rao, Chief Engineer (in charge) J. Karthikeyan, Traffic Manager Venkatesh, Chief Mechanical Engineer P. Rajendran, Deputy Conservator Captain K.C. Thomas, Financial Advisor G. Krishna Kumar, Deputy Financial Advisor K.G. Nath, and Deputy Secretary Unnikrishnan Nair, was authorised to negotiate with the KRL. After protracted negotiations and bickering that lasted several months, both sides reached an agreement, and a Memorandum of Understanding (MoU) was finally signed in June 2003 between Chairman Jacob Thomas and KRL CEO BK Menon, agreeing that the proposed SPM would be constructed and developed under Cochin Port itself.

Earlier, in the year 2001, the KRL was acquired by the BPCL and the merger was completed in about five years. The refinery itself was renamed as the BPCL Kochi Refinery. By the year 2006, the company successfully completed the construction of the SPM, investing approximately Rs 703 crores. This crucial infrastructure has been designed to accommodate mammoth oil tankers, including VLCCs, with a capacity of up to 300,000 Deadweight Tonnes (DWT). Realisation of this mega infrastructure was crucial for the BPCL itself, as it would bring about the economies of scale essential to ensure profitability of the refinery. Located at a water depth of 30 metres and 10 nautical miles (approximately19 kilometres) off the Puthuvypeen coastline, this SPM ensures that even during adverse wind and wave conditions, tankers with draughts exceeding 21 metres can remain securely moored. A network of modern submarine pipelines connects the SPM to the onshore tank farms comprising four tanks, each with the capacity of 80,000 kilolitres (KL), located in the Port-Based Special Economic Zone (PBSEZ), built in a land area of 70 hectares leased out by the port. This state-of-the-art facility achieved full operational status in December 2007.

Senior officers of the port admit that apart from the diligent efforts of the port management and the accommodating spirit of BPCL-KRL officials, it was the pressure from trade unions that averted a major existential and financial crisis for the port. Give trade unions their due!

Goshree: A Tale of Three Bridges

The stories of Cochin Port's growth are closely intertwined with those of the numerous Vembanad Lake islands of Vypeen, Vallarpadam, Bolgatty-Mulavukad, Thanthonni Thuruthu, Kadamakkudy, and a number of smaller islands that remain strewn over an area of about 200 square kilometres, located in and around Cochin Port's waters. For residents of these difficult-to-access islands, despite their physical proximity to the city of Cochin, connectivity with the mainland had remained a long-cherished dream. The conceptualisation of the three Goshree Bridges is believed to have been the brainchild of Sahodaran Ayyappan, the visionary social reformer and minister of the former Cochin State. Over the years, the demand for bridges linking the islands had become an increasingly emotional issue. Some local leaders claimed that the Cochin State had initially allocated a generous sum of Rs 12 lakhs for the construction of the Goshree Bridges, but the funds were eventually redirected to other projects. In the absence of any forward movement, an "Action Council" formed by the islanders and led by Advocate Majnu Komath, the Convenor, had been organising rallies and protests for several years, vigorously advocating for the Goshree Bridges project. In fact, in August 1989, the "Action Council" initiated a massive rally of 400 country boats to draw the attention of the authorities.

It was the creation of the Goshree Islands Development Authority (GIDA) in 1994, carving it out from the existing Greater Cochin Development Authority (GCDA) that marked a turning point for the islands. Some innovative thinking and strategic planning followed, as GIDA decided to reclaim 25 hectares of prime land adjacent to Cochin's marine drive, which would soon become some of the most coveted properties in the city. The reclaimed land was sold for an impressive Rs 340 crores, out of which Rs 80 crores was utilised for the construction of the three bridges, while the remaining funds were channelled towards the development of other infrastructure.

The Mumbai-based consultants, the City and Industrial Development Corporation (CIDCO), introduced the idea of land reclamation to support the project. Successive district collectors of Ernakulam provided leadership at various stages. The construction of the three bridges was managed by the Cochin Port Trust on a deposit work basis, with Chandramohan as the project director, supported by Superintending Engineer K.K. Gireesan. Following Chandramohan's transfer, the project was overseen by M.S. Jaya, whose expertise in urban planning ensured that the new infrastructure was integrated well into Kochi's urban landscape.

The construction of the GIDA bridges posed several execution challenges for engineers, primarily due to the complex and unstable geotechnical conditions that required extensive soil investigations and stabilisation measures. Additionally, the sensitive ecosystem of the area imposed environmental constraints, necessitating strict adherence to regulations and mitigation measures. Logistical difficulties in transporting materials and equipment to the construction site further complicated the project.

The Incredible Social Impact

The Goshree Bridges have had a profound social impact by providing the islanders with much-needed connectivity to the city. Constructed under the supervision of the Cochin Port Trust with funding by the GIDA and formally opened in 2004, the three Goshree Bridges, linking the islands of Vypeen, Vallarpadam, and Mulavukad with the main city to the east, was a watershed moment for the social and economic development of the area. From a social standpoint, the bridges brought about a dramatic improvement in connectivity, simplifying movement of people and goods, and helping to improve the quality of life for the inhabitants. The substantial integration of the islanders with the main city broke down some of the barriers that had previously isolated the island communities. Before the bridges, islanders faced many hardships, especially in medical emergencies, with pregnant women often giving birth on boats and even instances of deaths during boat journeys. The bridges have not only eased access to medical facilities but have also made essential services more accessible, improving the quality of life and dramatically reduced the isolation of these communities, particularly during the challenging monsoon season.

Economically, the bridges opened up new avenues for livelihood, providing easier access to the city markets for local people, farmers, and small businesses, including fishing communities. This has boosted economic growth and created new jobs, particularly in transportation and logistics. The bridges also opened a new direct road connectivity towards the suburbs in the northwest of the city and beyond. Some researchers say that the new connectivity has resulted in a reduction in migration from the islands and the northwestern suburbs to the main city, as people can now avail themselves of all services without having to relocate. The new infrastructure improvements have also led to an increase in tourism, which has generated additional revenue for the local economy and created employment opportunities for the local residents.

Today, the Goshree Bridges, spanning across the scenic backwaters of Kochi, have become an integral part of the city's landscape. The construction of these bridges was a strategic and visionary decision that has had a positive impact on the social integration and economic development of the region.

A Game Changer for Cochin Port's 21st-Century Development

While the Goshree Bridges were primarily built to enhance connectivity and infrastructure for the various islands scattered across the region, Cochin Port has, over time, derived significant benefits from their construction. These three bridges have contributed notably to the port's tremendous growth by improving access to port-owned lands located on the northern side of the navigation channels. In fact, they have played a crucial role in the development of Cochin Port during its millennial phase.

Although Cochin Port owned large tracts of land in the areas situated north of the navigation channels, the lack of direct road connectivity posed a significant logistical hurdle for transporting construction materials and cargo. Before the bridges were built, these areas could only be reached via waterways, which were time-consuming and less efficient. However, the situation changed significantly with the construction of the Goshree Bridges, which connected the islands to the mainland and provided much-needed access to these port lands. This, in turn, facilitated the smooth movement of container cargo and other materials to the hinterland, significantly enhancing overall logistical efficiency.

Thus, the Goshree Bridges have not only brought connectivity to the islands but have also been an unforeseen catalyst for the next phase of Cochin Port's development, like the ICTT, the LNG Terminal and Regassification Plant, the SPM and related tank farms, the Multi User Liquid Terminal (MULT), the Ro-Ro Terminal, the Cochin Marina and the new hotel projects on Bolgatty Island, and the two PBSEZs. The bridges have provided easy access to the port, which has attracted other activities like CFSs to set up their operations there. Much credit is due to the visionary efforts of local inhabitants, political leaders and government officials of the state government, district administration, and Cochin Port who envisioned this project and found the resources through an out-of-the box approach, finally executing it with great passion.

The land area that would eventually become the ICTT at Vallarpadam was created primarily using dredge spoils—the sand, silt, and mud generated during the deepening of the port channels in the 1980s and 1990s. This process merged the existing Candle Island and Ramanthuruth with the southern part of Vallarpadam Island, creating approximately 300 acres of land for future development. Vallarpadam, along with the neighbouring Mulavukad and Bolgatty, are part of a picturesque cluster of islands situated to the north of the port's navigational channels. This entire area is renowned for its stunning lagoons, estuaries, and the Periyar River system that flows into the expansive Vembanad Lake before joining the Arabian Sea.

Vallarpadam Church: A Symbol of Interfaith Harmony

The magnificent Vallarpadam Church, also known as the Shrine Basilica of Our Lady of Ransom, stands overlooking the ICTT site. Considering that this major pilgrimage centre attracts devotees from various parts of India and around the world, Cochin Port had helped build a direct approach connectivity to the church. The church, affectionately called Vallarpadathamma, has a history that spans over five centuries. The image of Mary and the Infant Jesus, installed at the top of the main altar of the Basilica, is believed to have been brought to the region by Portuguese missionaries who arrived in Cochin with Vasco da Gama. The original Chapel of the Holy Spirit, established by the missionaries in 1524, is thought to have been washed away during the massive flood of 1676.

According to a legend, an image of Mary and Jesus once adorned a chapel in the region. This sacred image was mysteriously found floating in the Vembanad backwaters and brought to the attention of the Dewan or Prime Minister of Cochin, Paliyath Raman Valiyachan. A devout and respectful individual, he got the image retrieved from the water, recognising its religious significance. It was Valiyachan who donated a parcel of land for the construction of the Vallarpadam Church. His generous act led to the building of the current Basilica, which stands as a symbol of religious unity and tolerance in Kerala. The Basilica has since become a major pilgrimage centre for Christians and a place of reverence for people from other faiths as well. As a gesture of goodwill and respect for the church, Valiyachan also gifted a *keda vilakku*, or perpetual lamp, to the church. This lamp has been kept burning continuously for centuries, symbolising the eternal flame of harmony, love, and respect among different faiths in Kerala.

The story of the Vallarpadam Church and the role played by Paliyath Raman Valiyachan in its establishment beautifully highlights Kerala's age-old tradition of harmonious living. Across the ages, Hindus, Christians, Muslims, Parsees, Jews, people from various races and subnationalities have peacefully coexisted in this region in brotherhood, respecting one another's beliefs and customs. The perpetual lamp at the church stands as a symbol of Kerala's rich history of religious accommodation and a reminder of the importance of nurturing understanding and respect among diverse communities.

This spirit of unity is deeply ingrained in Kerala's social fabric, where shared festivals, traditions, and celebrations often transcend religious boundaries. It is common to see Muslims and Christians actively participating in Hindu festivals, just as Hindus join in the joyous celebrations of Eid and Christmas with equal fervour. The state's legacy of interfaith dialogue, cultural exchange, and a steadfast commitment to communal harmony stands as an inspiring model, demonstrating that diversity and cultural pluralism can be a wellspring of strength rather than division.

2

CLEANING THE COBWEBS

Turbulence and Catharsis

Cochin Port is no stranger to labour unrest and strife. The labour movement at the port is deeply embedded in the region's sociocultural fabric, having played a pivotal role in the 1953 *Chappa Samaram* (Chappa Strike),[1] where workers united against and succeeded in dismantling the existing oppressive and exploitative systems. A certain culture of labour activism has always persisted since, which continues to shape the port's industrial relations. During my tenure as Chairman, substantial chunks of my time had to be devoted to dealing with trade unions and managing labour-related issues. This required a careful balance between constructive engagement and conflict

1. The Chappa Strike was a landmark labour movement in the history of Cochin Port that became a symbol of the struggle against an unjust labour system. The term "*Chappa*" refers to metal tokens that were tossed to casual labourers to determine who would get work for the day. This highly arbitrary and demeaning practice allowed contractors and middlemen to exercise control over the workforce, which led to corruption, favouritism, and poor working conditions. The strike, led by trade unions and workers, aimed to abolish the *Chappa* system and introduce a fair and transparent employment process. It became one of the most significant labour uprisings in Kerala, marking the rise of organised labour at Cochin Port and setting the stage for broader labour reforms across the region.

resolution—it would take an entire chapter to capture some of its complexities and nuances.

This chapter looks into the difficult labour and industrial relations at Cochin Port. It reflects on some of the deeply entrenched practices, rigid political ideologies, vested and engrained interests, and some undesirable and unacceptable customs. Addressing these issues and ushering in change required determined efforts to confront harsh realities and adopt a balanced strategy to manage resistance to change. It was a challenging journey for all of us, involving some painful processes of cleansing and reform.

This chapter recounts the collective efforts of port workers, senior officials, trade unions, business partners, and other stakeholders in their shared mission to eradicate illegal and undesirable practices within the system. Each attempt to confront disruptive and illicit activities or dismantle long-standing negative or undesirable practices inevitably provoked resistance, often in the form of labour strikes. In spite of proactive actions by the management, labour tensions persisted throughout my tenure, leading to prolonged strikes, sporadic picketing, and sympathetic wildcat work stoppages. However, despite intense political pressure, simmering anger, and mounting frustration, the port team remained unwavering in its commitment to the reform agenda and refused to budge.

As difficult as this period was, it was also a time of upheaval, catharsis, and organisational change. Ultimately, the unions understood and appreciated the need for change, often giving in and making amends. A notable strength of the Cochin Port unions was their ultimate commitment to the organisation's well-being and their willingness to embrace change once convinced, albeit often following initial and, at times prolonged, resistance. Ultimately, cleansing the organisation of past hangovers and cobwebs was seen as a win-win for workers, stakeholders, and the organisation itself. I now understand that the era of persistent strikes and work stoppages is behind us—for which Cochin Port trade unions deserve full credit. Looking back, I see this as a turning point in the history of the port. Despite the difficulties and excruciating exchanges, I feel fortunate to have been a witness to it all.

Labour Rights are Sacrosanct

The principles of freedom of association and collective bargaining reflect a recognition of human dignity and serve as essential enablers for fostering mutually beneficial collaboration between workers and employers. The right of employees to bargain collectively is steeped in our democratic traditions and our constitutional commitment to social justice. It plays a crucial role in protecting workers from exploitation, discrimination, and harassment. Recognising these rights and responsibilities is crucial not only for promoting productivity, industrial peace, and economic growth but also for ensuring that the consequent fruits are equitably shared.

Kerala's Saga of Securing Workers' Rights

> *Kerala's achievements in land reforms, education, healthcare and distributive justice, have been held up as a model for other States as a shining example in social development and justice...*
> *—Amartya Sen*[2]

A remarkable achievement of Kerala over the years has been its impressive social progress and respect for human dignity. Scholars attribute this to the state's highly literate and politically aware population, which has created an enlightened and participatory political process.

Kerala's labour unionisation movement, which began in the 1920s and 1930s, did much good to the state. The influence of labour in the state is considered significant, as workers wield substantial bargaining power, contributing to the state's forward-thinking approach. Over the years, the state has implemented progressive

2. Amartya Sen, *The Idea of Justice* (Penguin Books, 2010). See also Jean Drèze and Amartya Sen, *An Uncertain Glory: India and its Contradictions* (Princeton University Press, 2013).

labour policies to ensure fair treatment of workers. These include the effective enforcement of laws relating to minimum wages, the regulation of working hours, the provision of social security schemes, and the protection of the right to unionise. Kerala has also implemented various initiatives to empower marginalised workers, promote gender equality, and encourage education and skill development. As a result, the state has seen improvements in workplace safety, better regulation of working hours, the assurance of fair wages, and a rise in unionisation rates. Despite criticism of its relatively high labour costs, Kerala's labour policies have been instrumental in advancing worker welfare and promoting social justice in the state.

Kerala's labour-friendly policies have remained consistent over time, regardless of whether the ruling government is led by the left-leaning Left Democratic Front (LDF) or the Congress-led United Democratic Front (UDF). Successive state governments have supported labour movements by providing platforms for collective bargaining to secure fair wages, benefits, and job security. They have also championed workers' rights, strengthened safety regulations, and introduced social welfare initiatives such as healthcare benefits and education programmes. As a result, even unskilled labourers in Kerala enjoy significantly higher wages and better working conditions compared to their counterparts in other Indian states. This enduring commitment to social reform, driven by the principles of equity and fairness, has become a defining feature of Kerala's unique sociopolitical landscape. It is heartening to see that these principles have shaped the policies and governance decisions of both the LDF and UDF, affirming that no single political party can claim exclusive patent ownership of these principles.

While unionisation initially brought positive changes to Kerala, the aggressive nature of its trade unionism eventually led to detrimental consequences. Over time, hyperactive union activity—marked by frequent strikes and *hartals*—inflicted tremendous harm. Thus, militant trade unionism became a bane to the state's economic progress, perpetrating a negative reputation for being a 'labour problem state'. Many scholars and commentators have directly attributed Kerala's sluggish industrialisation and limited employment generation to the dominance of aggressive trade union politics that prevailed in the state. The culture of frequent strikes, protests, and work stoppages unleashed by hard-line trade unions in the State had stymied economic activity and industrial operations, resulting in decreased productivity and efficiency. Such instability had instilled fear among investors, deterring them from expanding their businesses. Consequently, the state witnessed a migration of labour-intensive manufacturing industries to neighbouring states, leading to a slowdown in industrial development and employment generation. The confrontational approach of certain trade unions had created an atmosphere of uncertainty and mistrust, seriously impeding the state's industrial and economic growth.

Cochin Port: The Crucible of Labour Movements in the State

The labour dynamics at Cochin Port have, in many ways, mirrored Kerala's own developmental challenges and policy dilemmas. Striking a balance between protecting labour interests and long-term progress has consistently remained a complex predicament. This tension has contributed to negative perceptions, some warranted, but many unjustified. Likewise, Cochin Port has long grappled with a similar labour conundrum. Unfavourable views of Kerala's labour situation have also affected Cochin Port, impacting its capacity to attract business over the years. To some degree, both the State of Kerala and Cochin Port have had to bear the cost and consequences resulting from the transference of negative perceptions about each other. In the following sections, I will provide specific examples of how these negative perceptions have manifested on various occasions and in different settings, and how they have adversely affected Cochin Port's business and growth. Unfortunately, any discussions about negative perceptions can unsettle many people, but I believe that such realities will not go away unless they are openly acknowledged and addressed directly.

In spite of the prevalent perceptions, I was firmly convinced that the port's management, its progressive employees, and trade unions could work together to break the vicious cycle of pessimism. Cochin Port had the potential to contribute significantly to Kerala's economic growth by leveraging its strategic location and modern infrastructure. Such a triumph of our collective strengths would be possible only if all stakeholders came together in the larger public interest, discarding outdated and counterproductive political doctrines and practices.

I took up my responsibilities, fully energised and optimistic about clinching that elusive balance. I believed it was possible to earn the trust of the workers and, together, work towards fostering a more business-friendly environment. My aim was to make sure that investors are provided with transparent, efficient processes, enable fair enforcement of labour laws, and establish a dialogue with labour unions to address their concerns, promoting a more collaborative relationship between port users, labour, and the port management. Some of my friends, genuinely concerned about what they saw as my naiveté and what they perceived as a disconnect from reality, could not help but laugh at my optimism!

A Word about the Governance Structure

The governance of major ports is primarily overseen by the Ministry of Shipping, which formulates policies and regulations. These ports enjoy significant autonomy in day-to-day administration and decision-making, allowing them to modernise infrastructure, improve efficiency, and enhance competitiveness in the global maritime sector. Like other major ports, the Cochin Port Trust is governed by a Board of Trustees, comprising representatives from Central and state governments—mostly senior IAS officers—officers representing the railways, customs, Coast Guard, Indian Navy, various chambers of commerce, BPCL Kochi Refinery, Cochin Special Economic Zone, as well as two representatives of the port's largest trade unions. Indeed, this diverse representation brings a wealth of expertise and experience.

The senior management team of the Cochin Port Trust is led by the Chairman, Deputy Chairman and the Heads of various administrative and operational departments (HoDs). These include the Traffic Manager, who oversees cargo handling and commercial operations; the Chief Engineer, responsible for civil engineering, infrastructure, and development projects; the Financial Advisor and Chief Accounts Officer, who manage financial planning, accounting, and budgeting; the Chief Mechanical Engineer, who supervises mechanical and electrical operations; and the Chief Medical Officer, who heads the port's 150-bed hospital and health services. The Secretary is responsible for administrative and labour-related matters and also serves as the Secretary of the Port Trust Board. The Deputy Conservator and Harbour Master ensure navigational safety, oversee marine operations, and safeguard environmental conservation. The senior management team works cohesively and collaboratively to ensure the port's day-to-day operations and strategies.

Discovering Employee Excellence

The port is managed by a dedicated team of professional and administrative officers and staff, including managers, finance professionals, engineers, technical staff, and marine personnel, who oversee infrastructure maintenance and vessel navigation. Specialised marine personnel operate the port's flagship dredger *MV Nehru Shatabdi*, tugboats, and mooring crafts, ensuring smooth port operations and safety, while pilots expertly guide incoming and outgoing ships. Supporting this complex ecosystem are the administrative staff, specialised personnel across various technical departments, cargo handling staff, and dockworkers—who constitute the largest component of the workforce.

During my early interactions with colleagues, I soon realised that the strength of Cochin Port as an organisation was its strong base of highly committed and dedicated employees, with a strong sense of work ethic and loyalty. In my interactions with the staff, I saw this permeating presence of brilliance, perseverance, and dedication. My task was easier with a strong team and together, even the most difficult aims looked easily achievable. I quickly sensed the underlying energy and enthusiasm within much of the workforce. It was clear that the average staff member and worker genuinely desired a transformation and shared in the excitement surrounding the implementation of the mega infrastructure projects, and were willing to work hard to make it a reality. This collective eagerness to usher in change and seeing their dedication and readiness to contribute, fuelled my own determination to push forward, knowing that the workforce was aligned with the vision of a modernised, thriving port. Their commitment became a source of motivation, reminding me that true transformation is driven by people who believe in it.

The Real Changemakers

In times when an organisation plans to bring about systemic changes, it becomes essential to inspire every member to assume the role of a changemaker. Transformative projects demand collective effort, and when each individual feels empowered and motivated to contribute, the momentum for progress grows exponentially. Engaging staff at all levels fosters a sense of ownership, responsibility, and shared vision, ensuring that changes are not merely implemented from the top. When employees see themselves as active participants in the change process, they become more adaptable, innovative, and committed to success. This collective mindset is crucial for overcoming challenges, maintaining morale, and ultimately achieving the organisation's long-term goals.

Most employees exhibited personal integrity, took their responsibilities seriously, and maintained a positive attitude. The energy and personal commitment on the part of some of our staff were truly inspiring. These persons ensured that daily targets were met and policies as well as projects were implemented on time. In this robust work culture, it became easy for me to communicate the vision of developing the mega projects on the agenda as well as rebuilding the port infrastructure and securing their commitment. Recognising the importance of an effective communication strategy, efforts were made to engage port workers and staff at various levels, customers, and port users, securing the buy-in of all stakeholders. Deputy Secretary Unnikrishnan Nair helped me in developing and implementing a communication strategy that effectively reached out to different sections of stakeholders.

One of our earliest strategies was to promote a culture of transparency and accessibility of employees with all echelons of the management. Workers were free to meet me anytime, be it to air a grievance or to communicate a suggestion. All HoDs were also encouraged to follow the policy. Right from the initial days, I began receiving letters and messages from the staff, suggesting what improvements were called for. I reached out to those who wrote to me personally and in confidence, and found that many had valuable and innovative ideas and suggestions to share along with understandable expectations. It quickly became clear that encouraging open and transparent communication between management and staff would be the way forward.

Interaction with Workers on the Shop Floor

As part of our commitment to improving working conditions, enhancing workers' safety, and ensuring better treatment, the HoDs and I made it a priority to regularly interact with employees at the shop floor. These interactions included discussions on their working environment, facilities, and job-related issues, which helped us to identify areas for improvement and implement corrective actions. Through these conversations, we gathered numerous valuable ideas for enhancing working conditions, boosting productivity, and modernising work practices. Ensuring the health and well-being of workers was a key component of labour reforms that we pursued, implementing a series of measures to reduce the risk of accidents and injuries in the workplace. The workers were genuinely pleased to have the opportunity to regularly communicate with the chairman and the HoDs. These personal interactions not only made the workers feel valued and heard but also allowed them to directly share their insights and concerns about their working conditions. Our willingness to engage in open discussions on job-related matters and act on the feedback we received was met with much appreciation.

Meeting with Political Leaders and Stakeholders

Given the intricacies of the political terrain, I was aware of the importance of building relationships and rapport with trade unions and political leaders as well as members of civil society. I had personal acquaintances among many political leaders from Kerala during my previous tenures at Delhi. I was hopeful that such pre-existing familiarity would help. Cultivating positive relationships and earning the trust of leaders across the political spectrum were paramount to maintaining industrial harmony and peace at the port. This would enable us to focus on the core objective of streamlining systems and processes, while also prioritising the mega infrastructure projects we were to embark upon.

One of the strategies considered to build rapport was to make proactive efforts to meet informally with as many political and trade union leaders as possible. These relationships would save the day on many occasions. Despite my differing views with some of them on many counts, I developed amicable ties with several trade union leaders over time. The most influential union leader of Cochin Port was Vayalar Ravi, a senior leader of the Indian National Congress, and a powerful minister of the Union Cabinet. I made it a point to meet him during my visits to Delhi. He was a patient listener and treated me with kindness whenever we met in the initial days, although subsequently he would become very critical of my "policeman's approach". His deputy, P.M. Mohammed Haneef, the working president of the Cochin Port Staff Association (CPSA), was effusive and cheerful, always friendly with me, at least when he was not in the *samara pandal*.[3]

---

3. *Samara pandals* are temporary tent-like structures set up by labour unionists during strikes and protests. These serve as rallying points where striking workers gather to demonstrate solidarity, engage in discussions, deliver speeches, and raise slogans advocating their demands.

Calling on the then Chief Minister Oommen Chandy and seeking his support was another top priority. Known for his affable nature and accessibility, Chandy was respected across party lines, widely recognised for his passion and tireless efforts toward Kerala's economic growth and his deep commitment to improving the quality of life for its people. He was kind, reassuring, and very forthcoming during our meetings. Given that some of the most influential trade unions of Cochin Port were affiliated with the Indian National Congress, I sought the support of other senior Congress leaders as well. Union Defence Minister A.K. Antony too promised his full support. Despite holding such a high office and his seniority, he was always approachable, friendly, and empathetic. In the days that followed, I would often rely on the Defence Minister's help, particularly in securing the assistance of the Southern Naval Command to manage port operations during the frequent strikes by the port's marine workers. I had developed good relationships with successive chiefs of the Southern Naval Command, and each one of them consistently lent support to Cochin Port, especially during strike-induced crises. However, this support was abruptly cut off when, under pressure from trade union leaders, A.K. Antony intervened, severing this vital lifeline. I shall recount details of this event later in this chapter. During this period, I also briefed many senior Congress leaders like Ramesh Chennithala, K.C. Venugopal, Kodikkunnil Suresh, M.M. Hassan, and others.

The Communist Party of India-Marxist (CPM) wielded substantial influence over Cochin Port's trade unions. It was imperative for me to engage with the party's top brass as well as with the leadership at various levels. It is commonly observed—perhaps not without reason—that the CPM tends to more actively promote industrial peace while in power than when in the opposition! In the days to come, it was through the active support of the CPM-led government, its ministers and leaders that the port was able to effectively deal with some toxic trade union practices.

One of my top priorities was to meet the senior-most CPM leaders of the state, like V.S. Achuthanandan and Pinarayi Vijayan.

Both were staunch proponents of the state's economic development and expressed genuine concern about the challenges confronting the port. V.S. Achuthanandan, who served as the Chief Minister of Kerala from 2006 to 2011, played a crucial role in resolving several contentious issues, which I will elaborate on later. Pinarayi Vijayan, who would later become Chief Minister, was guarded in the beginning, but later lent support to some of our initiatives. The then Home Minister and senior CPM leader, Kodiyeri Balakrishnan, was always sympathetic and extended all help, including cooperation from the police department. Several CPM leaders and ministers, such as Elamaram Kareem and P.K. Gurudasan, were supportive of efforts to clean up the system. I also enjoyed friendly relations with many CPM leaders, several of whom I had known since my college days.

Some of the CPM leaders and trade union activists were suspicious of our intentions in the beginning, but eventually relented and began supporting us. I made some attempts to meet M.M. Lawrence, the prominent trade union and senior CPM leader, but he did not respond. Eventually, I sought the assistance of a journalist friend in *Deshabhimani*, the CPM newspaper, who took me across to meet M.M. Lawrence. Our subsequent meetings were more cordial, although he frequently expressed dissatisfaction over how I conducted the affairs of the port, insinuating that I lacked adequate sensitivity to the trade unions. CPI general secretary Kanam Rajendran, widely known for his balanced approach, was an influential politician of Kerala, who was consistently supportive.

I frequently interacted with Chandran Pillai, CPM Member of Parliament in the Rajya Sabha, who also headed the CPM-led Cochin Port Employees' Organisation (CPEO). We would frequently engage in long and stimulating conversations. I received invaluable support from C.D. Nandakumar, the CPEO leader on the site. Both P.M. Mohammed Haneef and C.D. Nandakumar were members of the Cochin Port Board of Trustees and they encouraged our developmental initiatives. Even some of the leaders against whom I took strong disciplinary action became friends subsequently, like Bharatiya Mazdoor Sangh (BMS)'s K.K. Vijayan. By and large, the BMS supported management policies even when the other unions fiercely opposed us. The BMS, however, had a limited presence and influence those days. There were numerous other trade unions and their leaders who were generally friendly at a personal level. Abdul Aziz, a customs house agent and a very pious, religious person, used to help in establishing communications with some of the recalcitrant union leaders during times of industrial unrest.

Reaching out to civil society leaders and respected voices was a priority. I regularly interacted with editors, journalists, lawyers, former judges, bureaucrats, and academics. This approach helped me gain insight and guidance on critical issues. I frequently consulted P.C. Cyriac, a retired IAS officer and former chief secretary of Tamil Nadu, known for his independent, fearless stance on public affairs. One of the most respected figures I had the privilege to meet occasionally was the venerable Justice V.R. Krishna Iyer, the revered patriarch of social justice and a tireless champion of human rights. During times of uncertainty or when faced with complex issues, I sought solace in his inspiration and guidance. Despite his advancing age and declining health, he remained intellectually active and agreed to meet with me whenever I reached out. While he often expressed his reservations about the "dark side of neoliberalism", he believed in the necessity of positive labour reform. On one occasion, he even visited Willingdon Island as our chief guest to release one of our publications.

Periodic Meetings with Trade Unions and Port's Business Partners

To achieve and sustain industrial peace and growth, it was crucial to balance the interests of various stakeholders, including labour unions, port operators, and the diverse array of port users. While these interests might appear conflicting, they were ultimately mutually reinforcing, and a careful navigation of policies could help to reconcile them. With this in view, we began a series of joint meetings with trade unions and the port's business partners. The meetings with trade union leaders progressed well, at least in the initial days. Frequent meetings between trade union leaders and the port management helped in understanding each other better and to alleviate potential industrial tensions by allowing both parties to express their concerns in a constructive manner.

This was also the time when we were putting together our ambitious plans for implementation of the large infrastructure and modernisation projects of the port. While these projects were mostly at the conceptual or in the early stages of implementation, there was already a palpable sense of excitement. I regularly engaged with union leaders to discuss the management's vision for these initiatives. Obviously, without the support of employees and trade unions, none of these projects could take off. Indeed, involving port unions in these early discussions provided valuable suggestions beneficial to both the port and its workers. Regular communication and collaboration between management and trade unions was seen to foster a more productive and harmonious work environment.

Despite such initial bonhomie, however, I would soon discover that dealing with some of the union leaders could be emotionally exhausting, and progress was slow. At times when I was on the brink of losing my patience, I would remind myself that I should be more patient and persistent, considering that building good relationships would take time.

The Quest for Trust

From the outset, the port management embarked on a series of strategic initiatives aimed at cultivating trust-building between the management, employees, trade unions, and port's business partners. While the average employee was receptive to our efforts, gaining the confidence of trade unions was a more knotty task. To foster a positive relationship and an atmosphere of trust, the port management embarked on a policy of transparently sharing relevant information about the port's operations, finances, and future plans. We always made it a point to respond to all feedback and concerns from employees and union representatives. It was also our endeavour to establish consistent policies and procedures that were fair and equitable for all employees, regardless of their union affiliation, based on the belief that demonstrating a commitment to treating all workers fairly and impartially would foster trust.

Trust-building became the central agenda in all our communication and outreach strategies. As a matter of policy, all senior officers would proactively listen, showing respect for the dignity of the individual, recognising the rights of workers, always taking care not to take any discriminatory actions. With a view to creating a positive working relationship, the management made all efforts to adopt a collaborative approach to working with unions, seeking to identify areas of mutual interest and to find solutions.

In an industrial environment, disagreements and disputes between management and unions were inevitable. It was always our effort to establish clear and effective processes for resolving conflicts in a timely and fair manner, which was expected to help prevent trivial disputes from escalating and damaging the relationship between the management and unions. The port's secretary, Cyril George, was exclusively in charge of this responsibility, while also participating in tripartite fora between labour commissioners, trade unions, and the management.

This policy of building trust paid off well, especially in the first few months. Even during periods of unrest, an atmosphere of mutual understanding and respect largely prevailed among the union leaders. However, while trust is the cornerstone of harmony, it also serves as kindling for those who are always looking for a spark to start a fire. There were frequent attempts to undermine this trust through the spread of false narratives and claims.

So, how did the industrial situation begin to deteriorate?

The Elusive Synergy Between Unions and Port Management

Trade unions often present a continual clash of interests between "management" and "workers", creating a perception of perpetual conflict between the two. Some of our trade unions remained deeply influenced by outdated philosophies, their perspectives frozen in time and out of sync with contemporary realities.

On the positive side, such rhetoric can foster stronger worker solidarity. When employees feel empowered by having their interests represented by a union, it often leads to more equitable labour practices. Thus, in sectors where profit-making is the primary objective, maintaining a clear distinction between "workers" and "management" underscores the importance of collective bargaining and helps ensure the workers' rights and interests are effectively advocated.

However, in a public sector organisation engaged in public service—where employee remunerations and benefits are protected by well-established norms—the situation may be somewhat different. The unrelenting narrative of an adversarial relationship between management and workers, along with fabricated tales of worker exploitation appears out of place in the context of a government-run institution. In fact, such rhetoric has contributed to an entrenched adversarial mindset, making it difficult for workers and management to find common ground.

I often pointed out to trade union leaders how clinging to this outdated conflict-driven approach was lowering morale, hindering constructive dialogue and collaboration between workers and management, and even stifling innovation and productivity.

Based on these beliefs, I began urging union leaders to stop referring to management and workers as separate and opposing entities. I emphasised that such boundaries needed to be dissolved, especially at a time when every employee was expected to see themselves as a changemaker and to collaborate willingly as part of a motivated team. Above all, it was crucial for both employers and unions to work together to create a positive and inspiring work environment for the success of the entire organisation.

Expectations of organisational change and building a better future were in the air. Our aim was to bring about positive transformation by creating a new environment based on mutual respect, compassion, empathy, and trust. It was always our endeavour to respect union leaders, acknowledging them as representatives of the workforce and their concerns. For managers, maintaining transparency and receptiveness was crucial, as was attentively listening to the concerns of their subordinates and union representatives. Managers were expected to cultivate genuine empathy, striving to understand the perspectives of union leaders and the workers they represented. Such an approach was necessary in the context of the transformations that we were embarking upon. Importantly, the establishment of trust was deemed paramount.

Unfortunately, a section of the union leaders who believed that management and workers were destined to remain in perpetual conflict, did not agree to such a "preposterous" proposition. One union leader even joked that too much trust between management and workers might put all of them out of a job!

The Rhetoric of Victimhood

On the first day I landed in Cochin Port, I came across large billboards portraying the workers as being exploited by the port management. A sense of mistrust and animosity between workers and management seemed to be already in the air. On enquiry, I was told that there were no major, outstanding issues of contention. While conflicts and disagreements do arise from time to time, both workers' unions and management have been working together towards common goals such as improving productivity.

At the same time, the rhetoric about "exploitation of workers" by management and "denial of workers' rights" remained very much in the air. Apart from billboards and wall posters, the unions periodically circulated leaflets and publications that alleged different forms of denial of workers' rights by the management. As is wont in our political culture, it was normal to make personal attacks and character assassination of individual officials in the management. I could not believe that in a state like Kerala where people are aware of their rights, there could be such large-scale exploitation of workers and violations of labour rights, that too, at the hands of a public sector management, but I kept an open mind and decided to study and explore this.

It soon became clear that such rhetoric was merely one of the routine tactics some unions employed to stay competitive. With dozens of trade unions locked in fierce rivalry, many resorted to competitive sloganeering to attract attention. This approach helped build a sense of solidarity and support among members and constituents, and was occasionally used to highlight specific issues.

However, only a few unions had the organisational strength, the ability to identify real issues, negotiate effectively and deliver tangible benefits to workers.Many others focused on posturing and disrupting work, often relying on unrealistic promises or claims. This created a sense of hostility towards the administration, thereby undermining the overall morale and productivity of the workforce.

Within days of my arrival in Cochin, I became aware of the complexities of the relationship between workers' unions and management. So, I decided to work towards building cooperation and mutual understanding. I firmly believed that the interests of labour and administration were not necessarily mutually exclusive, and that they need not always be in conflict with each other. Investing in labour could lead to a more positive work environment and greater productivity, whereas neglecting workers' interests risked social unrest and disruption—both of which would be detrimental to the port's functioning and its overall health. A major consideration, especially in the context of the ambitious infrastructure projects we were embarking upon, was that cultivating an atmosphere of team spirit and mutual trust would be crucial.

An Antenna to Detect Wrongdoings

As a professional police officer with intelligence training, detecting and investigating wrongful or undesirable practices came naturally to me. So, it did not take long to understand the underlying reasons behind the façade of a number of industrial disputes and the "direct action" taken by certain persons claiming to represent workers' interests. I began getting valuable feedback from employees and members of the port-user community, who were often the best source of relevant information. Many employees were willing to openly share information in the broader interest of the organisation. These led to the unearthing of unbelievable levels of extortion and questionable labour practices that had been bleeding the port over the years, resulting in significant revenue loss and serious damage to its reputation. In the pages that follow, I shall provide more details about the specifics of these undesirable practices. I will also outline the strategies and actions undertaken by the port administration to effectively address and ultimately eliminate these issues.

Soon enough, it became apparent that numerous illicit practices were thriving under the guise of trade union activity. It was evident that for the greater good of the organisation and the public, it would be necessary to clean up the system, even if such action would be unpopular or involved the disruption of certain long-standing norms. I was aware that such a course of action would entail challenging the interests of powerful individuals or groups. However, it was crucial to adhere to ethical policies to ensure a fair and just workplace for all employees.

The Leadership Dilemma

How does one make a leadership decision when faced with two clear alternatives: one easy and comfortable, the other difficult and painful? The path of least resistance would be to maintain the status quo, to turn a blind eye, allow things to continue as they are, and not to rock the boat. The difficult choice, of course, would involve confronting the illegal practices head-on, and taking decisive action to cleanse the system, even if it would mean trampling upon some powerful toes. This path, however, was also bound to result in painful consequences like work disruptions and debilitating industrial unrest. The real question then became: What was more important—sustaining industrial peace, or opting for a painful surgery to remove the growing tumours of undesirable practices once and for all?

Obviously, upholding ethical standards and to take resolute action to address the illegal or corrupt practices would be paramount. Failure to do so would result in continued damage to the credibility of the organisation, continued erosion of business, and long-term harm to employees and stakeholders. When faced with a leadership dilemma of this kind, the leadership choice would need to be based on a careful assessment of the potential consequences of different courses of action.

The HoDs at the port supported the idea of a thorough reform initiative and the need to foster ethical, responsible conduct within the organisation while minimising harm to employees and stakeholders. However, they counselled me to judiciously weigh the potential risks and benefits of different approaches and to consider the long-term implications. Interestingly, even some union leaders were privately supportive of the difficult choice, endorsing the necessity for change.

The Elusiveness of Discipline

My first encounter with the strike culture occurred just weeks after my joining the port, when one fine morning, I was jolted by a sudden outburst of slogans and angry voices outside my sixth floor office room. I was intrigued as I could not think of any unresolved issue that could have triggered this uproar. I was counselled by my staff that this was only a routine demonstration and that I should ignore it. However, I found it unacceptable to tolerate such unruly behaviour inside the office, especially in the absence of any provocation. I promptly issued orders suspending the four individuals who were leading the uproar. Little did I anticipate the storm that would follow. Over the next two days, the entire port was engulfed in a strike, as tensions escalated and repercussions reverberated.

Having spent my entire professional life as a policeman, my approach towards unruly behaviour and disruptions was likely different from the prevailing norm and understandably unacceptable to many. In the days that followed, I would receive tons of advice from my colleagues, friends, and even senior trade union leaders not to "behave like a policeman". But I was perhaps too impatient and had a very low threshold of tolerance. What truly unsettled me were the phone calls from an important minister and a couple of other powerful political leaders, asking me to ignore what they described was "genuine expressions of legitimate union activity" and not to take drastic action. I respectfully explained the situation to them, but when the minister was insistent, I had to politely ask him not to interfere.

Strikes: The Elixir of Life!

Although my first encounter with a strike lasted only two days, many more were to follow. Often, any attempt to enforce discipline or halt undesirable practices would trigger some form of work stoppage, ranging from *dharna*s, go-slow or work-to-rule strikes, wildcat strikes, flash strikes, *hartal*s, lorry transport bans, drivers' strikes, and other solidarity strikes. These were not always instigated by the major unions—external entities like transporters' unions could also initiate actions that caused significant disruptions. Fortunately, in most cases, the majority of port staff remained loyal and continued working despite the constraints. Thus, while the Cochin Port teams managed to maintain productivity, the culture of strikes inevitably created inefficiencies in workflow. They undoubtedly resulted in the diversion of time and energy that could have been invested in more efforts of value. Ultimately, while the port team succeeded in completing all large infrastructure projects on time and without significant cost overruns, the reality remains that the port could have been even more productive had these strikes not occurred. The strikes introduced added layers of complexities that the organisation had to manage, impeding its ability to fully capitalise on the momentum and reaching its maximum potential.

At every stage, however, I believed that confronting each strike head-on was in the organisation's long-term interests. It was better to put an end to undesirable practices than to allow festering issues to worsen over time. In hindsight, I might even lay claim to the dubious distinction of having presided over the highest number of strikes, marked by unprecedented waves of labour unrest and militancy during this period. An unrelentingly ruthless and uncompromising approach certainly played its part. More on this in the coming pages.

How Many Are Too Many?

While the right to form unions is inviolable, it is equally important to consider how many employees should be engaged in full-time or part-time union activities. Naturally, there must be enough union leaders to effectively perform essential functions, such as negotiating with management, organising collective actions, and communicating with members. Ideally, the appropriate balance between union leaders and the broader workforce should be determined through a democratic process that genuinely reflects the needs and aspirations of the employees. At the same time, union leaders must also be able to fulfill their official duties and responsibilities. However, an excessively large number of full-time union office-bearers would undermine the very purpose of efficient representation and responsible functioning.

But then, how many are too many? The number of employees identifying themselves as full-time or part-time "union leaders" and "office bearers" was substantial. The presence of an unspecified number of trade unions—some officially recognised, others not; some with substantial memberships, others with very negligible subscribership; and all competing for space and attention—pointed to a high level of labour activism and advocacy, which had both positive and negative impacts on the operations of the organisation. While an optimum level of union activity is essential for safeguarding workers' interests, the proliferation of unions with a disproportionate number of office-bearers could negatively impact productivity and overall job performance.

An Unwelcome Visit to a Union Office

The land area of the port is spread over approximately 2,177 acres of land situated across Willingdon Island, Vallarpadam, Puthuvypeen, Fort Kochi, and other areas. It is customary for the port chairman and HoDs to make regular visits to these lands, buildings, and various port facilities that remain scattered over such a vast area. Along with other senior officers, I used to walk across these lands and inspect the progress of projects and spend time with port officials and workers in the field to understand their problems and get their suggestions. These visits played a vital role in closely monitoring projects and overseeing the port's day-to-day operations. One of those visits, however, generated much consternation, noise, and heat.

During one of our field inspections, we were in the process of identifying suitable locations for the installation of CCTV cameras and biometric attendance capturing devices as well as assessing access control options to office buildings. This was a crucial step in the implementation of the Enterprise Resource Planning (ERP) project, which mandated the deployment of these devices to streamline attendance tracking processes. The inspection team consisted of the secretary of the Port Cyril George, overseeing port administration, and leading the biometric project. Chief Engineer J. Karthikeyan provided civil engineering expertise, Chief Mechanical and Electrical Engineer Niteen Borwanker was responsible for installing the biometric and CCTV infrastructure while the CISF Commandant D. Shyamala brought in the security expertise and support.

In the course of this inspection, I noticed that within the main campus of the chief engineer's office, a prime building was occupied by one of the largest and politically powerful staff associations of the port. Finding a number of persons gathered in the hall, I got curious and walked inside only to be told that it was habitual for some union members and supporters to gather there every morning after signing the attendance registers in their respective offices. This came as a shock and personally, I was disturbed that such large numbers of staffers should be wasting their working time without any official purpose.

Following this episode, I gave the instruction that the union office be walled off from the rest of the office campus, with provision for a separate entrance. This arrangement, together with a biometric employee attendance system, would bring about some semblance of attendance discipline, I thought. But it was not to be so easy. Though unplanned and unpremeditated, my unannounced visit to the union office came in for much disquiet and outrage, with all trade unions protesting vehemently and writing to the state and Central governments as well as the labour commissioners complaining about the chairman's "illegal and unauthorised" visit to the union office. Interestingly, all unions, irrespective of the colour of their flags, expressed their outrage against the "invasion" of the union office by the port chairman. In fact, protest resolutions were adopted in far-off ports like Chennai, Mumbai, Visakhapatnam, and Kolkata. Delegations went to Delhi and Thiruvananthapuram to register their remonstration and demanding action against the chairman.

The installation of the biometric attendance system had already been planned as part of the ERP-based digitisation initiative. The data collected would be utilised to calculate salaries and overtime pay. The port had no other option but to proceed with the attendance automation programme and the management did not budge. However, since the biometric devices were spread geographically across multiple offices and areas of the port, there were numerous attempts to tamper with them and the

CCTV cameras monitoring them. Despite these initial setbacks, the majority of the staff and workers accepted the new system, ultimately leading to its successful implementation.

The Land of *Nokku Kooli*

A controversial labour practice prevalent in Kerala is *Nokku kooli*, where headload workers, mostly affiliated with trade unions, demand wages for overseeing the unloading of goods, even if they do not perform the task themselves. Traditionally, it originated as a legitimate wage for manual labour, but it has deteriorated into a form of extortion. Efforts to reform or abolish *Nokku kooli* have faced resistance from unions. I have described the ingenious practice of *Nokku kooli* in some detail in the final chapter.

One of the most challenging missions that the port management undertook during the period was to completely eradicate these undesirable practices, which had plagued the port for many years. Shortly after assuming my role at the port, I discussed this with senior members of our team, major unions and the port's business partners. All of them vowed to rid the port of this archaic practice, as it had become one of the biggest impediments to the port's survival. We were determined to confront this head-on, but little did I know how formidable a task this would prove to be.

The practice of *Nokku kooli* was as corrupting and obstructive as it was, at times, absurdly comical. For instance, during the construction of the highway connectivity to ICTT, a local union asserted their right to be paid on a per-cubic-metre basis for work that they did not perform and was being done entirely by a dredger. The union installed its flags in the entire reclamation area, several kilometres long, and asked the contractor to halt all work. For days together, they prevented the contractor from carrying out the reclamation work, until I became aware of the tensions that had developed there. The port authorities with the help of the CISF had to intervene decisively to stop the blatant extortion. This incident is just one of the many in a long list of such ludicrous practices.

Similarly, the cement packaging plants on Willingdon Island frequently faced persistent demands for *Nokku kooli*. In recent years, taking advantage of the booming construction industry in Kerala, some top cement manufacturing companies had set up bulk cement import and packaging plants within Cochin Port. Under this scheme, cement or clinker from factories elsewhere in India or abroad is imported in bulk cement carrier ships and at the port, the cement is automatically transferred to the onshore plants for packaging and further transportation for distribution in the hinterland. The entire process is fully automated and pollution free. No manual intervention is required for unloading or packaging. As soon as the first such plant was set up in Cochin Port by Gujarat Ambuja Cements Limited, some unions smelt an opportunity and began to harass the plant executives by demanding *Nokku kooli* for the unloading and packaging of cement. When the affected parties approached me, I sent for the union leader, who said that the automatic process was an "affront" to the rights of the labour class and they would not stop until the company agreed to "compensate" the workers. The company representatives were scared and were willing to effect a compromise and make a limited payment every month. But the port management stood firm on the principle that *Nokku kooli* had no place in the port's operations. This led to multiple skirmishes outside the plant.

Even after officially ending the practice of *Nokku kooli*, I once received a late night phone call about a largish gathering of union members at a cement facility in the wee hours. They demanded that the cement company halt all operations until all the "past dues" of *Nokku kooli* were paid up. I immediately went to the site, where Additional Traffic Manager Vipin Menoth and CISF Commandant (promoted later as Senior Commandant) D. Shyamala were already there, grappling with the situation, which was ultimately brought under control. I learned that union representatives had frequently resorted to intimidating the cement companies and some *Nokku kooli* used to change hands secretly in the initial days. The cement plant managers were too apprehensive about reporting the issue to port authorities or seeking assistance from the CISF, and would often succumb to the demands. Addressing this ongoing issue required persistent efforts over several months. A dedicated task force was set up by the port's traffic department, led by Additional Traffic Manager Vipin Menoth, Deputy Traffic Manager Jimmy George, and Assistant Traffic Manager Girish Thomas, along with CISF Senior Commandant D. Shyamala. This team tackled the situation vigorously, eventually succeeding in completely eradicating the menace of *Nokku kooli* associated with cement handling.

And then, there was this *Nokku kooli* with a twist. In the early years of containerisation, manual twist locks were used to safely mount and secure containers loaded on trucks and railway rakes. In the 1980s and the 1990s, workers used to manually fix these twist locks on all four corners of the container, after they were placed on the truck or railway rakes. However, with the advent of automated twist-locking technology, the need for manual twist lock application became obsolete. But even decades after the introduction of automatic-twist locks, the workers continued to charge *Nokku kooli* for the "lost opportunity" to manually set the twist locks. Abolishing this practice resulted in frequent strikes at the container terminal, but we eventually succeeded in eradicating the twist lock *Nokku kooli*, only to realise that the real twists were waiting to surprise us elsewhere!

Kettu Kooli: The Nokku Kooli as Organised Crime

While driving through Willingdon Island, I often encountered long queues of container lorries lined up at different approach roads of the port. It appeared as if every lorry driver knew what he was required to do. He would count and hand over either Rs 200 or Rs 300, depending on whether he was carrying a 20-foot container unit or a 40-foot unit, to the union person who walked up to the lorry. Occasionally, the unionist would even issue a "receipt" to the lorry driver. Curious, I asked my driver about this practice. He explained that the union was collecting *Kettu kooli* from container lorries. Intrigued, I enquired deeper into the matter and was startled to learn that this coercive collection of a "cess" from container lorries, in the name of a certain category of workers, had been going on for more than two decades.

Historically, before the era of containerisation, labourers would manually cover lorries with tarpaulin and secure them with ropes to safeguard the cargo from rain and theft. However, the introduction of containers rendered this labour obsolete. Arguing that a certain number of workers had lost their jobs due to containerisation, and to compensate for their lost income, one of the trade unions, the Cochin Thuramukha Thozhilali Union (CTTU), began the practice of collecting fees from every cargo container passing through the port. This practice, commonly referred to as *Kettu kooli*, which began in the late 1980s, had persisted ever since. *Kettu kooli*, a variant of *Nokku kooli*, purportedly "compensated" for the hypothetical loss of work of a certain group, who were once engaged in tying up open truckloads of cargo with tarpaulins and ropes. The union felt that every cargo container that passes through the port represented a case of job loss for those workers and that it was quite ethical to demand and extort that money. The leaders claimed that the funds so collected would be deposited into the Workers' Welfare Board, which would then make payments to the "displaced" workers. Despite the fact that most of the original beneficiaries of this practice had either moved on or passed away, a group of individuals continued to extort money from every passing container lorry.

The scale of this extortion was staggering. Given the large volumes of container traffic passing through the port, the illegal extortions ran into crores of rupees. This unlawful practice was not only adding to the cost of doing business for container cargo operators but also spoke poorly of the port's administration. I was appalled by this blatant criminal activity and immediately sent for CTTU leader V.H.M. Rafeeq, demanding that they put an end to this illegal practice. Rafeeq, however, was aggressive, defiant, and unrelenting, insisting that the collections were based on a labour settlement reached sometime in the early 1990s and were completely legal. He threatened that the workers would go on strike and the entire Willingdon Island would be "set on fire" if the port management "interfered with" what he insisted was legitimate union activity.

On my part, I was certain that any practice of forcible collection of money from container lorries entering or exiting the port was clearly illegal and had to stop. Moreover, on enquiry with the Labour Department officials, we also found that there was no process of documenting the money collected, although occasionally the union would deposit small amounts with the Welfare Board, while the lion's share collected remained unaccounted for. The port could not afford to allow this to continue and I passed orders to stop the practice at once. This obviously met with stiff resistance from the CTTU leaders. Despite intense pressures from the unions as well as from some senior political leaders, the port management refused to back down. We knew that what we were fighting for was right and just, and we were determined to see it through to the end. In spite of some showdowns and muscle flexing on the part of some union activists and powerful political leaders, Cochin Port finally succeeded in fully eliminating *Kettu kooli*.

Some of the young officers and staff of the port's Traffic and Administration Departments took on the challenge, even while facing physical threats, they were driven by a resolve to fight illegal practices. The CISF personnel, under the leadership of Senior Commandant D. Shyamala, played a pivotal role in eradicating the toxic practice of *Kettu kooli*, while simultaneously maintaining order, security, and safeguarding the port's assets. Special CISF squads conducted extensive patrols along the roads of Willingdon Island, diligently watching for any gatherings or extortion attempts. Cochin Police Commissioner Manoj Abraham provided invaluable police support, adeptly managing the crowds and averting any potential harm to drivers of container lorries. The synergy between the state police's local expertise and the CISF's specialised skills in industrial security created a robust defence against any threats to law and order. Despite the initial days of resistance, the collaborative efforts of the port management, the CISF, and the state police ensured a smooth and seamless transition, completely eliminating the noxious practice of *Kettu kooli* from Cochin Port.

The repercussions were, however, far from over. The CTTU leader was furious about the loss of one of the union's lucrative extortion schemes. He openly threatened revenge and began instigating a string of strikes. Rafeeq wielded considerable influence over some of the Lorry Operators' Associations and used his sway to trigger a series of crippling strikes that resulted in a near paralysis of cargo movement in and out of the port. True to his promise, the lorry operators would go on strike ever so frequently, demanding increases in different components of the lorry tariffs, drivers' wages, and so on. However, just as we were celebrating its eradication, we soon discovered that *Kettu kooli* was only a small tip of one of the numerous icebergs! Putting an end to all forms of extortion and illegal practices was crucial for the port's survival, and the management team was determined to make it happen. Every step toward abolishing the variations of *Nokku kooli* triggered strikes, some of which lasted several days. Nevertheless, the Cochin Port team stood firm against persistent political pressure from diverse directions, and their relentless efforts ultimately resulted in the complete eradication of *Kettu kooli.*

As reports of extortion in the name of *Kettu kooli* began surfacing in the press, the issue garnered substantial public attention, while also sparking reverberations elsewhere. Union Minister Vayalar Ravi resigned from his position as president of the CTTU, stating that he was unaware of the ongoing extortion practices. He also stepped down from the formal positions he held in other labour unions at Cochin Port.

Chairman Paul Antony, who succeeded me, enforced this policy even more rigorously, and today, Cochin Port stands free from the scourge of *Nokku kooli*, although this issue still persists in many parts of the state.

The Dark Side of Cargo Operations

The physical labour of loading and unloading cargo between ships and the shore and vice versa is primarily carried out by dockworkers. In other words, the right to handle cargo in the dock area is usually reserved for registered dockworkers. Their work typically involves manual labour, such as operation of cranes and other heavy machinery, loading and unloading cargo from ships, and moving cargo within the port area. They are also responsible for securing cargo on ships and ensuring that it is properly stowed for transport. Dock labourers are assigned to work for shipping companies, stevedores, or other organisations that operate in and around ports and dockyards. The work can be physically demanding and may involve long hours, shift work, and exposure to harsh weather conditions.

Over the years, the CTTU and its top leader V.H.M. Rafeeq had effectively taken control of the labour supply function in Cochin Port, essentially acting as a labour contractor while disregarding the legal obligations related to the workers' welfare. Beyond the ethical concerns of a labour union leader also functioning as a labour supplier, the monopoly of a single labour contractor created several issues. Without competition, the contractor held immense bargaining power with consumers of labour, dictating arbitrary rates for different types of cargo and leaving labour employers with no choice but to comply. Shippers, exporters, and importers were also at the mercy of this individual, who could capriciously deny them labour supply and force them to pay exorbitant and arbitrary rates. This, in turn, made export and import activities through Cochin Port significantly more expensive.

At the same time, in the absence of competition, the dockworkers themselves were at the mercy of the union leader, with little bargaining power regarding wages and working conditions. The vast disparity between the rates charged by the union leader to the industry and the actual payouts to the workers revealed extensive profiteering. It became clear that the loading and unloading operations at the port were effectively controlled by a network of gangs of middlemen.

This mafia-like influence extended to cargo transportation as well. The union leader and his associates established an extensive extortion network that infiltrated various aspects of the port's operations. Shipping agents negotiating cargo handling rates on-board bulk cargo ships were compelled to deal with the same union leader. Any businessperson, shipper, trader, or even officials who dared to challenge his authority faced severe retaliation or were silenced. Shippers who did not fall in line were denied the ability to move their merchandise for weeks. In one instance, several trucks belonging to a rival businessman were vandalised, with acid poured into their fuel tanks. Many others suffered similar fates, their businesses ruined by the wrath of this person. Many shipping companies, import-export businesses, and stevedoring firms approached me, seeking a comprehensive solution.

Kavadam Kadathu Kooli

The same union leader had a monopolistic stranglehold on the truck operations in the port as well. Every lorry that entered or exited the port's gates was required to pay an "entry fee" amounting to Rs 2,000 to the union. Unlike the open *Kettu kooli* extortions, the *Kavadam kadathu kooli* was discreetly charged as part of the truck hire charges, making it difficult for the port authorities to stop it. Trucks hired externally or outstation trucks coming into the port were also required to make the payment at the union office that openly ran a checkpost on the main approach road to the port. The scale of these illegal activities was staggering, especially considering that every year, several lakhs of trucks passed through the port. This implied that the union could potentially amass several crores of rupees every month.

The culture of unlawful extortions had led to a significant increase in the cost of doing business at Cochin Port. This, in turn, had made it more expensive for both traders and shipping companies to conduct their operations within the port. As a consequence, several businesses opted to relocate their operations to neighbouring ports, where they would not have to pay the illegal fees.

Despite a ban by the Kerala High Court on practices like the "turn system" in container lorry hiring in July 2002, extortion from trucks had persisted for a long time. The court's orders explicitly stated that no restrictive practices should be allowed, and that trade and truck movement should not be obstructed. However, in spite of the best efforts of port authorities, these gangs had continued their extorting operations with impunity, resorting to threats and violence against any individual businessman who dared to question them.

Taking Other Unions into Confidence

Adopting a zero-tolerance stance against gangsters and musclemen became an urgent necessity not only for the port's survival but also for safeguarding its integrity, reputation, and trustworthiness. As the port launched several ambitious infrastructure projects and attracted investments from both domestic and international stakeholders, it was imperative for the port administration to send a clear and unequivocal message to the world. Equally important was the need to reassure the shipping industry that it would be protected from unlawful activities.

As a first step, we initiated a series of discussions with all the major trade unions operating within the port, which included the Cochin Port Staff Association (CPSA), Cochin Port Employees Organisation (CPEO-CITU), the Bharatiya Mazdoor Sangh (BMS), and others. All major trade unions offered their full support to the administration's endeavours to eradicate malpractices. Simultaneously, we engaged in dialogues with trade associations, shipping lines, customs house agents (CHA), and Chambers of Commerce, all of whom also pledged their support and cooperation. The top political leaders in the Congress, CPI (M), and the BJP in New Delhi and Thiruvananthapuram, who controlled the port trade unions, were also taken into confidence and they pledged their support. I also met with Union Minister Vayalar Ravi, the top leader of some of the most influential trade unions in the port, in Delhi to brief him.

Throughout the entire campaign, the media played a crucial role in highlighting the extent and reach of undesirable practices, presenting the perspectives from the trade unions, while also showcasing the authorities' efforts to clean up the system.

Revamping Security and Seeking Police Protection

As tensions continued to escalate, it became clear that an urgent, renewed strategy would be needed to curb illegal activities, despite the continuing defiance of the perpetrators. Both the CISF and the Kerala police demonstrated their unwavering commitment to maintaining security. The CISF played a pivotal role amidst alarming intelligence reports of potential violence and sabotage by providing special squads and Quick Response Teams (QRTs) for relentless patrols around the clock. The CISF team's dedication was instrumental in preventing major security incidents, ensuring peace.

The initial strategy was for the port to take direct action against the criminal activities with the assistance of the district administration, the state police, and the CISF. State Police Chief Raman Srivastava and his successor Jacob Punnoose assured us of their full support, involving the port's contingency plans to address unforeseen incidents. Chief Secretary P.J. Thomas was equally reassuring. After extensive discussions and consultations with government officials, police, and other key stakeholders, a plan was formulated to once again approach the extortionists directly with the hope of resolving the issues without further conflict.

V.H.M. Rafeeq and the other CTTU leaders, however, refused to relent. During my subsequent interactions with Rafeeq, he became even more defensive and aggressive. He held a press conference at the Ernakulam Press Club, asserting that the money he collected was being used for the "welfare of poor workers". When it was evident that he was not willing to stop the illicit activities, a request was made to the city police commissioner to deploy police forces in Willingdon Island. Police commissioners and senior officers in

Cochin, including Manoj Abraham, P. Vijayan, R. Srilekha, Vinson Paul, and K. Padmakumar, collaborated closely with the port authorities. District Collector A.P.M. Mohammed Hanish and his successor M. Beena provided consistent support from the district administration at every stage of the campaign.

Meanwhile, with the help of the CISF and the state police, the port management successfully dismantled the structures and office rooms used by the extortionists, which practically resembled an elaborate checkpost, where trucks were stopped for money collection. However, despite our initial success in establishing some control and preventing overt acts of extortion and violence, it eventually became apparent that the gang had the capacity to inflict damage on the port by continually orchestrating strikes, with operators of trucks and trailers resorting to a series of flash strikes and work stoppages.

At every step of the way, the port management took care to meticulously document each development, keeping both the Central and state governments informed. I wrote detailed reports to the shipping secretary as well as the heads of Central intelligence and investigation agencies, ensuring that they were fully apprised of all pertinent details. We also kept in close contact with the state's Chief Secretary, Home Secretary, Labour Secretary, and the state's Police Intelligence Chief.

Political Support

At this juncture, I decided to seek assistance from the political leadership, as it was clear that the port administration alone could not find lasting solutions to these complex and deeply entrenched practices without political support. It was crucial to obtain the backing of both the Congress and CPM leaders, as both parties exercised significant control over trade union activities. I must say that we received tremendous support from both parties. Union Defence Minister A.K. Antony, known for his consistent stand against corruption, assured me that he would do everything to clean up the system. Chief Minister Oommen Chandy volunteered to visit Cochin Port with Vayalar Ravi to meet with the trade unions. Vayalar Ravi himself headed some of the powerful trade unions of Cochin Port, and without his help, no lasting solutions could be found. Unfortunately, by this time, my relationship with Vayalar Ravi had cooled somewhat, and he had become increasingly critical of my style of functioning. Simultaneously, I briefed other Cochin-based people's representatives, ministers, MPs, MLAs, and other prominent politicians like Professor K.V. Thomas, K. Babu, Dominic Presentation, M.M. Laurence, Sebastian Paul, and Chandran Pillai.

Meanwhile, I requested a meeting with the newly sworn-in Chief Minister V.S. Achuthanandan, and was granted an audience at his Cliffhouse residence in Thiruvananthapuram. There, I presented the entire situation to him. He patiently listened to my briefing although initially, he appeared sceptical. Nevertheless, he asked me to meet him at the state's Secretariat the following morning. At his office, he was joined by two other ministers, Labour Minister P.K. Gurudasan and Industries Minister Elamaram Kareem. After I provided them with detailed information about the situation, the chief minister subjected me to some rigorous questioning. Eventually, he seemed convinced of the severity of the issue and tasked the two ministers with visiting Cochin Port the next day to conduct a thorough investigation and formulate a strategy. He made it unequivocally clear that no corruption, extortion, or hooliganism would be tolerated.

The rest, as they say, is history. Ministers P.K. Gurudasan and Elamaram Kareem visited the port the very next day and conducted their own inquiries. They met with numerous businesspersons, exporters, representatives from shipping companies, and other port users who shared their experiences of harassment by extortionist gangs. The ministers eventually were convinced that criminal activities were indeed taking place. They subsequently made several trips to Cochin Port, holding a series of meetings with a spectrum of stakeholders, including chambers of commerce, trade unions, the Labour Department officials, police, and revenue authorities.

Some trade union leaders and affected businesspersons themselves narrated their accounts of the situation.

The two ministers displayed exceptional diligence and attention to detail in their efforts. They were methodical and impartial, conducting exhaustive investigations with determination and relentless efforts, and the port ultimately succeeded in putting an end to the nefarious activities of the extortionists, thereby restoring order and security.

Reorganising the Labour Booking Process

While dockworkers are crucial to port operations, they are not permanent employees of the port. Instead, they constitute labour pools informally attached to the Dock Labour Department, which leaves them without the benefits and securities afforded to permanent employees. Despite working in a highly unionised environment, their precarious employment status often subjected them to uncertainties and a lack of comprehensive labour protections.

At the same time, muscle power and highhandedness on the part of some unionists resulted in other toxic consequences. Over the years, the dominance of a single union leader with monopolistic control led to numerous irregularities, including erratic and unpredictable cargo handling rates and the outright denial of labour allocations to certain business operators. These arbitrary practices placed Cochin Port at a considerable financial and operational disadvantage compared to other Indian ports and nearby international ports, resulting in inflated and unpredictable handling costs, labour exploitation, and highhandedness.

A sad consequence of the stranglehold exerted by the union leader and middlemen was the exploitation of the dockworkers themselves. Ironically, while these illegal activities thrived under the guise of benefiting labour, the workers themselves endured considerable hardships. They had little bargaining power and access to social security, making their situation increasingly precarious. Obviously, there was an urgent need for corrective measures to address these injustices and ensure fair treatment and protection for them.

With the intervention of state ministers, the district administration and the police, the port management successfully dismantled the monopolistic labour booking system. However, a reliable alternative system was necessary to safeguard workers' interests and social security, while ensuring that businesses could access labour services freely and at predictable rates. A solution was found when it was proposed to bring in the services of an existing state government entity—the Kerala Headload Workers' Welfare Board (KHWWB). The welfare board units have been technically in existence across Kerala, established under the Kerala Headload Workers' Welfare Act of 1978. While this Act itself had come up for criticism for tolerating practices like *Nokku kooli*, the KHWWB's handling of the management of the labour pools appeared to be an acceptable solution. It transpired that a KHWWB branch existed on Willingdon Island, and it was decided to leverage and repurpose the scheme for the dock labour bookings. Under this scheme, dockworkers could register with the KHWWB to join the labour pool. Businesses needing the services of dockworkers could requisition the required number of personnel from the KHWWB's active list, after paying the stipulated charges. Interestingly, in the early 1990s, such a system had existed on Willingdon Island but had since become defunct. Recognising its potential effectiveness for constituting and running the labour pool, the port submitted a proposal to the State Labour Department in July 2006, and with the labour minister's direct intervention and support of the state administration, the system was successfully reinstated.

The transformation that followed has been one of the most significant labour reforms in Cochin Port, resulting in a complete reorganisation of the labour booking system. It achieved the liberation of hundreds of manual workers from the whims of a single, capricious union leader, transitioning to a democratic labour employment scheme. It assured fair wages, medical insurance protection, and other benefits of social security. This scheme has scope for further improvement, especially through the leveraging of today's digital technology and mobile apps.

Tipping the Manning Scales

One of the most debilitating episodes of labour unrest occurred in 2009, when the port management decided to implement the National Industrial Tribunal Award on Manning Scales. First, let me explain the significance of manning scales in port operations.

There was a time when loading and unloading of cargo from ships to shore and vice versa was performed manually by workers, and these operations depended solely on their physical strength. The process was time-consuming and laborious, and it required a large workforce to handle just a few tonnes of cargo. However, the realm of cargo-handling has transformed dramatically in the modern era. Technological advancements and containerisation have led to the deployment of sophisticated cranes, conveyor systems, and different kinds of forklifts that have drastically reduced the number of workers needed. What once took two dozen workers a full day to unload manually can now be accomplished by one or two operators using an efficient crane in just a few minutes.

In the world of shipping and cargo handling, the term "manning scales" is used to determine the number of workers required for various tasks such as loading and unloading of cargo, securing of cargo, operation of boats, tugs and other marine craft, repair and maintenance of equipment and so on. Manning scales help to ensure that there are enough workers to carry out the tasks safely and efficiently, while also minimising the risk of accidents or injuries. A manning scale is, therefore, an important tool for ensuring that cargo handling operations are carried out in compliance with regulations and industry standards. But imagine a situation where there is a demand for deploying as many workers for unloading a certain cargo as would have been required in the pre-crane days.

The modernisation of cargo handling equipment may have indeed revolutionised the industry, but legacy and cultural factors continue to play a role in the way things are done in many ports. Manning scales, which have existed since the days of manual cargo handling are a prime example of this. The real conflict between trade unions and management regarding manning scales in ports is typically related to determining the number of workers required. Specifically, trade unions often advocate for higher manning levels to ensure that their members have job security and are not overworked, while the management may want to reduce manning levels to cut costs and increase efficiency. Trade unions argue that higher manning levels ensure that there are enough workers to handle unexpected workloads and emergencies.

While safety and efficiency are paramount, legacy factors have played a role in shaping practices in many ports. For instance, the number of workers initially authorised to unload one tonne of cargo remained unchanged in some ports despite the arrival of sophisticated cranes. This adherence to outdated practices led to considerable inefficiencies and other undesirable practices. For example, when a crane could be efficiently operated by just a few individuals, surplus workers from the original team would still be shown on paper as being at work, while in reality, they were engaged elsewhere. Similarly, the number of authorised personnel assigned to operate a marine craft often exceeded those actually present and working. Those absent were occupied with personal matters, yet continued to be marked as on duty and, in some cases, even claimed overtime allowances!

Apart from the ethical issues involved, such practices not only resulted in inefficiencies but also compromised safety. It was crucial for ports to adopt modern manning scales that took into account the efficiencies of modern cargo handling equipment and marine craft.

For Cochin Port to survive, time had come to confront the cultural factors that contributed to such practices. This required a change in the mindset and the adoption of new practices founded on safety, efficiency, and transparency. Surely, a review of manning scales was needed. I raised this matter on multiple occasions during our interactions with the union leaders. However, we were unable to make much headway. I also discussed the potential fallout and practical issues with the HoDs and other senior officers. Our team was fully alive to the ethical dilemmas of fairness to workers as well as the issues of pragmatism. While it was important to prevent the wastage of manpower, we were equally mindful of the need to ensure that workers were not overburdened, that they received adequate rest, and that they were always treated with dignity and respect. These considerations were central to our ongoing discussions and efforts to reform.

National Industrial Tribunal Award on Manning Scales

It is important to provide some historical context here. It all began way back on 2 August 2000 when an MOU was signed as part of a settlement between the Secretary of the Ministry of Surface Transport and the Port Workers Federations to resolve issues related to wages and working conditions of port workers and dock labour. Under that settlement, it was mutually agreed that matters concerning manning scales would be referred to the National Industrial Tribunal in Kolkata, and that its award would be binding on both parties. The Tribunal eventually issued its award on 19 April 2006, which was subsequently published in the *Gazette of India* by the Ministry of Labour. At the same time, the Ministry of Surface Transport issued directives instructing all major ports to implement the award.

In the meantime, the award was challenged in the High Court of Andhra Pradesh by the Harbour and Dock Workers' Union of Visakhapatnam Port Trust. The High Court's initial order was to maintain the status quo, but on 18 April 2009, the court vacated the stay order, permitting the Visakhapatnam Port Trust to implement the award. The award recommended a need-based system of deployment of workers, depending on the specific job requirements and cargo types. It also suggested uniform manning scales for similar types of vessels and equipment across all ports. Immediately, following the lifting of the stay order by the Andhra Pradesh High Court, the government of India's Ministry of Labour and Ministry of Shipping once again issued orders to all major ports to implement the award.

We at Cochin Port were eagerly awaiting an opening of this sort and lost no time when the opportunity finally knocked! Complying with the Shipping Ministry's instructions, Cochin Port quickly notified the labour unions about the matter. The unions, however, were equally quick to oppose the implementation, arguing that the award would lead to a reduction in workers' strength, violation of labour laws, loss of employment, and deployment of outsiders by way of low-cost contract labour. Their argument was that the need-based system of deployment would lead to a decline in the number of workers employed, as only those workers with specific skills required for a particular job would be employed. This would, in turn, lead to job layoffs and violation of labour laws, they argued.

The port management provided assurances to the unions that no existing employees would lose their employment and that the new system would be used to streamline existing deployment schemes. The implementation of the award was anticipated to usher in significant changes in how port workers were assigned, prioritising need-based allocation over the previous practice of fixed gang sizes. Further, the Tribunal had put an end to restrictive practices that had been prevalent among workers, which had become a bane of the ports' work culture, leading to manpower wastage, disciplinary problems, and financial losses. The port management had no other choice but to implement the award, as mandated by the Tribunal and ordered by the government of India.

Implementation of the National Industrial Tribunal (NIT) award on manning scales represented the opportunity of rationalising labour deployments at the port and aimed at improving the port's productivity, efficiency, and competitiveness. Therefore, despite stiff opposition from the unions, the port management decided to proceed with the implementation of the award. However, as the efforts by the management to convince the unions proved unsuccessful, dark clouds of industrial unrest loomed over Willingdon Island.

Prolonged Strikes

It is important to note here that the Federations of Trade Unions were signatories to the settlement that led to the case referred to the Tribunal. Thus, the award was statutorily binding on all parties and could not be modified or disregarded by the port authorities. However, the unions decided to oppose its implementation. The first impact of their resistance was felt in the marine department, when a section of its workers went on a flash strike in protest against its implementation. Earlier, anticipating this problem, I had personally reached out to the flag officer commanding in chief (FOC-in-C) of the Southern Naval Command and requested the navy's assistance in maintaining essential services. A formal requisition was submitted to the Southern Naval Command and to the Ministry of Defence, through the Ministry of Shipping. The Southern Naval Command responded positively, quickly deploying the requisitioned number of naval personnel to run the port's marine operations. These included manpower support to operate the tugs, mooring vessels and manning of all critical marine operational sections to ensure the smooth functioning of the port. This support of the Indian Navy proved particularly critical, especially in ensuring uninterrupted shipping services to Lakshadweep and import operations of crude oil for the smooth functioning of the Kochi Refineries.

Meanwhile, a conciliation meeting convened by the Central Labour Commissioner on 11 May 2009 with representatives from various port trade union federations across India failed to resolve the issue of manning scales. In the aftermath, several trade unions at other Indian ports too announced their intention to go on strike. However, the strike materialised in only a few ports, with

Cochin being the most affected. At Cochin Port, workers from all departments joined the strike, significantly disrupting operations.

Intense Political Pressure

In the days that followed, the port administration came under intense pressure from various fronts. It must be remembered that, at the time, the management's full attention was directed towards the implementation of major infrastructure projects, such as the ICTT, the Vallarpadam road and rail connectivity initiatives, the LNG terminal and regassification plant, and the ERP rollout. Each of these demanded close monitoring, hands-on supervision, and active intervention. Simultaneously, protests were erupting in various parts of Ernakulam city against the land acquisition efforts tied to the road and rail connectivity projects. At such a critical juncture, when a flurry of developmental activities was already underway, a prolonged strike at the port was the last thing we were prepared to handle.

The port administration was already stretched to its limits, working hard to meet numerous project deadlines. However, the eruption of a major strike during this critical phase placed an enormous additional burden on the Cochin Port team. Frustration and anxiety over potential project delays were palpable. Leaders and project team members found themselves in a difficult position, torn between managing the strike and ensuring operational continuity for the successful completion of ongoing projects. Maintaining team morale became more pressing, especially as negotiation fatigue began to set in, with prolonged discussions yielding little progress.

Meanwhile, a pervading sense of negativism was in the air. The entire Willingdon Island was strewn with flags and banners. Every day, trade union leaders and political figures from various parties would gather in the expansive *samara pandals* that sprang up in front of the main administrative buildings and elsewhere on Willingdon Island. The tactics involved applying intense personal pressure on officers, with many of the insulting speeches blaring from the loudspeakers. On the other hand, the continuing disruption of port operations and the financial losses being suffered by the port and its business partners exerted enormous mental pressure on all of us. Nevertheless, the management team remained resolute as it was important to continue the process of cleansing the port of detrimental labour practices. We had already achieved considerable progress in cleaning out the cobwebs. There was no question of leaving the task unfinished.

While trade unions in other ports also voiced their protests and grievances against the implementation of the award, most refrained from engaging in protracted general strikes or causing prolonged disruptions to port operations within their jurisdictions. In a few ports, certain unions did resort to symbolic or brief strikes, but in many ports, there were no strikes at all. However, for Cochin Port, it seemed like an occasion for celebration of union rights, even as the agitation and work stoppages continued for nearly six weeks. Interestingly, some union leaders from other ports across India travelled to Cochin to partake in the strikes here, even as operations in their own ports went on smoothly!

During such times of crisis, the support of one's superiors becomes paramount. Both Shipping Minister T.R. Baalu and Shipping Secretary A.P.V.N. Sarma stood by us throughout this difficult period. While the Shipping Minister gave us complete operational freedom, I came under increasing pressure from several political figures, including Union cabinet ministers, top leaders of national political parties and several senior Kerala political leaders across parties. They urged me to put the implementation of the award on hold, citing its political inconvenience, especially with the parliamentary elections underway.

Interestingly, although the Labour Ministry had issued orders instructing the ports to implement the award, the Labour Minister himself wanted us to halt the process, though he stopped short of officially rescinding the ministry's orders. Oscar Fernandes, the Labour Minister, was known for his gentle and friendly demeanour and his reputation for simplicity. I held him in high regard, but during our numerous telephonic conversations throughout the strike period, he repeatedly asked me to delay the award's implementation until the ongoing parliamentary elections were concluded. With all due respect, but firmly, I told him that it would be difficult for me to comply.

The intense political pressure mounted by political leaders in Thiruvananthapuram, including by some state ministers, was no less. In my experience, most politicians of Kerala are cultured and well behaved, treating government officers with dignity, although there were a few "honourable exceptions". Throughout this strike period, I received numerous calls from various Kerala political leaders and I took the opportunity to explain our position to them and many of them expressed their appreciation. Some of them were aggressive, warning me of consequences. Shockingly, one of them even resorted to abusive language while on a telephone call!

A few days into the strike, the Cochin Thuramukha Samrakshana Samithy, a coalition of trade unions, held a press conference in Cochin, announcing that they had met with Defence Minister A.K. Antony who, they claimed, had ordered the withdrawal of the naval personnel from the port and stopping the Indian Navy from extending any support to the port. By the evening, the chief of the Southern Naval Command informed me that he had received orders to recall the personnel. This reversal was rather shocking because the naval personnel were under deployment with the port after an official decision of the Ministry of Defence. The withdrawal effectively meant that the port would no longer be able to maintain essential or emergency services. I was both pained and disheartened on hearing from the unions that a respected political leader of the state and one of the senior-most cabinet ministers, A.K. Antony had himself taken this decision, giving priority to political expediency rather than the requirements of governance and maintenance of essential services. After all, Cochin Port was only implementing the orders of the Government of India in the national interest. I felt personally disheartened because A.K.

Antony had always been very supportive and was an avowed votary of strict governance.

Following the withdrawal of naval personnel, the marine operations came to a standstill for a few days. During this period, the port received numerous humanitarian appeals from the inhabitants of Lakshadweep, urging the authorities to keep alive the shipping services to the islands. Prolonged strikes at Cochin Port often had a direct and severe impact on these island communities, leading to sharp increases in the prices of essential goods and restricting access to critical medical facilities on the mainland.At one point of time, an official of the Lakshadweep administration requested for an emergency evacuation of a few medical cases, including some pregnant women. I discussed the matter with the department heads and a team of the senior leadership of the marine department offered to man the mooring and tug operations to send off and receive the Lakshadweep ships. Following this, Deputy Conservator Captain Paul N. Joseph and Harbour Master Captain Joseph J. Alapatt, together with several senior pilots, handled the berthing and mooring of the Lakshadweep ships with the help of other officers of the port, assisted by CISF personnel.

Meanwhile, another potential crisis was looming, concerning the handling of crude oil and petroleum products. Continued denial of services to the BPCL's Kochi Refinery could trigger major disruptions in the refinery's operations that would have a cascading impact on availability of petrol and diesel in the state of Kerala and parts of Tamil Nadu, and could have ripple effects on the national economy itself. As the BPCL was one of our most valued customers, it became our moral responsibility to ensure that the refinery operations were not adversely impacted. Meanwhile, the successful handling of the Lakshadweep ships gave confidence to the senior leadership of the port and it was decided to attempt the berthing and mooring of the large petroleum tanker ships too, by similar teams of senior officers, with the active assistance and support of the CISF. And, it worked.

The success achieved by the marine department's leadership team under Captain Paul N. Joseph and Harbour Master Captain Joseph J. Alapatt in handling berthing and mooring of even large petroleum tankers, had a demoralising effect on the striking unions. Meanwhile, many workers who were against the prolonged and indefinite strike began to report for duty. Simultaneously, the port management continued their negotiations with the union representatives. Finally, after nearly six weeks of disruption of port operations, the unions agreed to call off their agitation, following discussions with the port's senior officers. Captain Paul, in his capacity as the deputy conservator and the head of the Marine Department, had a direct role in these negotiations, as marine operations were the most affected in this strike. Cyril George, in his role as the secretary, headed the Administrative and the Labour Departments of the port and had long experience and skills in negotiating with the unions.

In the end, the unions, too, acknowledged that the existing manning scales were excessively high and expressed their willingness to bring them down. Nevertheless, after such a prolonged strike, they needed a face-saving solution. The port management was open to making some concessions. For example, the existing practice of running the tugs with 25 personnel in a shift, would be brought down to 12, although the tribunal award had authorised only nine. Along these lines, the port management agreed to make minor concessions while re-assessing the revised manning scales in all areas of port operations. The management reached an understanding with the unions that the mechanics and practical issues regarding the implementation of the revised manning scales would be sorted through mutual discussions in the future. The port management maintained its stance that the implementation of the Tribunal Award could not be compromised in any way, but practical difficulties in its implementation could be discussed. Thus, ultimately, a solution acceptable to all parties was found.

Throughout the strike period, the Cochin Port management remained resolute in its belief that the ongoing wastage of manpower called for a resolution once and for all. They were steadfast in their determination to discard the archaic manning scales that the port had clung to, from a bygone era. If the implementation of the award was withdrawn halfway, it would have been very difficult to re-introduce the changes again in the future. Thus, even in the face of intense political pressure from both New Delhi and Thiruvananthapuram, the port management did not budge. They consciously opted for the difficult alternative and remained determined, fully aware of the hardships that both the organisation and its stakeholders, including the port staff, had to suffer. But then at times, it is crucial to look beyond band-aids and opt for painful surgeries.

No Bitterness

Although I had several skirmishes with the unions and some senior politicians, there was no lingering animosity. In fact, many trade union and political leaders with whom I had conflicts continue to remain friends to this day. Even V.H.M. Rafeeq, the CTTU general secretary with whom I had frequent confrontations, eventually appreciated the port management's stance and expressed a willingness to make amends. He once visited me at my office to convey his regret. (Sadly, a few months later, he was diagnosed with a serious illness that he succumbed to.)

In times of emergencies, crises, and challenging situations, trade unions closely collaborated with the management, supporting the administration's efforts in addressing various issues—whether it was managing marine accidents, responding to calamities like the collapse of the Mattancherry Wharf, or uniting as a team to prepare for major events like the Volvo Ocean Race. Yet, while I look back at the events with satisfaction that the entire port team handled matters with professionalism and mutual understanding, I still believe that we could have achieved much more and many losses could have been averted had there been better industrial peace, harmony, and mutual cooperation between the management and the unions.

Also, Some Humour

In an otherwise humourless world of a constant struggle for survival and competing interests, we were fortunate to have a few individuals who brought plenty of laughter to the table. Humour, in such a high-pressure environment, became not only a relief but also a bonding mechanism among colleagues. Many persons among us were blessed with a sharp wit and an infectious sense of humour, not only among our colleagues and board members but also within the ranks of politicians and trade union leaders. They always enjoyed a hearty laugh, even in the midst of conflicts, that helped to break the ice, lighten the mood, and diffuse tensions. In a setting where every decision was scrutinised and often met with resistance, the ability to laugh at ourselves, at the absurdities of the situation, or at shared frustrations, became a survival tool.

Humour also played a subtle yet meaningful role in bridging the gap between the management and labour. In moments of seemingly irreconcilable differences, a well-timed joke or a light-hearted comment could momentarily dissolve tensions. It wasn't just about cracking jokes; it was about using humour as a tool to soften the edges of difficult conversations, to acknowledge the shared disagreements. In those moments, humour acted as a balm for the inevitable frustrations, fatigue, and weariness. It served as a powerful reminder that, despite our challenges, we could still find common ground, joy and camaraderie in our work.

Cochin Port's Tryst with Labour Reform

Looking back at those tumultuous days, several important lessons emerged from our experience. The most significant was the leadership dilemma we faced from the outset—whether to face long-standing issues head-on with a confrontational approach or to turn a blind eye for temporary peace. Clearly, allowing matters to drift and avoiding tough decisions would have jeopardised the port's larger interests and long-term integrity. One crucial lesson was that short-term disruption is sometimes a necessary cost to be paid for a long-term transformation. Refusing to compromise on core principles eventually yielded positive outcomes.

The experiences shared here from Cochin Port offer valuable lessons for the entire state of Kerala. While all political parties have contributed to advancing progressive labour policies in the state, they must also accept responsibility for the indiscriminate and widespread weaponization of industrial action. More about this in the final chapter.

3

E-THURAMUGHAM: INDIA'S FIRST E-PORT

Digitalisation, Automation, and a Complete Organisational Transformation

This chapter is the story of how the employees of Cochin Port demonstrated to the external world what a determined group of men and women, with fire in their bellies, was capable of achieving. The vision of the e-*thuramugham*[1] Project extended far beyond a mere plan for digitalisation and automation. It aspired for and successfully accomplished a complete organisational and cultural transformation, turning the port into a fully digitalised and

---

1. E-*thuramugham* stands for the pioneering Cochin Port Enterprise Resource Planning (ERP) system, built on a SAP platform and integrated with customised systems, including the Port Operations System (POS) and the Port Community System. E-*thuramugham* encompasses all aspects of the port's operations, comprising various modules such as the Finance and Cost Controlling Module (FICO), the SAP Industry-Specific Utilities Module (ISU), the Cargo and Logistics Management System (CALMS, vessel and cargo-related), the Plant Maintenance Module (PMM), Materials Management (MM), Geographic Information System (GIS), Estate Management Modules (EMM), and the Human Resources Management System (HRMS). E-*thuramugham* also interfaces seamlessly with banking systems as well as with the systems of the Customs Department. In this book, the expressions "e-*thuramugham*" and "e-Port" are used interchangeably.

data-driven enterprise. This transformation involved re-imagining, re-engineering, and streamlining of the processes and workflows in every department, impacting and empowering every employee and every port customer, while braving, managing, and sailing through some gruelling bouts of headwinds, turmoil, and turbulence.

The magnitude of this complete digitalisation and automation of processes cannot be overstated, as it encompassed not only an across-the-board system overhaul, but also a profound organisational behavioural change of immense proportions. For a large and multifaceted government establishment interfacing with several Central and state departments, multiple regulatory authorities, and trade bodies, functioning in a heavily unionised atmosphere, with deeply entrenched work practices and cultures steeped in history that evolved over the decades, this transformation was a tremendous achievement.

The port infrastructure built by Robert Bristow was already showing signs of age, even as an array of new, modern facilities was coming up. As the port prepared for the construction and development of several mega infrastructure projects, it became clear that these state-of-the-art facilities would require a matching modern, automated, and integrated management and governance system.. This called for a carefully calibrated refinement of the operational model, accompanied by a comprehensive digital transformation that involved multiple stakeholders, processes, technologies as well as data and risk management frameworks.

The e-Port vision aimed to digitalise all business processes of the port, moving beyond traditional departmental boundaries. A core objective of the proposed automation initiative was to standardise and improve the processes across various units and departments of the port and integrate them into a unified system capable of interfacing with external systems as well. This meant that individual units and departments of the port would no longer function in silos, but instead, transform into interconnected, interdependent and well-functioning organs of a single, healthy system.

How Did it All Begin?

My first day at Cochin Port had begun with a jolt. After signing the joining papers, I was led to my first Board meeting of the Port Trust, which was already in progress. As the chairman's post had been vacant for nearly six months, an overdue Board meeting was scheduled to coincide with my joining. This being a first for me, I promised not to talk much, remaining on a "listening watch". Having had no experience in the port sector and with no prior experience of chairing a Board meeting, I thought some active listening would be better than opening one's mouth. But that was not to be.

One matter that came up for animated discussion was the audit report of the port for the previous years. The Comptroller and Auditor General (C&AG) in the report had pointed out the existence of numerous instances of financial transactions and outstanding advances drawn over the years that remained open and needed reconciliation and closure. Although many such transactions had since been reconciled after the C&AG report, there still remained numerous open transactions that could not be resolved. The port's officers informed the Board that efforts made to trace out details of some of the open transactions could not succeed "for non-availability of old records". The suggestion to write off some of the unreconciled and outstanding amounts, if deemed necessary, was met with strong opposition from several Board members, who were scathing in their observations. The Board was clearly displeased and hesitant to approve such a course of action.

For a newcomer, the entire situation was quite unsettling—truly a wake-up call. Although many of these cases may not have involved financial irregularities, the sheer number of open cases was alarming. The police instinct in me was immediately triggered by certain observations in the audit report. At that moment, I decided to intervene and gave an assurance to the Board that every possible effort would be made to track the relevant records and close the outstanding transactions. I also assured the Board that I would study the systemic issues to identify the underlying root causes of the current situation and promised to put in place robust systems and procedures to prevent the recurrence of similar non-standard financial practices.

The Mountain of Cash

During one of my morning rounds, I came across an incredible sight. Inside a large hall was a mountain of currency note bundles, surrounded by staff members meticulously counting the money and preparing individual envelope packets. I was informed that they were preparing salary packets for employees. In another hall, a similar exercise was underway for pension distribution. It was clear that manually handling such large volumes of cash would keep a significant number of employees occupied for several days each month. Right then and there, I ordered an immediate end to the practice of cash-based salary distribution, directing that all future payments be made through banks only.

The decision to ban cash transactions was met with much consternation and resistance. Soon enough, it was to bring me face to face with one of the earliest skirmishes with the trade unions, who argued vehemently that workers had an "inalienable right" to be paid in cash, directly at their workplaces. The existing policy required that every month, several teams of finance department personnel would be required to visit every nook of the sprawling port complex, including offshore sites, ships, dredgers, tugboats, and other marine craft for the delivery of pay packets to workers at their workplaces. Pensioners complained too, but with a valid argument that the cash distribution of pensions every month gave them the opportunity to visit the port and socialise with their fellow pensioners. It took several rounds of discussions and cajoling to persuade everyone that this outmoded practice had to go and finally, all concerned were convinced and the story ended happily.

Yet, computerisation was not new to Cochin Port. Several software systems were already in place, each addressing different needs. However, these were sporadic efforts, resulting in patchy, standalone systems that did not communicate with one another. This meant that the same data had to be entered and handled multiple times, for each department and for different operational transactions. Incongruencies in data entry caused not only duplication of work but also problems of interoperability of databases leading to unacceptable levels of inefficiency and confusion. Above all, repetitive data entries were resulting in fatal errors in our books.

Manual transactions were becoming too cumbersome for the business community as well. For consumers and port users, conducting business under the existing system involved navigating a complex maze of paperwork. This included manually filling out dozens of forms to be submitted to various departments, moving from window to window to reserve berthing slots, booking labour and equipment, making remittances, and obtaining multiple clearances from different authorities. Continuing with the archaic manual systems would be inconsistent with the ethos of the modern port terminals and facilities that we had started building. The inefficiencies, inadequacies, and bureaucratic red tape associated with manual systems could erode customer and stakeholder confidence, making them hesitant to do business with the port. This, in turn, could undermine the impact of the world-class facilities we were developing.

There were other administrative compulsions that demanded immediate attention. For example, the audit observed wastage and inefficiency in inventory management, with some departments having large stockpiles of certain items, while others continued to purchase fresh supplies of the same material. This, of course, was easily verified during visits to the departments.

All these called for urgent action to bring about efficient and error-free accounting, to usher in transparency and, above all, accountability in our financial and commercial transactions. Digitalisation and automation could be an effective safeguard against errors as well as potential fraud. This consideration prompted me to give an assurance to the Port Trust Board, right at the outset, to explore digital solutions to rectify the situation. This would call for a fundamental rethink of our systems and procedures. The vision was to build a single, integrated system that would allow files to be transferred digitally and securely, where decisions would be supported by data. Those in management positions would have access to all relevant information and track the progress of proposals. Above all, it would allow interoperability between all departments of the port and interfaces with systems of external business partners, customs and other regulatory departments, banks, and port-users.

Looking Within and Developing the Shared Vision

The obvious question that arose was whether we had the digital skills, requisite talent, and capabilities within the organisation to drive the project forward. I set out to explore this through extensive interactions with employees across various departments—discussing diverse issues and assessing their willingness to learn, experiment, and take risks. Within just a few days, I became personally convinced that the organisation already had a significant number of senior and middle-level officers and staff with the necessary digital skills and the passion to overhaul the archaic system. Many others were eager and willing to learn on the job. All that was needed was a clear vision, adequate resources, and strong leadership.

Obviously, the future ERP project had to be a shared vision of not only the port's top management and employees but also of its multifarious external stakeholders. I engaged in a series of sittings with the senior officers to develop the big picture, the key issues concerning the envisioned transformation as well as the pros and cons of the project. The senior leaders of the port administration were unanimous in their view that some undesirable practices needed to be stamped out, while simultaneously introducing new, modern, and robust systems that would prevent archaic practices from raising their heads again. The top team, comprising the deputy chairman and HoDs, was convinced that ushering in a transparent and accountable system could be our best protection against potential malpractices, negligence, abuse, or fraud. The enthusiasm and commitment of the officers inspired and motivated me.

Within a month, I approached the Port Trust Board to report on the actions taken in response to the C&AG's audit observations. I emphasised the importance of strengthening financial accountability and the urgent need to re-engineer our largely manual business processes. I pointed out how a digital transformation could automate workflows, streamline repetitive tasks, reduce errors, and eliminate guesswork, ultimately leading to a fundamental shift in the organisation's work culture.

This transformation would require moving to an automated system, ideally a robust and comprehensive ERP, especially as the port's business volume and operational complexities continued to grow rapidly. The vision I presented to the Board focused on achieving operational efficiency, transparency, and governance through a holistic digital transformation. The Board gave "in principle" approval, but it was clear that further groundwork and greater clarity were necessary before we could approach the Board with a comprehensive proposal.

Defining the Project's Scope and Depth

While it does not cost money to dream, we soon realised our project would involve substantial expenditure. After a few sittings with the team to understand the costs and benefits, the projected Return on Investment (RoI) was very clearly in favour of taking the plunge. I was convinced that an efficient ERP would help the port prevent revenue leakages, ensure timely billings and revenue realisation, which alone could help us recover the investment in a few years. Other benefits would be the built-in operational efficiencies that an ERP would bring along, simplification of processes, the ability for better informed decision-making, error-free operations and, above all, ushering in a transparent work culture. Speed, Transparency, Reliability, Efficiency, Accuracy, Accountability, and Meticulousness (STREAAM) would soon become the byword of the project.

Engaging a consultant from the market would be expensive and possibly out of our reach. So, we began scouting for a consultant from within the port system and soon we zeroed in on a highly experienced systems professional, Victor Thangadurai, a retired Information Technology (IT) head of Tuticorin Port, who was promptly appointed as our IT advisor and project consultant.

The Vision Document

As a first step, the consultant was tasked with conducting a comprehensive study of the port's existing IT systems, assessing the system requirements, and preparing a document that would define the scope and objectives of the proposed ERP project—detailing its design, structure, and key internal processes. A series of brainstorming sessions, seminars, and workshops—engaging port officers from all departments and across various levels of seniority—helped in drafting the vision document, ensuring a mapping of all functional requirements of the project. The new ERP was intended to replace the existing manual processes across all functional areas, including finance, marine, engineering (civil, electrical, and mechanical), traffic, commercial, real estate, HR, administration and project management. At the time, these functions were being managed through paper files, manual workflows, spreadsheets, and standalone PC systems.

Democratising Decision-Making

Our internal brainstorming sessions and workshops helped in deciding that the organisation had to automate its business processes and implement a full-fledged ERP system connecting every department and functional area as well as all major activities of the port. Since the existing mix of manual and partly computerised systems was inadequate to cater to the current and emerging requirements of governance, the team was sure that an all-encompassing ERP solution was necessary together with the development of a comprehensive Port Operating System (POS).

This required extensive consultations with a diverse range of stakeholders, including the port-user community and regulatory authorities, such as customs, Central excise, mercantile marine departments, port health authorities, and banks. Efforts were made to understand the views of customers, import-export businesses, the shipping industry, and key stakeholders, including Customs House Agents (CHAs), Container Freight Stations (CFSs), and business partners such as DP World's India Gateway Terminal Private Limited (IGTPL), the upcoming Petronet LNG (PLL) terminal, Kochi Refinery Limited (BPCL), and the Lakshadweep administration.

What began as a modest strategy of internal discussions, consultations, and brainstorming soon evolved into a virtual parliament—an open forum where people shared ideas and demonstrated impressive problem-solving skills. A good measure of original and independent thinking was on display, while others conducted their own research and offered fresh insights, often pointing out gaps and inefficiencies in existing processes, systems, and workflows.

There was a palpable sense of excitement in the air, as employees from all levels—including junior officers and shop floor workers—contributed a wealth of out-of-the-box ideas on how tasks could be done differently, more easily, efficiently, or cost-effectively. After several brainstorming sessions and spirited debates, the team produced a document outlining the scope of what was initially called the Integrated Port Information System (iPINS), integrating the proposed ERP into the project.

Choosing the Right ERP and the Birth of the e-Port Project

The next step was to choose the right ERP platform that suited our unique and specific requirements. Again, we witnessed senior officers as well as youngsters spending long hours of research, trying to find out what the global practice was and what the most efficiently run ports in the world had chosen. What were the strengths and weaknesses of the major, globally recognised products? The energetic ERP committee—by now known for its decentralised approach to thinking and decision-making—was soon to come with its recommendation: SAP would be the most suitable solution to meet our needs.

By the end of August 2006, presentations were made to the Port Trust Board, and a comprehensive proposal for establishing the iPINS was approved by the Board in its meeting held on 30 August 2006, nine months after my initial promise to it. The iPINS was subsequently rechristened the e-Port, or e-*thuramugham* in Malayalam. The conceptual, preparatory stage was thus marked by positivity, transparent communication between port officials and stakeholders as well as democratisation of both information and decision-making. This distribution of the function of visioning and ownership of the project generated an innate energy of its own, which would drive the project further.

The next major step was to understand the functional features and requirements of the proposed ERP product from the perspective of every department of the port. This task was assigned to Departmental Working Groups, chaired by the respective HoDs but largely driven by young, middle-level managers and their teams. Their decision-making process involved cross-departmental and cross-organisational consultations, ensuring that the final product achieved the level of interoperability essential for the all success of the project.

Typically, the Departmental Working Groups would begin their work late in the evenings after the regular day's duties, led by the HoDs. Many of the youngsters used to sit late into the night—or even into the early morning hours—working with remarkable energy, precision, and passion. Within three months, the Departmental Working Groups identified the functional requirements and key processes to be incorporated into the application software. Based on their inputs, the IT advisor, in consultation with the respective groups, prepared the draft tender documents for the application software, data centre, and data communication network by early January 2007.

Tenders for a large ERP project posed some unique challenges, particularly because no other major Indian port had set out on this venture before. A tendering process in the corporate IT industry would be very different from requirements in the government sector. As a pioneering project, there was no precedent or prior experience within the port sector to draw upon. Luckily, I was able to take the help of some senior friends in the National Informatics Centre (NIC) in Delhi, who assisted in going through the maze of documents and giving their suggestions, informally. Finally, the port was able to complete and release the tender announcement in January 2007.

The tender process attracted considerable attention, but there were only two valid bids—one from Tata Consultancy Services (TCS) that quoted a lower quote than the only other competing bidder, Wipro. TCS's competitive pricing reflected a strategic understanding of the project's business potential; success in this pioneering project would not only establish their expertise in the port sector but also open the doors for them to similar ERP implementation projects in other ports in India and abroad. After a thorough evaluation process, conducted in full compliance with tendering norms, we finally selected TCS and awarded the project work to them. They responded swiftly, assembling a dedicated team of experts, each responsible for the development of individual modules.

Clearly, the stakes were equally high for the TCS as they were for us! Recognising the importance of effective communication in the local language, TCS made a conscious effort to deploy resource personnel from Kerala wherever possible.

Team Building and Project Implementation

Financial Advisor and Chief Accounts Officer (FA&CAO) K.G. Nath was nominated as the project director and chief coordinator. I was told it was the first time that a project would be headed by the Finance Department's HoD. Considering that the entire ERP would be centred around the finance function, this decision proved to be appropriate. Meanwhile, M.V. Paul, who headed the Electronic Data Processing (EDP) Division, was promoted as the Deputy Director of the EDP. Paul would be assisted by C. Vinod and would do all the ground work for the project.

A high-level Steering Committee, initially led by Deputy Chairman Captain Subhash Kumar and later by G. Krishna Kumar, was tasked with monitoring the project on a weekly basis. However, such was the enthusiasm that the committee ended up meeting almost daily! I personally participated in the proceedings of the committee as well as the Departmental Working Groups. During this period, all infrastructure facilities required for the project like the data centre, the enterprise-wide-optical-fibre network, servers, computers, and peripherals were procured.

Each functional module was to be headed and driven by the Module Implementation Teams, handpicked from the best-known talents in each department. Accordingly, B. Bhagyanath, Deputy Financial Advisor, K. Poothapandi, Additional Financial Advisor, Captain J.J. Alapatt, Harbour Master, Vipin Menoth, Additional Traffic Manager, Girish Thomas, Assistant Traffic Manager, K.V. Bhagawat Singh, Executive Engineer, and K. Ramesh, from the Stores Division (M), A.G. Sathyan, Executive Engineer, T.P. Thadevus, Assistant Executive Engineer, and C.P. Varghese, Estate Manager, were to head these teams. The HRMS was supervised by Secretary Cyril George, Unnikrishnan Nair, and B.K. Jha, and assisted by C. Premakumari, C.N. Santamma, Shyamala Kumari, and A.R. Radhakrishnan as well as representatives from individual departments. While I may not recall all the names, there were many other key officials who played crucial roles in the overall scheme.

The progress of the project was reviewed on a weekly basis by the project coordinator in the presence of the TCS team, the project manager and heads of functional working groups. The project advisor attended the review meeting once a month, in addition to making independent monthly visits to the port. By this time, leadership of the TCS team had been taken over by Anil Pai, a highly competent professional. His exceptional oratory skills played a key role in effectively communicating with the teams and motivating them with clarity and harmony.

Decision-Making and Policy Clarification

The interesting aspect of ERP implementation is that it necessitates a deep introspection within an organisation. Areas where policies were previously ambiguous are scrutinised for clear definitions and evaluations. This process is crucial for determining the most efficient policies for the future. This introspective exercise is invaluable in achieving policy clarity and ensuring the organisation is aligned with best practices. This comprehensive process of evaluation of existing organisational policies unfolded in distinct stages, each contributing to the refinement of policies. It began during the planning phase, where existing practices were meticulously examined to pinpoint areas requiring adjustments or realignment with the port's overall policies. As the ERP project advanced into the design and development phase, policy refinement continued, ensuring that each policy would seamlessly integrate with the upcoming system. An important step was the workflow analysis, which allowed for a meticulous review of current processes and workflows. By the time the ERP system was fully deployed, policies had undergone scrutiny and clarification, ensuring their alignment with the port's policy framework and their optimisation for efficient operations within the ERP ecosystem.

Policy decisions on issues were taken almost on a real-time basis by the project coordinator, K.G. Nath, who was fully empowered by the Chairman for doing so. In fact, very often, decision-making had to be done on the spot during the daily meetings. K.G. Nath exhibited commendable initiative in resolving issues by taking instant decisions, after consulting the chairman, deputy chairman, and HoDs where necessary. This scheme expedited the resolution of issues that could have otherwise led to stalemates. At no point was there any significant delay in policy decisions.

SAP Modules and Areas Covered by the e-Port Project

SAP, the German Enterprise Resource Planning (ERP) system, is globally renowned for its robust capabilities in enabling integrated management of business processes. SAP comes with more than two dozen software modules, out of which, Cochin Port selected some of the important modules like Finance & Controlling (FICO), Human Capital Management (HCM), Project System (PS), Real Estate Management System (REMS), Plant Maintenance (PM), Office Management System (OMS), Material Management (MM), Industry Solution for Utilities (IS-U), and Business Intelligence (BI-Executive Information System). SAP Netweaver PI was used as the integration tool in the project. The solution also included the Geographic Information System (GIS) for integration from the ESRI for spatial asset management.

Among all the modules, the FICO, as the name suggests, handles the core functions of recording all financial transactions and generating both internal and external financial reports. It covers all aspects of financial management, accounting, pre-auditing, and controlling through budgets. As this finance-related module has a coordinating and integrating impact on all other SAP modules, it was decided that the FA and the CAO of the port should oversee the entire ERP implementation, a decision that turned out to be very valid in the days to come. Another important module that we opted for was the Human Capital Management (HCM) or the HR Management System, covering the full lifecycle of HRM activities including Pay Roll, Employee Self Service (ESS) and Manager Self

Service (MSS). The ESS would facilitate employees to make requests using the system for leave, advances, and other facilities without having to go through any paperwork. The HCM would also integrate the Access Control System with biometric functionalities for recording attendance, thereby regulating the pay bill.

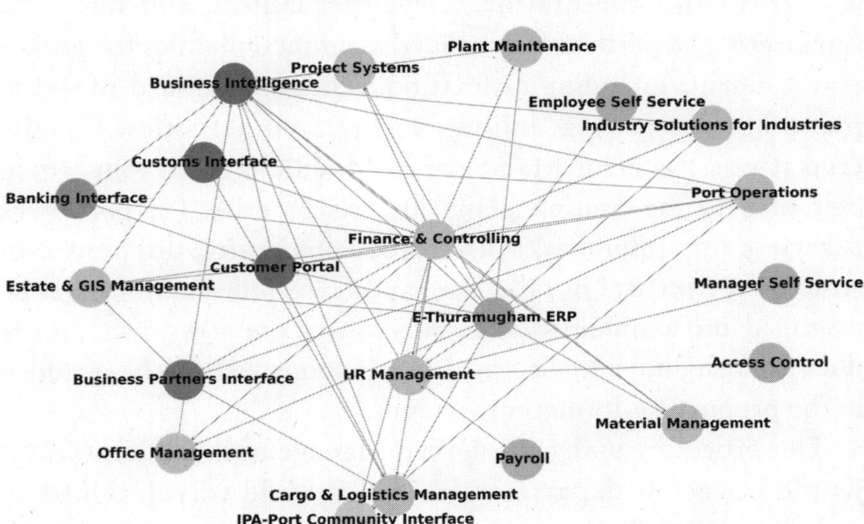

Real Estate Management System (REMS)

The port owns several hundred acres of land in Willingdon Island, Vallarpadam, Puthuvypeen, Fort Cochin, Mulavukad, and many other areas in the Cochin city. Large parts of these land parcels, as well as building and marine structures are regularly leased out to port users for a variety of business purposes. The manual processes used for monitoring the lease contracts and realisation of the resulting revenue were proving to be cumbersome and inefficient. The REM module was expected to bring about error-free transactions in this area. It would deliver digitalised and accurate information, along with graphical visualisation of the port's entire land and water assets, through a GIS software seamlessly integrated with lease management processes—including allotment, occupation, vacation, renewal, rent collection, and recovery of financial dues from lessees and users. The proposed GIS software would also provide storage, retrieval, and management of different layers of the port's infrastructure and utilities.

With the port almost ready for a slew of mega infrastructure projects, the Project Systems (PS) module was expected to play a vital role for the Marine, Civil, Mechanical, and Electrical Engineering Departments. It offered key functionalities for project management, including estimation, tendering, award of work, planning, monitoring, billing, and related activities. Equally crucial was the Plant Maintenance Module (PMM) that would help manage the multiple plants and machineries. The port owns a variety of equipment, a fleet of marine crafts, different civil structures, electrical installations, and IT facilities that need to be managed and maintained. Processes carried out at workshops, dry docks, IC engine[2] and electrical repair shops were to be included in the proposed information system.

The processes under the Office Management System (OMS) would cover all departments. This module was designed to include a full-fledged document management system for storage, retrieval as well as tracking of files and movements. It would also automate the workflow of operational processes related to obtaining administrative and financial sanctions. The MM system would handle the entire cycle of material management operations, starting with the collection of requirements from various functional departments, followed by the purchase process, receipt and issue of materials, inventory management, and the final disposal process of surplus stores.

Similarly, the Industry Solutions for Utilities (IS-U) module was designed to manage the sourcing and distribution of electricity and water within the port area to its tenants and business partners, as the port holds a licence for providing these services. The module covered the entire utility management cycle—from the procurement

---

2. Repair shops for internal combustion engines

of electricity and water to their supply to consumers—including metre reading, billing, charge realisation, and tax remittances.

The Geographic Information System (GIS) module envisaged control over various assets of the port like lands, buildings, cargo sheds, roads, railway lines, water tanks, electric installations, water lines, oil pipelines, and storage tanks by plotting them as different layers on a satellite image procured by the port from the National Remote Sensing Agency (NRSA). The port's Enterprise Portal—its official website—was envisioned as a vital interface for employees, customers, stakeholders, and the wider public. As business transactions moved online, it became essential for the portal content to be dynamically updated from backend databases, reflecting real-time internal and external processes. Accordingly, as part of the ERP implementation and integration, TCS agreed to develop a dynamic, enterprise portal tailored to meet the needs of both internal users and external stakeholders.

Business Intelligence (Executive Information System)

The cardinal objective of the proposed system was to provide summarised, timely, and accurate information to the top management to aid them in their day-to-day decision-making process and their long-term strategic planning. The different modules described above would have the necessary reports and outputs of the transaction processes. For a holistic view of the entire operation and management of the port, the top management would be required to access data from these modules and view them in a meaningful way. On top of all these, the Executive Information System (EIS) module was proposed to be built which would present a view of the entire gamut of activities of the port to enable the effective planning, monitoring, controlling and review of activities of the port. The EIS would include extensive reporting options to address the needs of the operational, middle, as well as top management levels. The system was expected to provide drill-down options and alert facilities for the various levels of management.

Port Operations System (POS)

Meanwhile, the Indian Ports Association (IPA) was developing the Port Community System (PCS) to facilitate real-time information sharing among ports and stakeholders across the country. From the outset, we were aware that SAP did not have an existing module tailored for port operations. However, a well-designed software was crucial for our needs. TCS informed us that a software developed by their strategic partner, the CMC, would ideally meet our requirements, and TCS offered a modified, customised version to suit the port's needs. We had outlined several operational functionalities that were essential, including processes related to vessel operations, cargo operations (export and import), handling of hazardous cargo, booking cargo-handling equipment, scheduling workers, and managing documentation and filing of customer applications. Other processes included cargo truck movements, vehicle tracking, entry and exit gate monitoring, management of shipping berths, storage areas, cargo sheds and CFSs. Under the contract, TCS agreed to customise and integrate the POS, including related financial transactions, with the SAP finance module.

The Port Community System (PCS)

The objectives of the proposed centralised web-based PCS included the development of a centralised and intelligent electronic message switching facility to and from the community members including ports, shipping lines, shipping agents, terminal operators, customs house agents, importers/exporters, stevedores, CFS, Container corporation of India Limited (CONCOR), surveyors, road transport operators, banks, insurance, customs, Port Health Organisation (PHO) and Immigration, which would provide a single, integrated and standardised process for information exchange. We had planned that Cochin e-Port would be integrated with the PCS when it was ready.

One of the objectives of this project was to improve the service quality and experience of the customers and it, therefore, needed to be oriented towards them. The e-Port would provide a single window for the users to transact business with the port and also an option to transact business through the internet. It was intended to provide one gateway for access to port e-services and information to port users under Cochin Port. The services ranged from ship schedule information to berth applications, to declaration of import and export of cargo, and related information.

Interface with Other Internal and External Applications

The e-Port project required seamless integration with external systems to optimize its operations. Collaboration with the private BOT (Build, Operate, Transfer) operator, the IGTPL of DP World, was essential for exchanging operational data such as container traffic, vessel schedules, revenue assessments, and productivity metrics. This necessitated establishing a robust interface between the port's e-Port system and the container terminal's management system for real-time data exchange.

Similarly, integration with customs systems was vital. The existing Port Operations software facilitated message exchanges, such as the Import General Manifest (IGM), at the national level. The e-Port system implemented a Message Broker to receive, validate, and process incoming messages from customs, while also generating and sending necessary data back to customs servers at specified intervals.

Furthermore, implementing an efficient e-Payment System was vital to enable online payments by port users. This involved secure web-based financial transactions between the port and selected banks through web forms or message exchanges, and was a key requirement in the tendering process.

Cochin Port operates a 150-bed hospital offering various specialty services. Earlier, its management processes were using a Hospital Management System (HMS) software, based on

Oracle and PowerBuilder, which now was integrated with the e-Port system, ensuring seamless data exchange and streamlined healthcare services. Similarly, the port's Security Management System (SMS), which encompasses access control and attendance monitoring, was also integrated with e-Port to facilitate efficient security management, real-time monitoring capabilities, incident tracking, and heightened security awareness to prevent potential violations.

Business Process Mapping: Knowing Where We are and Where We are Going

Soon, the entire organisation was drawn into this existential question—understanding and mapping our existing systems and workflows while envisioning the restructured systems we aimed to create. Analysing the current processes was the first crucial step towards a new future. The first step of developing and mapping the "As Is" situation turned out to be an extensive exercise in organisational introspection. Officers spearheading this effort engaged with relevant staff to gain a process-level understanding of every workflow, identifying existing efficiencies and inefficiencies, strengths and weaknesses as well as bottlenecks and delays.

The next step was the "To Be" process mapping—an equally daunting task of envisioning systems and process flows that would lead to the promised land! Crucial to this was the need to ensure that the new system would not replicate the operational inefficiencies and bottlenecks of the legacy systems.

Due to the complexity of existing manual systems and processes, many situations of potential logjams arose during the mapping discussions. These were mostly due to conflicts between the existing manual procedures in vogue vis-à-vis standard international protocols followed in SAP globally. It required acceptance of a different protocol in the "To Be" system, by taking people out of their current comfort zones. At the same time, we recognised that blindly adopting so-called international best practices would not be a panacea in itself. It would be necessary for us to do our own homework, understand, and define our unique work processes and business requirements.

The adoption of global best practices and workflow principles became necessary from an economic standpoint as well. Since the new ERP system was intended for long-term use, we needed to make provisions for its continuous upgrade in the years to come. Being ready for receiving those updates (patches) from time to time from SAP was crucial for the continuous and automatic upgrade of the software. If made according to the existing processes, every future upgradation would involve additional expenditure on account of "change requests". Thus, the biggest challenge before the project team was to adhere to the global best practices of SAP, which would mean agreeing to re-engineer the prevailing procedures. This transformation had to be acceptable to all concerned: the employees, regulatory authorities, business partners, and port customers. Achieving this was a stupendous task, requiring not only an in-depth understanding of processes and their real-world implications but also tremendous negotiation and persuasion skills. Nevertheless, the team successfully completed the mapping of the "To Be" processes on schedule.

According to the contract, only a certain number of change requests were to be done by TCS without additional payment over and above the contract price. Keeping this in mind, the port team carefully structured the "To Be" processes, ensuring that the change requests arising during implementation remained well within the permitted limit.

Change Management and Messaging Strategies

Very soon, we realised that the "To Be" mapping process itself could be very unsettling to many. As harbingers of the massive changes in the offing, it would affect them personally in duties, work contents, possible relocations to other departments, or additional training requirements. What was worse was that the ERP implementation could result in making job positions less powerful or even totally irrelevant, leading to disruption. The fear of the unknown turned out to be the biggest enemy, leading to suspicion and acrimony.

We adopted some subtle change management strategies, observing that computer-literate and tech-savvy employees would welcome changes while others would balk. Employees who had family members proficient in using computers also became champions of technology. The overall change management strategy was jointly driven by the port management and the TCS implementation team. A series of interactive sessions were carried out, aimed at influencing the attitude of employees towards the project and their acceptance and ownership of the operational changes in the offing. As we had begun operationalising our communications strategy very early in the project, there was considerable understanding and cooperation between the management and employees. In fact, the excitement was already palpable.

Meanwhile, TCS had suggested the creation of a Central War Room for the final push of the newly developed system. A recently constructed building used as the Media Centre for the Volvo Ocean Race was converted to the ERP War Room and it was quickly furnished with computers and peripherals. The entire TCS team worked there and it soon became the hub for all operational meetings related to the ERP. Apart from the senior management team, the working groups, and functional teams of the port, together with their counterparts from TCS, would assemble there on a daily basis, where every outstanding issue would be discussed and thrashed out.

What was extremely gratifying was that the port officers driving the project in their respective departments and their TCS counterparts made efficient teams fully aligned to the strategic aims and the scale of the envisioned change. Their enthusiasm, excitement, and energy levels were truly infectious and I could see even the cynics getting transformed!

In a highly unionised environment, the need for a carefully calibrated change management strategy was felt right from the conceptual stage of the project. It was clear that the organisation as a whole—and its employees in particular—needed to be thoroughly prepared. Leveraging their extensive experience in ERP implementation, the TCS also guided us in formulating an effective strategy to ready the organisation.

One of our first steps was to establish clear and transparent communication about the project with employees at all levels, trade unions, business partners, and customers. We used printed leaflets, brochures, and interactive meetings to explain the project's importance, its benefits, scope, and the various stages and timelines of implementation. In addition to routine departmental interactions, I made it a priority to regularly meet with trade union representatives in an effort to address concerns and dispel any apprehensions.

One of the underlying reasons for resistance to change was the fear that the new systems, workflows, and responsibilities may be too difficult for them to grasp, or too complicated to operate. Some would suspect that the new system would bring more work, beyond their comfort levels. But the elephant in the room was, of course, a genuine fear of losing jobs and related insecurities. This is where the change management strategy had to assure such persons that there would be no adverse consequences and that they would be adequately trained and prepared. On many occasions, the resistance was due to miscommunication and misunderstanding. In some cases, those who resisted did not understand the objectives of the project or its pressing necessity. Of course, there was also ideological disagreement with the philosophy of automation itself, anxiety about how the changes would affect one's job or how powerless one would be rendered. Involving employees at every level and as part of every process became crucial.

Labour movements have always looked at digitalisation projects with trepidation. The popular assumption is that computerisation would lead to unemployment and economic inequality. However, it is widely recognised that for knowledge workers and managers, the problem-solving capabilities of digitalisation would significantly enhance the quality of their work, enabling them to accomplish much more in less time. While this was bound to bring about efficiencies and help in getting rid of the drudgery of repetitive work profiles, some change in skills was necessary. Some types of jobs were bound to become obsolete and some job losses would definitely happen in the long run. While those without adequate computer skills would be at a disadvantage, new employment profiles befitting the new technologies would also increase. In fact, the ERP project would also provide opportunities to many employees to improve their skills for their professional growth.

In the background of these job-related apprehensions, it became crucial on my part to communicate clearly to the employees and trade unions, reassuring them that the management was committed to protect their interests. To begin with, I promised employees that no one would lose her or his job as a consequence of implementation of the ERP. The real challenge was in convincing the unions about the long-term implications. Personally, I knew that certain types of jobs that require human decision-making would only increase. Thus, job displacements could become a price to be paid for efficiency and productivity, while such advancements could also help new enterprises to proliferate, requiring new workers to move in.

The interactive sessions with union leaders were mostly held in a friendly atmosphere. In fact, at the function organised to signify the project "kick off", many senior union leaders spoke sincerely and frankly, and some even praised the management's initiative and volunteered many practical suggestions. This event had led to positive dialogues and sharing of information. Consultation with the major trade union leaders built mutual trust and genuine cooperation between the unions and the management as far as the ERP project was concerned. Deputy Secretary Unnikrishnan Nair, who was later appointed the joint director of the PBSEZ), exclusively dealt with change management and communication strategies. He focused on designing the multiple forms of messaging for the benefit of employees and the unions. To reinforce the transformation message, *Cochin Saga*, a fortnightly journal, was introduced, featuring the chairman's communication on e-*thuramugham*. Malayalam slogans were prominently displayed, resonating with employees and even inspiring a trade union leader to seek assistance for design of his union's slogans! Engaging employees further, a suggestion competition was held, offering mementos as rewards.

One important message was that the project would not only modernise the current processes but would also enhance the employability of officers and staff post-retirement. E-*thuramugham* was about creating entirely new systems, and employees would be playing a pivotal role in this transition. This initiative not only equipped officers with the necessary knowledge and skills but also fostered a sense of ownership of and contribution to the transformative journey. Eventually, many former employees made lateral migrations and today, some of them hold influential positions in the industry.

Resistance to Change?

There was a mix of excitement and apprehension, along with fear of the unknown, resistance, and even outright hostility in some cases. Most of the port's trade unions supported the e-Port project at various stages. Labour trustees on the Port Trust Board, C.D. Nandakumar and P.M. Mohammed Haneef, voiced their support whenever the matter came up for discussion and approval. However, there were also waves of resistance and work stoppages orchestrated by some unions. It is often said that organisations produce "antibodies" that reject anything new, especially when it involves large-scale, complex changes that would require people to adapt, mainly in their behaviour. This was somewhat true during the ERP implementation phase as well. Although the management did not face any major resistance or protests from the unions in the early phases of the implementation, as the project team neared the successful completion of mapping, we began to sense some clouds of resistance gathering, leading to a palpable increase in tensions.

Meanwhile, labour tensions were escalating in other areas of the port. The lack of trust and growing adversarial relationships in various sectors began to spill over into the ERP project, fuelled by a rising fear of losing existing rights and benefits. The immediate spark came when the management decided to introduce a biometric attendance monitoring system as a precursor to the ERP implementation. This required the staff to use fingerprint-enabled identification software when reporting to work and when checking out at the end of their duty hours. Under the ERP system, accurate attendance information would be a crucial component of the workforce management system. Naturally, both management and clients expected the staff to be present during their scheduled work hours to ensure the smooth and efficient operation of the organisation.

Then came the time to test the ERP process. As a preparatory step, the new protocol was given widespread publicity and discussions were held with unions prior to its introduction. In fact, a majority of the employees quietly followed the new rule, but some persons who were not used to signing in for their attendance so far, felt threatened and went on a warpath. Similarly, while some of the trade unions understood the logic and even cooperated with the management, a few vociferous ones began to mobilise the cadre, calling upon them to openly defy the new system.

One of the refrains of the demonstrators was that the biometric system was a symbol and measure of the distrust that the management had for the workers. To counter that premise, we took great pains to explain to the unions that the daily recording and automatic capturing of employees' attendance into the ERP system would be a compulsory requirement under the HR management system and fundamental to many other functions, including the software that controls the payment of salaries. What really sparked off this open defiance was not far to seek. It was a fear of "loss of control" on the part of some, especially those who had exercised a certain element of impunity in flouting the requirements of attendance. Some were simply "habituated" to walk in and out at will, and here again, the loss of control must have infuriated them.

In the meantime, while the major trade unions supported the management in this project, the demands for an indefinite strike against the ERP project began to get more vociferous and started to gain acceptability within some splinter groups. This could have been part of some tensions which were developing in certain other areas and due to causes very different from and unrelated to the computerisation project. And one day, there was a sudden outburst manifesting in violence, involving vandalisation of biometric installations and some computers. The sudden change of stance on the part of some of the unions left us stunned, but the implementation teams were not deterred. Every member of the team continued with the fierce focus and determination that was already motivating them. The work never stopped.

The Business Blueprint

The ability to meet the organisation's business needs efficiently and economically is the ultimate purpose of the ERP implementation. Mapping the business processes and creating a blueprint provides the much-needed clarity and understanding of the business itself. Clearly defining these processes paves the way for several activities, such as establishing system security profiles, providing end-user training, defining roles and responsibilities, and setting performance metrics. This required a thorough understanding by all employees of the detailed workflows, from start to finish.

Once the "To Be" processes reached some finality, the team started the work on the Business Blueprint Document. Along with this, creating an organisational chart also started. The real value of these exercises lay in the depth and extent of the introspection that we were able to undertake, on the organisational structure and operational culture, throwing light on deficiencies and shortcomings that had remained unnoticed so far. Obviously, the need for the employees to understand, accept, and own the business process, their operational roles and responsibilities in the new system emphasised the importance of a clear Business Blueprint. This document was expected to help the team plan out the details about the ultimate goal of the business transformation that we were aiming at and how to reach it. This would include the project milestones, deliverables, timelines, details of team members and their operational roles, details of user documents, and business scenario descriptions. Happily, the Blueprint development process too turned out to be a democratic one, involving the workers in each department. Being the ultimate end-users, the working group members brought much more practical understanding and insights into the "As Is" and "To Be" exercises.

Another extremely crucial milestone for us was the integration of the newly established e-Port ERP with important external software systems. One of the most central of these was the Port Community System (PCS), which was still being developed by the Indian Ports Association (IPA). The only catch was that the PCS was not yet ready, and Cochin Port, on the threshold of introducing its full-fledged ERP system, was obviously in a hurry.

Meanwhile, the TCS had already custom-built the Cargo and Logistics Management System (CALMS) for the Cochin e-Port ERP. Without loss of time, TCS was able to provide the interface between CALMS and the EDI system of the customs on the one hand and the upcoming PCS on the other. By early 2009, the e-Port experiment was nearing completion, ready to provide a seamless customer experience to the port's business partners and stakeholders through a full-fledged ERP platform. This meant that port-users would be able to log into the system from anywhere in the world and transact business with the port.

User Acceptance Testing (UAT)

By this time, we were ready for the User Acceptance Testing (UAT) stage, the next crucial phase. UAT plays a critical role in ensuring that the software aligns with the organisation's requirements and functions correctly. It allows the HoDs and their teams to validate these customisations, ensuring that the ERP system is tailored to the unique processes of each department. This validation would guarantee that the system would effectively support the port's operations. UAT also provides an opportunity for the HoDs and their teams to verify that the ERP system's functionalities aligned with their departments' objectives. They could test various features and processes as well as identify any discrepancies or issues that needed to be addressed before the system's final deployment.

In other words, the UAT phase actively involved the end-users and administrators from different departments in testing the ERP system, allowing them to interact with the software and provide valuable feedback on its usability and functionality. The users could identify any areas where the system fell short of their expectations or where improvements were needed, ensuring that the final product would be user-friendly and effective. UAT also served as a quality assurance checkpoint, helping to identify and rectify errors, bugs, or inconsistencies in the ERP system. This phase was meant to test data accuracy, system reliability, and overall system integrity. Any issues detected during UAT could be addressed before the system went live, minimising disruptions and errors in the production environment.

UATs played an important role in building confidence among the HoDs and their teams regarding the ERP system's capabilities. By actively participating in testing and validation, they could see first-hand how the system would support their daily tasks and operations. This increase in their confidence was essential for a smooth transition to the new digital environment. This phase ultimately served as a vital quality control and validation process, ensuring that the system met their specific needs, functioned correctly, and remained user-friendly.

Of course, the UAT phase was no cakewalk. Even as some of the employees came face to face with the new system for the first time, there was some visible resistance to change in the air, leading to some initial hesitancy and reluctance to work in the new system.

Ambiguities and inadequacies in test plans and documentation created some instances of confusion among the users. There were some data migration issues, including some mismatch and inaccuracies between the legacy and new systems, which raised a large number of concerns.

Being a pioneering venture among all Indian ports, our project faced several unique challenges, such as interfacing of the software with those of the banks and regulatory authorities like the Customs and Central Excise departments and the POS which was still under development by the IPA. Similarly, some of the software systems of some other interfacing agencies were also at different stages of development, leading to various teething troubles that caused us major worries throughout the ERP implementation, particularly the UAT process. The IPOS was the brainchild of the then Managing Director of IPA, Dr A. Janardan Rao, who was also a former Deputy Chairman of Cochin Port.

Interestingly, inadvertent data entry errors led to some discrepancies in accounting, initially causing alarm until they were identified as genuine mistakes. Resource constraints, such as staff shortages and competing priorities, frequently impacted testing timelines. Managing identification of bugs and their resolution became the biggest challenge, particularly when there were disagreements regarding the severity or priority of identified issues. Problems were encountered in incorporating feedback from the users into the system. Careful assessment of requested changes and their prioritisation within the project scope became essential since too much of change in the projected scope would also result in unexpected financial burdens. Very often, incomplete records and data inconsistencies delayed matters considerably. Nevertheless, the UAT process was a hugely important learning phase for us. This was also a period when our attention and priorities were pulled in various directions, with requirements of numerous mega infrastructure projects, trade union conflicts, and internal upheavals demanding our time. Despite these formidable challenges, the dedicated teams at Cochin Port demonstrated exceptional perseverance and determination, successfully overcoming the hurdles. Very soon, we were ready for the "Go Live" launch.

The Big Bang Launch

There were extensive consultations between the TCS and port teams about the modalities of implementation and the strategy for "Go Live". The entire team was in favour of adopting the "Big Bang" approach, deciding on a starting date for the new system to go live without doing a parallel run. The confidence level of team members was so high that they decided to take on the challenge.

"Go Live" was declared on 7 February 2009 at a function organised by the port with some fanfare, involving its employees and trade unions and inviting stakeholders from different spheres, regulatory authorities, business partners, port users, major industries in the area, and citizens' representatives. Cochin was to become the first e-Port in India, among all Indian major ports, implementing a comprehensive ERP involving all its operations and business verticals. This was the culmination of more than three years of frenetic but diligent work on the part of the port and TCS teams.

What Did We Achieve?

For Cochin Port, the ERP project was key component of our broader strategy for organisational survival—an idea that also formed the cornerstone of our communication efforts. In an era of shrinking business opportunities, it was imperative to make determined efforts to improve operational efficiency across the board. With several mega projects in the offing, effective project and task management had become critical to eliminating bottlenecks and improving coordination with business partners, contractors, and external agencies. Equally important was the need to boost productivity, strengthen problem-solving capabilities through data analysis, and empower employees to perform better by leveraging digital tools.

One major attraction was the lure of data-driven decision-making. The ERP's business intelligence function was found extremely useful in crunching numbers and understanding the complex trends. Recently, while interacting with the present chairman, I was told that Cochin Port is able to provide any information and data that the government asks for in minutes. This was a welcome change from the past when it would take several days to glean data from manual records and put them together in a presentable form. Today, it is possible to obtain deeper understanding of how the departments are functioning, and through dashboards, it is now easy to have detailed and accurate visibility of all important information at the click of a button.

Of all the benefits, I would say that the drastic change in customer experience was the most rewarding. There was a time when an importer or exporter was required to visit the port to obtain clearances for ship-berthing or cargo-handling. After filling nearly 40 different kinds of forms, they had to stand in front of multiple department windows to pay tariffs, visit the offices of the customs commissioner, and nearly half a dozen other offices before securing clearances. Today, the port's customers can transact their business online, sitting anywhere in the world, seamlessly and efficiently.

The one beautiful benefit of the ERP system has been that all internal processes are now integrated and are consistently and continually communicating with each other and sending updates to each other on a real-time basis, in contrast to the silo-like functioning of the past. Another well-recognised benefit has been the savings achieved in terms of operating costs, leakage of revenues, and enhanced efficiencies. Overall, the new system ensured absolute clarity on business processes, transparency in transaction, and efficiency in utilising resources. Another important advantage of the new system was that it eliminated the need for repetitive data entry.

A Win for Cochin Port's Image

Over the years, Cochin Port has been a victim of a negative image about its industrial climate and productivity losses. These perceptions had done much damage to the reputation, thereby, to the growth of the port. The successful completion of the Cochin e-Port project, making it a pioneering success story in the entire country without any time or cost overruns, has proved Cochin's critics wrong. In fact, the e-Port has been only one of the several complex projects that the port had taken up in recent years and was able to complete in record time.

Teamwork and Collaborative Vision

It must be emphasised that the implementation of the ERP was taken up during an era when the port officers were extraordinarily busy with the implementation of numerous mega infrastructure projects, which kept them busy throughout their working hours. This meant that the teams were required to work for the ERP implementation mostly beyond office hours, often late into the night, meeting multiple deadlines and working against all odds.

Cochin Port's ERP implementation experience stands as an excellent example in team-building, teamwork and decentralised efforts in achieving process re-engineering and ultimately culminating in a remarkable organisational change. The project and its implementation was entirely conceived, developed, and executed by the port's HoDs and their teams. Picture each Head of Department seated with their teams, working closely alongside team members from TCS, the implementation partner.

It is worth noting that while we were able to do the "Big Bang" launch in three years, the entire implementation work was done by the teams over four years, very often labouring late into the night. It was very much like rebuilding a house while continuing to live in it.

From conceptualisation onwards, the HoDs immersed themselves in project planning, assessment of needs, and goal setting, laying the groundwork for what lay ahead. Their leadership was crucial, as the project progressed through "As Is" and "To Be" analyses and gap identification exercises, setting the stage for reshaping the port's future structure and operations. During the design phase, the HoDs collaborated with their teams, configuring the ERP software to seamlessly align with the envisioned "To Be" processes.

Data Migration

It was now time for the challenge of data migration. Senior leaders worked closely with their teams to ensure the accurate transfer of diverse legacy data forms into the ERP. It must be remembered that the legacy data was in different formats and sizes. Much of the legacy data was on stand-alone computers in Word documents, spreadsheets, and databases in other formats. A substantial part of legacy data was in manual registers, which needed to be typed out and re-entered into the system. In terms of the sheer size of the work, this transition from legacy data to the ERP was one of the most time-consuming exercises, requiring very dedicated and meticulous attention to data integrity and error-free data entry.

The leadership and teamwork of our HoDs and their staff became even more visible during the subsequent phases of development and testing when the joint teams meticulously carried out the "test and integrate" customisations with the ERP system. Their journeys continued with the UAT, validating the ERP's link with each department's unique requirements.

The training needs of every department had been identified and the end-users and administrators trained to provide them with the necessary skills to effectively utilise the ERP system and work in the new data-driven environment. As the project neared completion, senior leaders played key roles in the rollout of the ERP system in their respective departments. At this stage, the teams were actively involved in data validation exercises, meticulously verifying data integrity and consistency within the live environment.

At every stage of this transformational journey, the officers exhibited remarkable leadership, engaging closely with their teams, encouraging their staff to think beyond the status quo. This collaborative vision on the part of our officers was the driving force that propelled the ERP implementation project forward. They and their teams not only understood the intricacies of the port's operations but also envisioned how the ERP system would seamlessly integrate into daily practices. It also laid a robust foundation for a more agile, efficient, and competitive port operation, ready to meet the demands of the modern maritime industry. Such visionary teamwork ensured that the ERP implementation went far beyond a mere digitalisation project, evolving into a strategic initiative that fundamentally changed the organisation itself.

Support of Trade Unions

Initially, trade unions were sceptical of the ERP project, fearing job losses, process disruptions, and a loss of their influence. However, as discussions progressed and the port management clearly communicated the long-term organisational benefits of the ERP system, the attitudes of union leaders and members began to change. Gradually, they came to recognise that the adoption of technology was inevitable and that the new system would ultimately serve the best interests of the port—and, by extension, those of its employees.

Project Leadership

From the early stages of the project, K.G. Nath, the Financial Advisor and Chief Accounts Officer of Cochin Port, assumed the responsibility of leading the entire mission as Project Director. He not only provided the overarching leadership but was also directly in charge of the development and implementation of the FICO module. His indefatigable dedication and commitment deserve special mention. He was enthusiastically assisted by his deputies,

B. Bhagyanath, K. Poothapandi, M.K. Radhakrishnan, and P. Kumaran. Many others also played exemplary leadership roles. They included Deputy Chairpersons Captain Subhash Kumar and later, G. Krishna Kumar; Chief Engineer J. Karthikeyan; Secretary Cyril George; Deputy Secretaries B.K. Jha, Jijo Thomas and C. Premakumari; Deputy Conservator Captain Paul N. Joseph; Harbour Master Captain Joseph J. Alapatt; Chief Mechanical Engineers Niteen Borwankar, A.K. Gadkari and M.S. Renjith; Traffic Managers Rajendra Paibir, Damodar Nayak, and Rajendra Paibir, Additional Traffic Manager Vipin R. Menoth and Deputy Traffic Manager Jimmy George. There were also those who were involved in the project implementation for shorter periods as they got transferred in between.

Equally significant were the contributions of Unnikrishnan Nair,[3] joint director of the PBSEZ, who was one of the pillars of the project from inception to completion. In addition to his responsibilities in handling the HR and CALMS modules, he played an important role in the change-management initiatives, which included communication with employees and stakeholders, identifying potential areas of resistance, and taking proactive measures to address them. He stood by me at every stage of this implementation and his dedication and diligence cannot be praised enough. Apart from the assiduous implementation of the project, the essential preparatory work, which provided its grounding, was carried out by the team of Cochin Port's Electronic Data Processing (EDP) Department led by Deputy Director M.V. Paul. They played a crucial role by providing reliable support, ensuring smooth coordination, technical readiness, and uninterrupted assistance throughout the implementation process. Their painstaking efforts were instrumental in establishing the necessary foundation on which the edifice was built.

---

3. Unnikrishnan Nair, JD PBSEZ, was subsequently appointed Traffic Manager of the port in September 2010.

While the HoDs played their leadership roles, the true magic happened at the middle and junior levels of operational leadership. The Working Group officers developed an in-depth understanding of their domains, enabling them to determine the practicality of new work processes or systemic changes and evaluate their actual operational impact. Their domain expertise was truly remarkable, showing a keen awareness of the problems that required attention and the necessary solutions. They understood how the proposed re-engineering efforts would shape the future. Their enthusiasm to embrace new technologies, digital tools, and processes, coupled with their eagerness for change and their ownership of the transformation process, was exceptional.

A valuable takeaway of this story is about the power of collaboration and partnership between the teams from the implementing organisation, Cochin Port, and the system integrator and implementation partner, TCS. The story is not only about the competence of individual members of the teams. It is about how their seamless partnership and collaboration produced extraordinary results and true magic. The highly competent members of the TCS team worked in such close coordination with the port officers that it often became difficult to distinguish between members of the two teams. Their interface and collaboration with the port personnel were so harmonious that it paved the way for a remarkable transformation.

The strategic direction provided by the TCS project leadership, led by Dinesh Thampy, Sujatha Madhav Chandran, and Anil Pai, contributed to the success of the project. Their unrelenting passion, dedication, and guidance played a vital role in driving the project forward. It was always a learning experience for us when we interacted with the highly competent TCS team members who interfaced with the port officers and drove the ERP implementation project. The collective work of these men and women from the port and TCS made all the difference. They were indeed the champions of change!

This story stands as a powerful testament to what can be achieved when members of the implementing organisation and system integrators come together as a synergistic team. Their combined efforts highlighted the immense value of collaboration in driving transformative change. Success was hard-won—the challenges were significant—but the journey became a source of immense pride. The team became pioneers in implementing an ERP system at Cochin Port, despite most officers and staff having had no prior exposure to a digital transformation initiative of such scale.

The port sector in the country had no prior experience to draw upon—no established roadmap to guide us through the complex terrain we were about to navigate, nor any clear indication of the opportunities and risks that lay ahead. Once we took the plunge, we were swept into a whirlwind of crazy work schedules, marked by periodic bouts of excitement and frustration. We faced resistance from formidable quarters, further compounded by our own missteps along the way. The speed at which change descended upon us was unpredictable and, at times, overwhelming.

Yet, in the end, we won! We prevailed because we had a clear vision of where we wanted to go. We succeeded because our employees and trade unions recognised the inevitability of technological transformation and understood the long-term benefits of what we were trying to achieve. Across all levels of the organisation, there was a shared understanding that radical changes were imperative to efficiently manage the ambitious, modern port we envisioned. The systems and processes we implemented were designed to bring us in line with the world's leading ports, enabling us to compete confidently on the global stage.

4

THE STORY OF VALLARPADAM

India's First International Container Transshipment Terminal

A historic day for Kerala, Cochin city, and Cochin Port, 11 February 2011 was also a proud moment of accomplishment for the entire team. On this day, Prime Minister Manmohan Singh inaugurated the Vallarpadam International Container Transshipment Terminal (ICTT) under Cochin Port, in the presence of Kerala Chief Minister V.S. Achuthanandan and a distinguished gathering of dignitaries from India and abroad. This was India's first integrated port project, comprising the Container Terminal, a 17-kilometre-long national highway from Vallarpadam to Kalamassery, a 9-kilometre-long-rail connection from the new port to the national railway network joining at Edappally, suitably deepened navigation channels, and other critical infrastructure. Each of these components was a large infrastructure project in itself, and the simultaneous commissioning of all these facilities symbolised the aspirations of India's maritime sector and those of the people of Kerala. The new terminal was designed to accommodate larger container ships with up to 14.5 metres draught, offering state-of-the-art infrastructure, efficient cargo handling, and seamless connectivity via road and rail.

The galaxy of dignitaries who graced the event included Union Defence Minister A.K. Antony, Shipping Minister G.K. Vasan,

Union Ministers Vayalar Ravi, C.P. Joshi, K.V. Thomas, K.C. Venugopal, and Mullappally Ramachandran, UAE Executive Council Deputy Chairman Sheikh Ahmed bin Saeed Al Maktoum, UAE Foreign Trade Minister Sheikha Lubna Bint Khalid Al Qasimi, and DP World Chairman Sultan Ahmed Bin Sulayem.

Vallarpadam was conceived and built as India's first International Container Transshipment Terminal and holds immense significance for the country's export-import trade. The project aimed to reduce India's reliance on foreign transshipment hubs like Colombo, Singapore, Port Klang, Salalah, and Jebel Ali, which, in turn, would potentially cut costs and transit times for Indian cargo. Cochin Port's strategic proximity to major east-west global shipping routes would enable mainline ships to call at Cochin, allowing Indian exports and imports to bypass foreign ports, resulting in substantial cost reductions, improved efficiency, and enhanced competitiveness for India's export-import trade, while strengthening its position in the global maritime trade network. The new terminal heralded the potential for big improvements in maritime logistics, aligning with India's national maritime strategy and commitment to modernising its logistics infrastructure. The successful construction and commissioning of all components of the integrated Vallarpadam port project, completed without time delays or cost overruns, generated optimism about its long-term impact. The Prime Minister hailed it as a triumph of public–private partnerships.

The Journey to Vallarpadam

Following the signing of the Concession Agreement between Cochin Port and the Dubai Ports Authority[1] (later Dubai Ports

1. At the time of submitting its tender for the Vallarpadam project, the company operated as Dubai Ports International (DPI), the international arm of the Dubai Ports Authority (DPA). In 2005, the two entities merged to form DP World, unifying domestic and international operations under a single global brand. DP World rapidly expanded its global footprint after acquiring the Peninsular and Oriental Steam

World), Prime Minister Manmohan Singh visited Cochin on 16 February 2005 to lay the foundation stone for the ICTT project. From the day I assumed office as Chairman of Cochin Port, I wholeheartedly dedicated myself to what was then the port's most ambitious flagship project. In its early stages, however, the project remained merely a visionary concept on paper, and the road ahead looked hazy and shrouded in uncertainty.

The primary challenge stemmed from the terms of the Concession Agreement, which stipulated that while the PPP concessionaire—Dubai Ports International (later DP World)—would be responsible for investing in the construction of the Transshipment Terminal, Cochin Port was contractually obligated to develop critical infrastructure such as road and rail connectivity and to undertake the deepening of port channels. These were the prerequisites for success of the ICTT. Unfortunately, the port lacked the financial resources to undertake these costly projects.

Nevertheless, I was driven by an inexplicable conviction that the necessary funds would somehow materialise. I was determined to see the project through within the five-year span of my tenure. Before long, I found myself immersed in the container terminal project—so much so that my life began to revolve around the world of cargo container boxes, prompting my wife to quip that it was time I started "thinking out of the (container) box".

For the Cochin Port team, the next five years were a rollercoaster of ups and downs, unexpected twists, and a seemingly unending interplay of hope and despair. Successes came often, but so did setbacks: fiascos, failures, disputes, confrontations, and the ever-present fear of falling short. Nevertheless, through it all, a strong sense of unity and shared purpose kept the team going. Throughout this tumultuous journey, there was an underlying sense of confidence, bolstered by steady support and encouragement from both Thiruvananthapuram and New

---

Navigation Company (P&O) in 2006—positioning it among the world's leading port operators.

Delhi. Surprisingly, support and endorsement often came from unexpected quarters as well.

By February 2011, the entire integrated Vallarpadam port project, and its rail and highway connectivity and deepened navigation channels were constructed, developed, and delivered within the scheduled timeline of five years, defying the heavy odds and challenges encountered along the way. This accomplishment brought immense euphoria, pride and satisfaction to every employee of Cochin Port as well as the leadership and teams of DP World, Rail Vikas Nigam Limited (RVNL), National Highways Authority of India (NHAI), their construction partners and contractors, and a plethora of other organisations and authorities who toiled hard for these five years to achieve the target. It was the realisation of the dream, the vision and the perseverance of numerous chairpersons of the port and their dedicated teams. For me personally, it brought immense professional satisfaction. After completion of my Cochin Port tenure and five days after the inauguration of the ICTT and other projects, I relinquished charge and returned to my IPS home cadre, Assam-Meghalaya, initially to take up one of the vacant positions in the rank of a Director General of Police (DGP) in the State of Assam.

To begin with, I will briefly narrate the efforts of my predecessors and their teams, shedding light on the circumstances that led to the envisioning and design of the Vallarpadam ICTT project. I shall outline the circumstances and events that led to the seeking of public investments, the agonies and challenges associated with land acquisitions and other related events. There will be some brief insights into the process of construction of the different components of the integrated ICTT project and its supporting infrastructure. For implementation of these projects, the Cochin Port teams gave their best. These are, of course, tales of success, achievements, goof-ups, failures, and setbacks. Talking of the container transshipment terminal, it is also important to bring in some context here. For a better appreciation of its significance, particularly for the benefit of those who are not familiar with the industry, an understanding of the container logistics and transshipment processes is essential and I will try to explain them. Towards the end of the chapter, I shall also try to explain how a flat-footed and inflexible application of cabotage law (explained later in this chapter) has effectively prevented India from breaking free from the stranglehold of neighbouring country ports in the transshipment business. Lastly, there will be some musings about the future of Vallarpadam, particularly in the face of the relentless expansion of container ship sizes, the race for deep water ports, and the anticipated competition from the upcoming Vizhinjam port.

The Advent of Cargo Container and Its Logistics

There was a time when cargo handling and transportation at ports was an incredibly arduous and time-consuming process. Goods were loaded and unloaded manually, often requiring large numbers of workers and long hours of backbreaking labour. Prior to the widespread adoption of shipping containers, cargo was manually handled in bulk or break-bulk form, packed in sacks, barrels, wooden crates, or slung in mats, with each item managed individually. This system was not only labour-intensive and inefficient but also prone to accidents, damages, losses, and theft. Shipping was slow, expensive, and frequently delayed. Cargo had to be carefully packed into various types of vessels, often resulting in significant logistical challenges and high risks of damage.

The concept of the TEU[2] container originated in the 1950s when American trucking entrepreneur Malcolm McLean revolutionised

---

2. The Twenty-Foot Equivalent Unit (TEU) is a standard measure used in the shipping and logistics industry to indicate container capacity. One TEU represents a 20-foot-long standard shipping container with a width of 8 feet and a height of 8.5 feet. It is commonly used to describe the capacity of container ships, terminals, and ports. Larger containers, such as 40-foot containers, are considered 2 TEUs. The TEU metric helps standardize multi-modal transportation and global trade while also making it easier to compare shipping volumes and port throughput across different regions and operators.

the shipping industry by envisioning a more efficient system—using standardised containers that could be seamlessly transferred between trucks, trains, and ships without the need for unpacking. In 1956, McLean introduced the first intermodal shipping container, which was 20 feet long. This standard-sized container became the foundation for global shipping.

This innovation drastically reduced transportation time and costs, and set the stage for the explosive growth of international trade in the decades that followed. It is amazing how one simple idea reshaped global logistics and trade!

The introduction of the standardised cargo container revolutionised the global shipping industry, making international trade more streamlined, efficient, and cost-effective. By packaging goods into large, uniform containers, cargo could be easily transferred between ships, trucks, and trains, drastically reducing handling time and labour costs.

This breakthrough, known as containerisation, stands as one of the most transformative advancements in global trade. It not only improved logistical efficiency but also enabled the smooth, large-scale movement of goods, thereby driving economic growth worldwide. Today, shipping containers ensure that cargo remains safe from pilferage and damage. Typically, the shipper loads and seals the container at their premises, after which it is securely transported by truck or rail to the port.

Modern ports are equipped with standardised infrastructure such as advanced cargo handling software and gantry cranes at the quay and yard, which facilitate the automated or semi-automated processes of lifting, stacking, retrieving containers from the stack, transporting them to the quay, and loading them onto ship and vice versa at the destination. These technological advancements have drastically improved turnaround times and overall port efficiency.

Since the widespread adoption of containerisation in the latter half of the 20th century, the logistics landscape has been completely reshaped. Today, around 95 per cent of global trade moves by sea, with an estimated 20 million containers in transit at any given time. The durability of containers, combined with modern port infrastructure, continues to safeguard cargo and optimise the lifting, storage, and transportation processes.

Globalisation and containerisation have also led to significant changes in the labour sector, dramatically enhancing the port workers' efficiency and productivity. This, in turn, has transformed the management of dock labour. The relative ease of moving containers between different modes of transportation, coupled with the increasing size of container ships, has not only improved economies of scale but also continually challenges the port workers' cargo handling expertise and efficiency.

Competition among ports and the drive to achieve higher productivity—measured in terms of Gross Moves per Hour (GMPH)—have further intensified the pressure on ports and their workers to complete cargo handling operations and vessel turnaround as quickly as possible. In this context, containerisation has played a pivotal role in enhancing interconnectedness and driving efficiencies across global logistics. Today, it is hard to imagine how difficult it once was to transport cargo from one part of the world to another before the advent of the standardised shipping container.

Container Transshipment: The Hub-and-Spoke System in Maritime Logistics

In today's shipping industry, direct transportation of containers from the point of export to the point of import using a single vessel is rare, typically occurring only over short distances with smaller vessels. Due to non-availability of direct shipping services between countries, containers often need to be unloaded and reloaded at multiple transshipment ports along the route. For instance, in the absence of a direct shipping service between Kolkata and Rotterdam, an export container may initially travel on a smaller feeder vessel from Kolkata to Colombo or Singapore, where it is then transferred onto a larger "mother ship" heading to Rotterdam. Similarly, when importing a container from Germany to India, it may begin its journey on a mother vessel to a nearby transshipment hub like Singapore, Colombo, or Jebel Ali. From there, it would be transshipped onto a feeder vessel that transports it to its final destination, such as Mumbai or Chennai.

Factors like economies of scale and efficiency concerns in maritime logistics have led to the development of colossal "mother vessels" capable of carrying several thousands of cargo containers. These mammoth vessels sail along major shipping routes, connecting vast seaports worldwide. This phenomenon has given rise to the "hub-and-spoke" system, where "mother vessels" dock at transshipment hub ports and smaller feeder services transport containers destined for regional ports.

Transshipment containers are typically unloaded from incoming vessels, temporarily stacked and stored in designated storage yards, and finally loaded onto outbound vessels. Modern transshipment terminals use advanced software and algorithms to efficiently manage and control transshipment flows from the quayside to storage spaces and back. Such software also support temporal planning by assigning servicing time slots to vessels. Simultaneously, it is crucial to effectively manage compliance and regulatory processes, such as customs and security clearances, as well as the requirements of the labour and health authorities.

Why Container Transshipment Terminals are Crucial for India

While a large part of India's export-import containers move directly from the port of origin to the port of destination, nearly 25 per cent of the country's container traffic is transshipped through foreign ports en route to its final destination. Nearly 75 per cent of this transshipped cargo is handled at foreign ports like Colombo, Singapore, Salalah, Jebel Ali, and Port Klang.

Every transshipment increases the cost of container freight due to extra handling charges, port fees, and taxes that are applied each time a container passes through a port. Each transshipment also incurs terminal handling charges, documentation costs, and fuel surcharges, particularly when the routing becomes less efficient. Moreover, transshipment can cause delays, resulting in storage and demurrage fees. For Indian exports, this is especially significant, as routing through hubs like Jebel Ali, Colombo, or Singapore raises freight costs, making Indian products less competitive in international markets compared to those shipped directly from larger transshipment hubs. In contrast, if the container were shipped directly from Cochin to Rotterdam, it would avoid these intermediate transshipment costs, reducing the overall freight expenses and transit time.

Developing a robust container transshipment sector in India is expected to generate significant economic benefits to the country, as it reduces dependency on foreign transshipment hubs, potentially lowering shipping costs and transit times. Secondly, transshipment ports have the potential for job creation, increased port revenues, and the stimulation of ancillary industries such as logistics, warehousing, and ship maintenance. Lastly, it can lead to improved infrastructure and greater investments in port facilities, further bolstering India's competitiveness in the global trade arena and contributing to its overall economic growth.

At the time of its conceptualisation, the Vallarpadam ICTT exemplified this vision, offering direct connections to various parts of the world and promoting seamless trade. A transshipment hub in Cochin would provide direct connections to various parts of the world, including the Far East, Southeast Asia, Australia, the Mediterranean, Europe, and the Americas. Such enhanced connectivity would facilitate seamless trade with these regions, promoting economic growth and regional development. Further, the establishment of a transshipment facility in Cochin would help attract investment from both domestic and international players, for the development of related industrial and commercial infrastructure and enhanced connectivity. Developing efficient transshipment facilities within the country would help reduce transportation time and save precious foreign exchange that would otherwise be spent on transshipping our goods through foreign ports. At the time of its conceptualisation, the ICTT was designed to accommodate the largest container vessels then in service, with capacities ranging from 8,000 to 8,500 TEUs. Since then, container ship sizes and capacities have increased drastically.

The Cochin ICTT: An Idea Whose Time Had Come

Cochin's strategic geographic location near the east-west maritime trunk route makes it an ideal choice for a transshipment hub. Its proximity to both the Suez Canal and Middle Eastern shipping routes allows mainline vessels to access the port with minimal deviation and without significant loss of sailing time. Importantly, Cochin is a natural harbour with minimal tidal variation, which enables uninterrupted cargo operations year round. This enhances operational efficiency, reduces delays, and helps lower cargo handling and inventory costs.

While envisioning the ICTT at Vallarpadam, it was considered important to fully capitalise on Cochin's inherent advantages by developing modern infrastructure tailored to the needs of larger vessels. This included ensuring sufficient draft depths, state-of-the-art quayside facilities, and seamless connectivity via rail, road, and inland waterways. Such infrastructure would position Cochin as a highly attractive destination for global shipping lines, ultimately boosting trade and enhancing economic prospects for both Kerala and the nation at large.

The development of an international container transshipment terminal at Vallarpadam under Cochin Port had long been a cherished vision. Such a facility would enable Cochin to fully capitalise on its strategic geographic location along key international maritime routes. However, despite multiple studies highlighting the port's advantageous location and commercial potential, the project remained confined to the drawing board for over two decades due to various challenges.

Feasibility Study

In the early 1990s, the Cochin Port Trust commissioned a feasibility study to evaluate the potential of Vallarpadam Island as a container transshipment hub. The study examined the suitability of the location, the infrastructure requirements, and the overall economic viability of the proposed project. Its findings suggested that the development of an ICTT at Vallarpadam would be strategically important and economically viable.

The market assessment considered several key factors: the rapid growth of India's maritime trade, the potential to attract international transshipment traffic, and the benefits of reducing dependence on foreign ports. At the time, a significant share of India's container transshipment traffic was being handled by ports in Sri Lanka and Singapore. The study indicated that the ICTT at Vallarpadam could capture a substantial portion of this traffic.

From a technical standpoint, Vallarpadam offered several advantages. Its strategic location along major international shipping routes, proximity to the Indian hinterland, and the potential for achieving the required draught through additional dredging made it ideal for accommodating larger container vessels. Moreover, the availability of land for future expansion and modernisation reinforced its suitability as the site for India's first dedicated ICTT.

Successive Cochin Port chairpersons, including C. Babu Rajeev and Jacob Thomas, were committed to realising the long-cherished vision of establishing the ICTT at Vallarpadam. Under C. Babu Rajeev's leadership, the port formulated a concrete framework for the construction and development of the terminal. The project was conceived as a Build-Operate-Transfer (BOT) initiative, aligned with the government's emerging PPP policy.

BOT Contract with Dubai Ports International

The initial tendering efforts, led by Chairman C. Babu Rajeev, failed to generate an adequate market response—largely due to the fluid market conditions prevailing in the region at the time—resulting in two unsuccessful tendering attempts. Undeterred, his successor, Jacob Thomas, continued to push the project forward. Drawing on the feasibility study, comprehensive market assessment, and various technical evaluations that underscored the strategic and economic significance of the ICTT for both the region and the global maritime sector, the Cochin Port Trust launched a fresh round of tendering. This new global tender sought a private partner to develop and operate the ICTT under a BOT model. The tender attracted several bids, with Dubai Ports International (DPI) emerging as the successful bidder.

In the presence of Kerala Chief Minister Oommen Chandy and Union Shipping Minister T. R. Baalu, the Cochin Port Trust signed the Concession Agreement for the development and operation of the ICTT with the successful bidder DPI on 7 February 2005 in Thiruvananthapuram. The agreement, structured under a BOT model, was for a period of 30 years, for which the DPI had offered the highest revenue share of 33.30 per cent—a figure considered highly competitive and favourable for the port.

In the first phase of the project, the DPI, through its subsidiary, the IGTPL and a Special Purpose Vehicle (SPV) involving other potential investors, committed to invest Rs 2,118 crores. Among the investors was Cochin's own Chakiat Agencies Private Limited, which held a minor stake. As per the terms of the agreement, the DPI would hold exclusive rights to handle container cargo at Cochin Port until the ICTT's throughput exceeded 2.5 million TEUs. As a first step in this direction, the existing Rajiv Gandhi Container Terminal (RGCT) at Cochin Port would be handed over to the IGTPL for container handling operations. It was also agreed that the DPI would complete the construction and development of the ICTT within four years and move operations to Vallarpadam, after which the existing RGCT berths would be returned to Cochin Port.

The agreement also placed several critical obligations on Cochin Port. Foremost among these was the responsibility to construct and commission both railway and highway connectivity to the ICTT as well as to deepen the navigation channels to provide a draught of 14.5 metres, enabling large mainline vessels of up to 8,000 TEU capacity to access the terminal. The agreement also stipulated that the area under development would be declared as a Port-Based Special Economic Zone (PBSEZ)[3] to facilitate international transshipments and related value-added activities.

Cochin Port was also tasked with obtaining all necessary environmental clearances for associated infrastructure projects. The Concession Agreement between the Cochin Port Trust and the DPI marked a significant milestone in the journey towards establishing the ICTT at Vallarpadam. It laid the groundwork for a world-class container transshipment terminal with the potential to boost trade and economic growth in the region.

The collaboration between the Cochin Port Trust and the DPI aimed to create a facility that would strengthen the region's connectivity and competitiveness in the global shipping sector. As mentioned earlier, following the signing of the Concession Agreement, Prime Minister Manmohan Singh laid the foundation stone for the ICTT project at Cochin Port on 16 February 2005.

---

3. The rationale behind the PBSEZ was to create an integrated logistics and trade ecosystem that would facilitate transshipment operations. The SEZ was envisioned to attract investment in value-added activities such as free trade warehousing, container freight stations, and port-based industries. The SEZ framework offered fiscal incentives, streamlined procedures, and customs benefits aimed at enhancing the terminal's competitiveness.

Preparing Employees and Labour Unions for the Transition

Even as Cochin Port prepared to sign the Concession Agreement with the DPI, the management had already recognised the importance of involving employees and labour unions in the decision-making process. There were genuine apprehensions that transferring the existing container terminal to DPI's management could bring significant operational changes, potentially triggering resistance or disputes if not handled sensitively. To ensure a smooth and conflict-free transition, the port management initiated several rounds of dialogue with the unions. These discussions aimed to address concerns of the workforce and create a transparent environment where all stakeholders felt heard and acknowledged. The management's proactive and inclusive approach helped build trust and promote cooperation.

Efforts were made to communicate the details of the Concession Agreement and modalities of the subsequent transition in a transparent and inclusive manner. During these discussions, the management highlighted the benefits that the collaboration with the DPI would bring—not only to the port and the state's economy, but also to the workforce. Emphasis was placed on the potential for skill development, improved working conditions, and greater exposure to international standards resulting from improved port efficiency and competitiveness. Importantly, the management also offered clear assurances regarding job security.

The labour unions, appreciating the need for change, entered into negotiations with the management to ensure that their members' rights and interests were protected. Subsequently, agreements were reached between the labour unions and the management, addressing issues such as job security, retraining, and skill development. These agreements played a crucial role in reducing unnecessary friction and disputes during the transition to the DPI management. By involving the labour unions in the decision-making process and addressing their concerns, the management demonstrated their commitment to open communication, mutual respect, and understanding when navigating significant changes within the organisation. This progressive approach of my predecessor, Jacob Thomas, paved the way for a smooth transition to the new management, ultimately contributing to the transformation of the RGCT into one of the more efficient port terminals in India, during the project's pre-stage arrangement itself.

The Beginning of Container Handling at RGCT

With the advent of containerisation in the global shipping industry, Cochin Port needed to adapt to the evolving demands of container handling. In the early 1990s, the port began operating a container terminal at the Q8 and Q9 berths of the Ernakulam Wharf. This initiative was launched under the chairmanship of G. Krishnan and later actively championed by his successor, C. Babu Rajeev, who assumed office on 15 November 1993. The development of the container terminal was funded through loans from the Asian Development Bank, backed by guarantees from the Government of India.

To facilitate container-handling operations, the port procured two specialised gantry cranes from Ansaldo, Italy, along with other handling equipment from various sources. The commencement of this terminal marked a significant shift in the port's focus from the traditional oil and bulk cargo handling towards container-handling operations. Despite its successful launch, the container terminal faced several structural and operational challenges. One major constraint was the height restriction imposed by the nearby Cochin Airport located on Willingdon Island, which was under the jurisdiction of the Indian Navy. This limitation prevented the installation of state-of-the-art gantry cranes at the terminal. In fact, this was one of the limitations to the container terminal's growth, requiring its re-location away from Willingdon Island.

Another significant challenge was the limited draught of 12.5 metres at the RGCT terminal, which proved inadequate for attracting major container lines. Nevertheless, the Cochin container terminal rapidly emerged as the port's primary profit centre. Under the leadership of Chairman C. Babu Rajeev, the management teams of the day ensured efficient operations by deploying skilled engineers and staff to the terminal. Despite its operational limitations, this arrangement remained in place for the next 12 years.

IGTPL and the Transition to Vallarpadam ICTT

As required under the Concession Agreement of 2005 between the Cochin Port Trust and the DPI, the operation of the existing RGCT at Ernakulam Wharf was handed over to the private operator as a pre-stage for ICTT's operationalisation. Meanwhile, the DPI had established a subsidiary company, IGTPL, to manage their container terminal operations. The Concession Agreement with the DPI included the unique provision of deputing 240 port personnel to the DPI, until the container handling activities migrated to Vallarpadam. This model, unprecedented in other port terminals in the country, proved highly successful and was later replicated in the port's contract with Cochin Shipyards Limited (CSL) for managing the workshop and dry dock.

The management transition of the RGCT to the new operator, IGTPL, marked a significant milestone in the port's growth and development. DP World aimed to enhance the terminal's efficiency and capacity by introducing new cranes, equipment, specialised staff, and advanced operating software. To their credit, the workers quickly adjusted to the new environment, acquiring new skills and learning new protocols. However, this transition was not without its challenges, particularly in the area of labour relations.

Even as the workforce of the port accepted this transition, one of the primary challenges faced by DP World was resistance to change from the existing work culture. The introduction of new equipment and advanced technology required the workforce to adapt and to learn new skills. This transition was met with apprehension and resistance, as the employees were concerned about job security and their ability to master the new technology. Further, the acquisition brought in a management team from Dubai, which led to cultural differences between the management and the local workforce. This created some communication barriers and misunderstandings, further complicating the smooth integration of the new management and technology.

The change in management and the introduction of new working practices led to frequent labour unrest, with employees demanding better working conditions, higher wages, and job security. The labour unions played a significant role in voicing these concerns and organising protests and strikes, frequently disrupting the operations of the terminal. To overcome the resistance to change and ensure a smooth transition, the DPI–IGTPL resorted to some retraining and skill development programmes for the existing workforce. This required additional time, effort, and resources to help the employees adapt to the new technology and working practices. The IGTPL had to navigate these complexities to ensure compliance with local laws while implementing the desired changes in the terminal's operations.

Despite these challenges, the IGTPL and its reconstituted workforce was able to transform the operations of the RGCT, making it an efficient port terminal. The introduction of additional cranes, equipment, specialised staff, and advanced operating software had significantly improved the terminal's capacity and productivity, contributing to the overall growth in container throughput.

The Construction of Vallarpadam

By the end of 2005, the BOT operator, the DPI, underwent an existential transformation of sorts, following its acquisition of the CSX World Terminals and P&O Ports, leading to its rebranding as "Dubai Ports World" (later, DP World).

It established its new subsidiary company at Cochin, christened as the IGTPL, to carry out construction of the new container terminal and all their port operations in Cochin. Meanwhile, just a few months after signing the licensing agreement, DP World appointed former Indian Railway Traffic Service officer Suresh Joseph as the general manager to head the IGTPL and also lead the construction and development of the ICTT. I joined Cochin Port Trust two months later and had the privilege of closely working with Suresh Joseph and his team throughout his tenure as the head of the IGTPL. Suresh exhibited outstanding brilliance and dedication, not only in overseeing the RGCT operations but also in his fierce commitment to the meticulous planning and construction of the ICTT, playing a pivotal role in ensuring the project's timely completion. Despite our not so infrequent disagreements and disputes during our collaboration, Suresh remained consistently cheerful and was a joy to work with.

The implementation of the Vallarpadam project began to gather steam when in June 2006, DP World appointed Royal Haskoning (RH), London, as the design and supervision consultant. Suresh Joseph, in his illustrative coffee table book *From Reclamation to Exclamation*, describes how the teams of RH, DP World, and Cochin Port had several brainstorming sessions in the early years of formulating the modular Master Plan for Development of the ICTT. Subsequently, as technical topography data, geotechnical information, and simulation study findings became available, Cochin Port began the application process for obtaining the necessary environmental clearances for the ICTT and associated connectivity projects. Concurrently, the port also submitted applications to the Government of India for the establishment of two PBSEZs, one in Vallarpadam and one in Puthuvypeen.

In February 2007, DP World finalised the Master Plan for the project and presented it to Cochin Port for approval. The project was to be realised in two separate phases, the first one being further split into Phases 1A and 1B. Phase 1A aimed to construct a 600-metre berth along with a container stacking yard designed to accommodate 1.2 million TEUs, while Phase 1B involved the addition of an extra 300 metres of berth length, resulting in a total handling capacity of 2 million TEUs. The full berth length, spanning 1800 metres, was slated for completion by the end of Phase 2, along with adequate stacking yards, thereby achieving the full annual capacity of 4 million TEUs. By October 2007, once the preliminary designs were approved by Cochin Port, DP World awarded the construction contract to Simplex Infrastructures Private Limited. The *Bhoomi Pooja* was held on 3 December 2007 and was attended by a distinguished gathering, including Union Minister K. V. Thomas, MLA K. Babu, District Collector A. P. M. Muhammed Hanish, Police Commissioner Manoj Abraham, Customs Commissioner Donald Ingty, previous port chairmen Babu Paul and Jacob Thomas, DP World officials Ganesh Raj and Suresh Joseph, and numerous other government officials, trade union leaders, and people's representatives.

Since the Vallarpadam site was created through land reclamation from dredge spoils, the foremost challenge for the construction teams was the exceptionally soft and slushy soil. In fact, consolidating the soft soil in Cochin Port's marshy reclamation area to facilitate the construction of heavy-duty facilities like port terminals, industrial plants, super-heavy storage tanks, railway tracks, and highway connectivity was a recurring obstacle. The primary objective involved stabilising the loose, water-saturated soil to establish a robust foundation capable of supporting such structures and heavy loads. This required different techniques, including soil improvement, ground reinforcement, implementation of effective drainage systems, and the use of deep piling-based foundations. Given the ecological sensitivity of the marshy terrains and the adjacent backwater and marine areas, environmental considerations were paramount. Striking a balance between engineering requirements and environmental preservation was of utmost importance, taking into account the conditions stipulated by the environmental ministry and related authorities. These measures were crucial for ensuring the long-term stability of the infrastructure and minimising potential risks to both the structures and the surrounding ecosystem.

Vallarpadam's marshy terrain presented all these challenges. To transform the land into a suitable foundation for a container port, it became necessary to drastically strengthen it, enabling the operation of heavy machinery and mammoth cranes as well as the high stacking of fully loaded containers. A railway station, complete with yards and railway tracks, was needed too. Suresh Joseph's book vividly depicts the engineers' efforts, involving a combination of innovative technologies and methods for soil improvement and stabilisation. This process entailed the installation of closely spaced stone columns and band drains to compress the soil and expel subsoil water. Interestingly, the band drains were inserted to depths of up to 22 metres. Layers of gravel aggregates were then applied over the band drains and covered with geotextile material. Subsequently, red earth was compacted atop the geotextile material, reaching a height of 4 metres before being left to consolidate. The piling for construction of the berth deck went as deep as 50 to 70 metres!

Meeting the Port's Contractual Obligations

The Concession Agreement between Cochin Port and the DPI outlined an array of contractual obligations and preconditions to be fulfilled by Cochin Port. These included many critical components such as the construction of a four-lane highway linking Vallarpadam to the national highway at Kalamassery, construction of a railway line connecting the ICTT terminal to the main railway network converging at Edappally, undertaking capital dredging to deepen the approach channels and the ICTT basin, securing the requisite environmental clearances for the ICTT and its associated road, railway, and dredging projects, and, lastly, the creation of a PBSEZ at Vallarpadam. Each one of these obligations would be integral to the successful completion of the ICTT and its efficient operation. The road and rail connectivity would facilitate seamless transportation of containers and connect the terminal with the national transportation network. Capital dredging[4] was aimed at deepening the navigation channels to reach a draught of 14.5 metres that would enable the largest mainline vessels of the day with capacities of up to 8,000 TEUs to operate at the ICTT. Obtaining environmental clearances was another requirement, not only for the ICTT development, but also for its associated road, railway, and dredging projects to assure the project's sustainability and minimise their ecological footprint. Another significant component of the port's obligations was the declaration of the project area as a PBSEZ as this would enable container transshipment, export-import-centric value addition industries, and related commercial activities.

But Where's the Money?

The directive from the Government of India was that the port should raise its own resources, establishing separate SPVs to construct and operate the highway and rail connectivity facilities. The prescribed funding model for the highway and rail connectivity projects was that one-third of the project costs be borne by the port, another one-third by the relevant authorities (the NHAI and the Indian Railways), and the remaining one-third to be sourced through public debts and bank loans. Moreover, the understanding was that the entire financial burden for capital dredging would be borne by the port. Altogether, meeting these financial obligations for the three infrastructure projects would require approximately Rs 1,600 crores or more.

In the first few days after assuming office, I held a series of stocktaking meetings in which it soon became clear that the port was already grappling with a severe financial crisis. The port's management teams began a series of brainstorming sessions,

4. *Capital dredging* refers to the initial deepening and widening of navigational channels, basins, or berths to create new maritime infrastructure or accommodate larger vessels. In contrast, *maintenance dredging* involves the periodic removal of silt, sand, and debris, which accumulate over time, to preserve the depths achieved through capital dredging and ensure safe, uninterrupted navigation.

seeking ideas for potential avenues for securing funds. From the series of presentations made by the financial advisor and his team, the precarious finances of the port was evident, already saddled with the responsibility of providing pensions to a growing number of retirees, with no pension funds or actuarial mechanisms in place. It soon became evident that there were no internal funds available to establish the SPVs or invest in the essential infrastructure projects. Adding to the complexity, the port was expected to shoulder the burden of the entire cost of dredging. Compounding these challenges, it transpired that obtaining bank loans would be difficult, due to the port's substantial outstanding government debts, being carried forward from pre-Independence days. Efforts to restructure the outstanding government loans made in the past did not reach anywhere.

Realising the extent of the financial shortfall to implement the Vallarpadam project was rather disturbing. Where could we find the necessary funds? Would the ICTT become just another unrealised dream in the port's history? These troubling questions weighed heavily on the team's mind.

Seeking Government Support

After several sessions of brainstorming, it became clear that the ICTT project would not take flight without a full financial backing from the Government of India for all the three crucial infrastructure components. The SPV approach was simply unfeasible for the reasons described above. This was a truly challenging situation for the survival and credibility of the port. We found ourselves in a predicament, practically unable to fulfil our contractual commitments. Meanwhile, newspapers had already started writing that Cochin Port lacked the financial resources to implement the connectivity projects, casting doubts and uncertainties on the future of the Vallarpadam project.

The only way forward would be to approach the Central government for financial assistance. There were apprehensions whether our requests would be entertained. Moreover, we all knew how difficult and complex it would be to get such large sums of money sanctioned. But we were determined to try. Our first step would be to prepare a strong and compelling proposal outlining the port's contractual obligations and the potential consequences of a possible default with a foreign entity. But the strategy was to emphasise the positive benefits that the ICTT would bring to the country and the region's development. We had to present a forceful and convincing argument emphasising the critical need for Central government funding for the successful implementation of the ICTT project, for which Prime Minister Manmohan Singh had himself laid the foundation stone in February 2005.

The strategy involved the preparation of three distinct sets of proposals, one seeking funds for the national highways project, another set for the rail connectivity project, and a third set seeking grants for the dredging project. This would involve some extensive groundwork. And this was when the entire port team rose to the occasion. Over the next few days, I witnessed some extraordinary teamwork in action by officers and staff from different departments of the port. Very soon, our teams diligently developed the entire paperwork, supported by relevant commercial and financial data, for submission to the Central government in the Shipping Ministry. Armed with the three proposals, my next mission was to meet Shipping Secretary D.T. Joseph and Shipping Minister T.R. Baalu. Their invaluable guidance and unwavering support were instrumental throughout the Vallarpadam project's implementation. They offered critical support at every stage, addressing challenges with their expertise and strategic insight and direction.

During the same visit, I also called on T.K.A. Nair, the Principal Secretary to the Prime Minister. As the highest-ranking bureaucrat in Manmohan Singh's PMO, Nair was widely respected for his strong sense of integrity and work ethic, his remarkable dedication to public service, his deep understanding of the intricacies of the country's developmental issues, and his ability to devise pragmatic solutions to complex challenges. Above all, he was friendly, empathetic, and eminently approachable.

Since T.K.A. Nair was one of the earliest protagonists of the project, he was already familiar with the ICTT proposal from its conceptualisation and he quickly appreciated the situation when I explained the predicament of the port's financial crisis to him. He posed many questions and raised several concerns regarding the port's inability to invest in the infrastructure projects, but ultimately, given his familiarity with the project's details and his conviction in our case, he promised to convene a meeting with senior officials of the government to discuss the matter. The crucial meeting, held at the PMO on 12 December 2005, was attended by secretaries and representatives from the Ministries of Finance, Railways, Road Transport and Highways, and Shipping. This meeting proved to be a watershed point in Cochin Port's history. I was asked to make a detailed presentation on the significance of the ICTT project, the terms of the Concession Agreement with DP World, and the financial situation of the port. After discussions, it was decided that the Government of India would meet the entire cost of the road and rail connectivity projects. The National Highways Authority of India (NHAI) would build the road connectivity, covering the entire cost of the project from the fuel cess funds, while the Indian Railways would assume the responsibility for constructing the rail connectivity, for which special budgetary provisions would be made available by the Government of India.

While approving these expenditures, it was repeatedly emphasised that the port should find its own resources to carry out the capital dredging work. At that juncture, our first priority was to begin construction of the road and rail connectivity projects, and the dredging requirement would arise only at a later stage. Consequently, I chose to remain silent, with a certain sense of *mens rea,* knowing fully well that I would eventually have to return to the same authorities for funding the dredging project as well.

By the time the meeting was over, I was overwhelmed with a sense of elation. It was too good to be true, but there could still be slips between the cup and the lip. As I knew that there should be no ambiguities about the decisions taken, I requested Nair to allow me to prepare the minutes of the meeting, which he readily agreed to. Sitting in an adjoining meeting room of the PMO, I typed out the draft on my laptop and showed it to him. At the end of the minutes, I had added a sentence: "The minutes have been seen and approved by the Prime Minister." After reading this, Nair looked at me questioningly, but without saying a word, he took me along to meet the Prime Minister. Manmohan Singh listened to Nair's briefing, went through the minutes, and promptly approved them. I got the document duly issued by his office and returned jubilantly to Cochin, brimming with an immense sense of accomplishment.

The Central government's decision to allocate funds for construction of the connectivity projects brought an end to the uncertainties that had loomed over the ICTT project, at least for the time being. This galvanised the entire Cochin Port team as well as our external stakeholders. This was only the beginning of the journey, but we were now definitely on our way!

The Port Connectivity Projects

For the ICTT Vallarpadam, seamless connectivity would be crucial for attracting global shipping lines and enabling the smooth flow of cargo into and out of the country. Good connectivity shortens the transit time for cargo that could make the ICTT Vallarpadam more appealing as a transshipment hub for shipping lines. This, in turn, would boost the terminal's competitiveness in the global market. What is more, well-developed connectivity infrastructure attracts investments, leading to the expansion of ancillary industries and the overall growth of the region.

The construction of road and rail connectivity, along with the deepening of the navigation channels, were not just pre-conditions outlined in the Concession Agreement—they represented far more than compliance with licensing requirements. These projects were envisioned as public assets that would benefit the nation for decades to come. Although initially touted as exclusive infrastructure to support the ICTT, the newly developed national highway, railroad and deepened navigation channels evolved into common-user facilities. These now serve a wide range of stakeholders, including the LNG terminal, the BPCL's SPM tank farms, the upcoming MULT, associated facilities at Puthuvypeen, and the two PBSEZs. Furthermore, Cochin Port's navigation channels are also used by the Cochin Shipyard, the Indian Navy, and the Indian Coast Guard, although the port alone bears the entire expenditure for maintaining them.

With the resolution of the funding issue, three significant challenges continued to loom. Our focus quickly shifted towards addressing them: finalising the alignment of the road and rail routes, securing essential environmental clearances, and acquiring the necessary land for the construction of the road and railway lines. These tasks were intricately interconnected, and navigating through them proved to be among the most complex and persistent challenges we would encounter in the days ahead.

Finalising National Highways Alignment

While finalising the alignments, our primary focus was on two critical factors: minimising the environmental footprint and reducing land acquisition to limit the adverse impact on local inhabitants to the extent possible. The port officials held extensive consultations with the National Highways Authority of India (NHAI) to identify the most suitable alignment while keeping these considerations in mind. By aligning the road along the edges of backwaters and riverbanks wherever feasible, it was aimed to avoid heavily inhabited areas and reduce land acquisition from residents in the region. This strategy entailed dredging the backwaters and marshy lands and reclaiming land along the water bodies' edges using dredge materials. This plan not only aimed to protect local communities but also to avoid large-scale land acquisition and displacement. By occupying the backwater edges, the strategy also sought to deter further encroachments into the water bodies.

However, despite their best efforts, they discovered that this balancing act also had limitations, and some land acquisition and displacement of settlements became inevitable, which we shall come to later. Moreover, this plan required some land acquisition from the Fertilisers and Chemicals Travancore Limited (FACT), a Central PSU. This strategic choice was extremely important because alternative alignments passed through densely populated areas of Kalamassery. Given that FACT was a Central government entity, acquiring its land was expected to be less painful and more straightforward than acquiring land from private owners. The proposed alignment would not disrupt any of the critical installations of the FACT.

However, acquiring the land from FACT proved to be far more challenging than initially anticipated. Despite several rounds of discussions with FACT's Managing Director, Gopalakrishna Pillai, the negotiations dragged on for several months and disputes remained unresolved. As differences persisted and threatened to cause project delays, we had to ultimately invoke the *sudarshan chakra* of dispute resolutions. In situations where two Central government organisations quarrel, a resolution mechanism exists under the purview of the Cabinet Secretary's office. It was a kind gesture on the part of Cabinet Secretary K.M. Chandrasekhar to personally intervene to resolve the deadlock. He made sure that the land for construction of the highway was made available after payment of due compensations.

Rail Connectivity: Choosing from Three Alternatives

The process of determining a railroad alignment acceptable to all parties for the Vallarpadam connectivity project turned out to be a far more difficult task. The authorities had to consider various factors, such as the impact on the local population and the environment, together with the overall cost of the project. After extensive land surveys and study of the ground conditions, they proposed three possible alignments to choose from.

The first alignment, being the shortest and most cost-effective, passed through a patch of the biodiversity park—Mangalavanam. This option was abandoned due to concerns over the potential environmental impact and the irreversible harm it could cause to the ecosystem. The second alignment passed through an end corner of the Lourdes Hospital campus, which was not acceptable to the hospital authorities. Earlier, Chief Minister Oommen Chandy had intervened in this case and, after discussions with various stakeholders and public representatives, decided that the third and the longest of the three alignments should prevail.

After my joining, port officials informed me that the second alignment, passing through a property belonging to Lourdes Hospital, could be far less disruptive, shorter, and a less costly option, potentially saving an estimated Rs 150 crores. After internal discussions to understand the implications, I travelled to Thiruvananthapuram, met Chief Minister Oommen Chandy and requested him to reconsider his earlier decision, citing all the advantages. While appreciating our point, the Chief Minister explained that his earlier decision was based on certain objections from the Lourdes Hospital and the church authorities. He asked me to meet the Archbishop of Verapoly and discuss the matter with him. In an earnest attempt to address the issue while also considering the hospital's concerns, I sought an audience with His Eminence, the Archbishop of Verapoly. Following the Chief Minister's advice and equipped with detailed drawings, maps of inhabited areas, and calculations, I, along with a delegation of officers from Cochin Port, met the Archbishop to seek his approval for the second alignment. However, he was unwilling to accept our proposal. I offered that in addition to the compensation amounts, the port would fully fund the construction of a new, modern hospital building for Lourdes Hospital. Such reconstruction would involve only a fraction of the savings we could achieve by opting for this shorter alignment. Not only would this alleviate the hospital's apprehensions but it would substantially reduce the environmental impact of the much longer alignment crossing the backwaters and result in much fewer disruptions to people's lives. However, the Archbishop was unwilling to consider this proposal. Following this, we reached out to some influential political leaders in Cochin, including Members of Parliament (MPs) and Union and State Ministers, seeking their assistance. Clearly, the politicians we got in touch with did not want to touch the hot potato in an election year. Consequently, the Railways had no alternative but to opt for the third and the longest alignment of 9 kilometres, including 4.6 kilometres of bridging. Thus, India's longest railway bridge came to be built across Cochin's backwaters.

Environmental Clearances

The two connectivity projects, one involving the construction of a 17-kilometre-long highway and the other a railway line, measuring 9 kilometres, both passed through ecologically sensitive regions. Securing environmental clearances necessitated comprehensive Environmental Impact Assessments (EIA) to minimise potential adverse effects on the environment. Most importantly, it was essential to preserve the ecological balance of the area. The process of obtaining environmental clearances for the main ICTT project as well as the road and rail connectivity and dredging projects proved to be a formidable task, involving in-depth studies, impact assessments, and consultations with diverse stakeholders.

In pursuing environmental clearances, the port adopted a proactive and fully transparent approach. Comprehensive Environmental Impact Assessments (EIA) were conducted, ensuring the involvement of all relevant stakeholders in the decision-making process. Environmental management plans were developed with the support of expert consultants and implemented with diligence. The project teams in the Civil Engineering and Marine Departments of the port were fully charged up while obtaining environmental clearances. To ensure compliance with environmental norms and guidelines, they painstakingly prepared all the necessary documentation required for submission to the regulatory authorities. The port authorities consulted an array of experts, both individual and institutional, in this process. These included several scientific studies by individual professors of IIT Madras, National Institute of Oceanography, Cochin, apart from ongoing consultations with the Kerala Coastal Zone Management Authority (KCZMA). Care was also taken to adopt environmentally sustainable construction practices.

The overall environmental clearances involved several steps. At the first stage itself, in the early part of 2005, the Coastal Regulation Zone (CRZ) clearances had to be obtained from the KCZMA. Simultaneously, the port applied to the Kerala State Pollution Control Board to obtain the No Objection Certificates (NOCs) and what is called the "Consent to Establish". After obtaining these clearances by early 2006, applications were submitted to the Ministry of Environment and Forests (MOE and F).

Our proposal was considered by the High-Level Expert Committee for Infrastructure Development of the Ministry of Environment through a series of meetings. The committee conducted multiple site visits to the project area, physically verifying the entire length of the proposed road and rail alignments before granting final environmental clearances. The committee members were rather stringent in their standards during the field assessments and asked us to conduct several additional scientific studies and documentation at different stages, before ultimately approving the project.

Mangroves play a crucial role in land preservation and environmental equilibrium. While the road and rail alignments were carefully chosen to avoid areas with any existing mangroves, care was also taken to avoid any disturbance to mangrove vegetation elsewhere. It was equally critical to prevent the new constructions from obstructing the essential saline water circulation crucial for mangrove preservation in the project region. Since mangroves were highly sensitive to alterations in their environment, especially changes in water flow, salinity levels, and sediment deposition, there were apprehensions that the construction of road embankments in coastal regions might interfere with the natural hydrological balance of the mangrove ecosystem. Consequently, during the design phase of the road and rail projects, meticulous attention

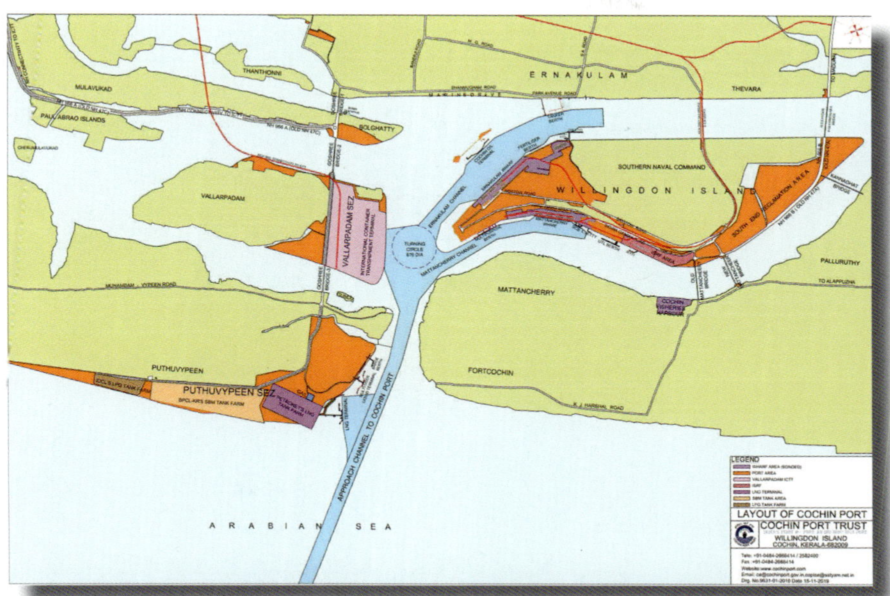

A layout map showing the land and port waters under the jurisdiction of the Cochin Port Authority, including the twin cities of Ernakulam and Cochin, Willingdon Island, Vallarpadam, and the surrounding islands

An aerial view from Willingdon Island of a mammoth cruise ship sailing into Cochin Port

T.K.A. Nair, Principal Secretary to the Prime Minister, being briefed at the ICTT project site in Cochin. Also seen (from left) are Kerala Government Additional Chief Secretary Tom Jose, Ernakulam District Collector M. Beena, Secretary (Roads & Highways) Brahm Dutt, and others

A.P.V.N. Sarma, Secretary, Ministry of Shipping, Government of India, during a visit to the ICTT project site in Cochin

Shipping Minister T.R. Baalu at a review meeting with state and district officials in Cochin. Also seen are (clockwise) Tom Jose, Additional Chief Secretary of Kerala, Ernakulam District Collector M. Beena, DP World official Suresh Joseph, and the author

The author, along with other Port officials, in discussion with DP World executives in Cochin

Shipping Minister G.K. Vasan, Union Minister K.V. Thomas, and Shipping Secretary K. Mohandas at the Vallarpadam site, just weeks before the inauguration of the ICTT

The author at the *Bhoomi Pooja* ceremony for the national highway port connectivity project from Kalamassery to Vallarpadam. From left: District Collector Mohammed Hanish, Cochin Port Chief Engineer J. Karthikeyan, IGTPL General Manager Suresh Joseph, and RVNL General Manager Keshav Chandran

Land reclamation through dredging and consolidation is in progress for the four-lane National Highway connectivity project from Kalamassery to Vallarpadam, aimed at minimising land acquisition wherever possible

The Vallarpadam Rail Connectivity project under construction across the Vembanad Lake. Both the highway and rail connectivity projects were commissioned by Prime Minister Manmohan Singh on 11 February 2011

An aerial view of the railway line soaring over the backwaters and weaving through multiple islands

A container train in operation, making its way to the Vallarpadam ICTT | Photo credit: A. Sanesh, *The New Indian Express*

Prime Minister Manmohan Singh dedicating the Vallarpadam International Container Transshipment Terminal (ICTT) to the nation on 11 February 2011. Also seen are Kerala Chief Minister V.S. Achuthanandan, Defence Minister A.K. Antony, Shipping Minister G.K. Vasan, Union Ministers Vayalar Ravi and K.C. Venugopal, Shipping Secretary K. Mohandas, Vice Chairman of the Dubai Executive Council Sheikh Ahmed bin Saeed Al Maktoum, and DP World Chairman Sultan Ahmed bin Sulayem

Images above and below: Container vessels berthed at the Vallarpadam ICTT

The author handing over possession of Cochin Port land to P. Dasgupta, Managing Director & CEO of Petronet LNG Ltd, for the construction of the LNG terminal on 6 February 2006

Cochin Port and Petronet LNG Ltd (PLL) formally sign the Licence Agreement on 12 March 2009

A section of the Port-based SEZ under construction at Puthuvypeen, featuring the LNG port and regasification plant

Construction work in progress at the Cochin LNG Terminal

A view of the Cochin LNG Regasification Facility at Puthuvypeen

A Very Large Crude Carrier (VLCC) anchored at the Cochin Single Point Mooring (SPM). These massive vessels can transport up to 3 lakh tonnes of crude oil, which is transferred via submarine pipelines to onshore storage tanks and then sent to the BPCL Kochi Refinery for processing

Post-commissioning, an LNG tanker anchored at the Cochin LNG Terminal, which has an installed capacity of 5 million tonnes per annum | Photo credit: Vipin Chandran

On the eve of the Volvo Ocean Race's arrival in Cochin: The author with Justice K. Narayana Kurup, Secretary (Industries) P.H. Kurian, Financial Advisor and Chief Accounts Officer K.G. Nath, and Joint Director (PBSEZ) Unnikrishnan Nair

The Cochin to Singapore leg of the Volvo Ocean Race was flagged off by Union Tourism Minister Ambika Soni, KeralaTourism and Home Minister Kodiyeri Balakrishnan (right), Leader of Opposition Oommen Chandy (left), and Kerala Sports Minister M. Vijayakumar (extreme right)

A moment captured during the Cochin stopover of the 2008 round-the-world Volvo Ocean Race. The mast of each of these boats reached the height of an 11-storey building!

Race boats undergoing maintenance at the Volvo Ocean Race Village, halfway through the competition

The author at a business meet to brief participants of the Volvo Ocean Race. Also seen are Kerala Industries Minister Elamaram Kareem (centre), and Principal Secretary T. Balakrishnan (second from right)

The e-Port Go Live event with active participation from Trade Unions. (From left): Dinesh Thampy (TCS), Victor Thangadurai (Project Consultant), C.D. Nandakumar (CPEO), K.G. Nath (FA&CAO), M.M. Lawrence (CPM leader and President, Cochin Port Labour Union [CPLU-CITU]), Mohammed Haneefa (CPSA), Donald Ingty (Commissioner Customs), and C.J. Mathew (Commissioner, Cochin SEZ)

A group photo after an e-Port meeting: K.G. Nath, Victor Thangadurai (Consultant), C. Vinod, T.K. Madhavan, M.V. Paul, N. Ramachandran, Girija, Ebenzer, Gayatri Devi, Annie Jacob, Dinesh Thampy (TCS), Anil Pai (TCS), and Nebu George(TCS)

Michael O. Leavitt, United States Secretary of Health and Human Services, with the author and his team during his visit to Cochin Port and Cochin Fisheries Harbour on 8 January 2008

The author receiving the National Tourism Promotion Award 2009 from Home Minister P. Chidambaram and Tourism Minister Ambika Soni in New Delhi in February 2009

The author receiving the Designer Sthapatheeyam Award from Dr Shashi Tharoor, Member of Parliament, at Thiruvananthapuram in November 2012. Also seen is architect L. Gopakumar, MD of Designer Publications

was given to preserving the natural water flows to maintain the delicate balance between saline water circulation and distribution of freshwater and sediment transportation within the mangrove habitat. Cochin Port's engineers as well as the NHAI and Rail Vikas Nigam Limited (RVNL) teams deserve accolades for their careful and proactive approach to minimise any adverse impacts on the existing fragile mangrove ecosystems.

Dealing with Sensitive Issues of Land Acquisition

Acquiring land for the construction of road and rail projects presented some of the most harrowing challenges in the ICTT Vallarpadam connectivity implementation.

It is important to mention here that Cochin Port had a limited role to play in the land acquisition process. Its involvement was primarily focused on coordination and facilitation. Initially, the NHAI and the RVNL, as the executing agencies, conducted field surveys in collaboration with the Cochin Port Trust and finalised the alignments after due consultations. Subsequently, after completing the necessary assessments, the NHAI and RVNL authorities submitted requisitions to the District Collector, the statutory authority responsible for executing the land acquisition process in accordance with the law.

Although the alignments were chosen to avoid inhabited areas to the extent possible, some displacements of dwelling houses became inevitable. The road project required the acquisition of 43.75 hectares (110 acres) in seven villages, affecting 183 families and the rail line construction needed acquisition of 4.36 hectares (10.77 acres) in which 144 families lived. The 327 families affected were spread over different areas like Moolampilly, Mulavukad, Kothad, Cheranalloor, Vaduthala, Kalamassery, Eloor, Manjummel, and Edappally.

The port officials worked closely with officers of the state and district administration in connection with the land acquisition and rehabilitation of affected families. Apart from the support of top officials and political leadership at Thiruvananthapuram, the entire land acquisition was spearheaded by the Ernakulam District Collector and their team of revenue officials. The land acquisition began during the tenure of District Collector A.P.M. Muhammed Hanish, but when he was transferred, the newly appointed Collector M. Beena continued the efforts. The contributions of these two officers were invaluable in navigating the complexities of land acquisition, energetically supervising the process, addressing each case individually, and eventually making sure that the land was made available for construction activities. Officers associated with the land acquisitions, at the state and district levels, were fully sensitive to the situation of the affected inhabitants and endeavoured to ensure that the compensations remained as liberal as possible. As the cost of land acquisition was already included in the Central government's financial support to the projects, we had budgeted a compensation and rehabilitation package, which was jointly worked out with the district and state administration. In due course, the state government announced a compensation package that was considered most generous and ground-breaking for its time. Many inhabitants submitted their consent notes and voluntarily moved out.

Resistance Movements against Land Acquisition

Evictions, rehabilitation, and resettlement of displaced persons are highly emotive and sensitive issues that inevitably arise during land acquisition for large development projects. The human and emotional costs of land acquisitions and evictions can be deeply troubling. Displaced individuals lose not only their homes but also their sense of security and belonging, leading to significant emotional and psychological distress. For those who depend on land for their livelihoods, displacement often results in income loss, pushing families into poverty. And for someone whose land is suddenly and forcibly taken, the experience could be a lingering nightmare. The relocation of families disrupts social ties, fragments communities, and isolates people. It also takes a toll on mental and physical health, exacerbated by disruptions in children's education.

In many ways, it becomes impossible to fully compensate the affected persons for what they have lost.

Local people strongly opposed land acquisitions, fearing displacement, loss of livelihoods, and disruptions to their daily lives. Emotional attachment to ancestral land and possible mistrust of the authorities made consensus difficult. Resistance campaigns led to the formation of village-level "struggle committees". To their credit, the prolonged agitations remained peaceful. These campaigns were not against the project itself but were aimed at securing fair compensation and proper rehabilitation, with essential amenities and support systems.

In the meantime, the district administration and the state government worked actively to address the concerns of the affected families. They were doing everything possible to implement the rehabilitation package and help those displaced rebuild their lives. However, despite all the efforts of the district administration and the political leadership, resistance movements against land acquisition continued over a long time. While political leaders and administrators were alive to the demands of the affected persons, the ground realities were multi-layered, complex, and challenging, with many competing interests at play.

For instance, the road and rail projects had vastly different impacts on local inhabitants. The proposed four-lane arterial road, passing through previously inaccessible areas, drastically increased land values, benefiting many landowners. However, the marginal landholders who were uprooted by the road project would only receive the official compensation and rehabilitation package benefits, while others with land in the vicinity stood to benefit from rising property values. This not only created a disparity but also led to some social tensions. In contrast, the railway project, while displacing many, provided little immediate value to locals and did not offer direct benefits.

The alignment traversed both low-value land areas and urban regions where land was expensive and scarce. Compensation for low-lying, marshy areas was relatively low, determined by prevailing land prices in these underdeveloped and poorly connected regions. As a result, such compensation was often inadequate for acquiring new property or alternative housing elsewhere. Even the seemingly generous compensation packages determined by the District Level Purchase Committees (DLPC) were tied to the prevailing land valuations, putting some affected persons at a disadvantage.

Adding to the complexity, allegations surfaced that some businesspersons and property brokers had acquired large tracts of land in the area at low prices from unsuspecting landowners, even before the local peasant owners were aware of the rising trends in land prices.

Moolampilly village, through which the proposed national highway alignment would pass, witnessed one of the most protracted agitations. The local inhabitants, mainly comprising peasants and fishing communities, opposed the acquisition of their land. Agitations were witnessed at Mulavukad, Kothad, Cheranalloor, Eloor and Manjummal. Similarly, land acquisition for the railway line project too faced prolonged protests in different areas in the city. The agitation in some areas like Vaduthala went on for beyond 1,000 days. From the point of view of affected persons, the Moolampilly agitation indeed demonstrated the effectiveness of community mobilisation and advocacy in drawing public attention to what they perceived was injustice. The Moolampilly agitation drew big media coverage and garnered support from various civil society organisations, human rights activists, and political figures.

Judicial Intervention

At one stage, some of the affected persons sought legal recourse by approaching the High Court of Kerala. The court issued two key directives: first, asking the families involved to promptly give their consent for acquisition, and second, directing the administration to uphold the right to life under Article 21 of the Constitution, ensuring fair compensation and proper rehabilitation.

Many affected individuals believed that the compensation offered for their land was inadequate and did not match the true market value, fuelling dissatisfaction and unrest. They alleged that their rights and interests were being ignored and drew attention to the broader issue of land acquisition for large-scale infrastructure projects.

In such circumstances, when local communities are under immense pressure, affecting their very survival, it becomes crucial for political workers and leaders at all levels to engage with them, understanding their concerns and serving as a bridge between the affected people and administrative officials. When politicians fail to maintain a strong presence on the ground, it creates a vacuum that is often filled by various activist groups, including civil society organisations, who play an important role in raising awareness about the people's issues. However, such movements often end up in the hands of individuals who may be more focused on advancing their own interests by prolonging the agitation rather than working towards practical and constructive solutions.

During this period, several senior ministers and representatives from the ruling LDF, the Opposition UDF as well as a few leaders from the BJP and other political parties made multiple visits to the affected areas. While all parties were committed to ensuring the project's success, they also had a genuine interest in addressing the people's concerns. However, with the upcoming Legislative Assembly elections in sight, most parties were seen walking a careful political tightrope.

Despite their attempts to engage with local communities, the political parties were only partly successful in persuading inhabitants to voluntarily move out. Many affected persons remained unrelenting and refused to move. Meanwhile, some affected persons, who had earlier consented to the acquisition, withdrew their consent notes. A communication gap prevailed, until events took a drastic turn. Between February 4 and 6, 2008, the revenue officials demolished the houses of 12 families who had earlier given their consent notes. This was indeed a low point in the land acquisition saga.

Wisdom of Hindsight

It is important to note that during the land acquisition for the Vallarpadam project between 2005 and 2010, the colonial-era Land Acquisition Act of 1894 was still in force. Nevertheless, the state government introduced a reasonably generous rehabilitation package, offering compensation at market rates through negotiated settlements—far exceeding the provisions of the 1894 Act—and incorporating several additional benefits. However, several reasons contributed to the discontent among the affected persons. The compensation, while generous for its time, may still have fallen short of actual market dynamics and future potential value in certain cases. In retrospect, the Vallarpadam land acquisition saga provided valuable lessons for administrators and political leaders, both successes and shortcomings.

How can Displaced Landowners be Stakeholders in Development?

When local inhabitants are displaced to make way for large infrastructure projects, numerous ethical and practical considerations arise. Respecting human rights, maintaining transparent communications, fair compensation and proper rehabilitation, including alternative housing and livelihood opportunities, should be the most important considerations. Addressing the long-term social, economic, and psychological impacts on displaced populations is crucial to ensure that the benefits of development do not come at the expense of the displaced persons' well-being.

Above all, when people are displaced for infrastructure projects, they must be made true stakeholders of the upcoming assets. There are two ways of approaching this. One way is to resettle them in proximity to the project site, if necessary, by acquiring more land nearby. Only if they are rehabilitated in proximity to the project site, will they benefit from future appreciations in land value resulting from the new developments.

For example, after the new national highway project materialised, the land value in the area shot up. But those who have been displaced and sent to far-off areas could never have benefited from the development. Kerala has set several good examples in the past. In Cochin Port too, we had a successful, recent example of an on-site rehabilitation scheme during the construction of the Kalamukku PBSEZ road connecting the Puthuvypeen SEZ area, where the LNG Terminal is located. As many as 28 families were affected. In addition to providing liberal compensation packages for the land acquired, Cochin Port also provided alternative plots of land for the resettlement of all the 28 families near the project site itself, for which land was created through reclamation. This process was enabled by the active involvement of District Collector Muhammed Hanish, the local MLA and Minister S. Sarma, and other people's representatives from the area. Cochin Port Chief Engineer J. Karthikeyan and his team of officers deserve appreciation for executing this project which stands out as a model of just rehabilitation of the displaced.

Buoyed by the above experience, Cochin Port explored the possibility of reclaiming land to rehabilitate some of the families affected by land acquisitions for the ICTT road project. Many affected persons wanted such a resolution and both District Collector M. Beena and Minister S. Sarma were supportive of this scheme. Cochin Port's Executive Engineer Susamma Xavier and her team promptly sprang into action in an earnest effort to create land adjacent to the affected areas for rehabilitation. However, due to the poor soil quality in the area, the reclaimed land was prone to collapse and sinking. Although some affected families took charge of the reclaimed plots, they were unable to construct houses due to extensive soil subsidence. This obviously became another reason for dissatisfaction although I learnt that the port authority subsequently made efforts to strengthen some of these reclaimed plots, by soil consolidation and piling.

Another way to ensure that the project-affected people remain engaged and invested in the development is by offering them employment opportunities within the new ventures. The Vallarpadam rehabilitation package included a provision for providing employment opportunities to at least one member from each displaced family in one of the upcoming projects. While this was not a contractual commitment, it was indeed a promise under the government's rehabilitation package. Given the sacrifices made by the uprooted families, it was a pledge that should have been politically followed up. It should have been possible for the newly built ICTT, LNG terminal, and various other new facilities that came up in the area to extend employment to some of the people who were uprooted from the project area. The Vallarpadam ICTT, PLL's LNG Terminal and BPCL Kochi Refinery installations were the largest direct beneficiaries of the highway connectivity. Similarly, the large hotel-cum-convention centre, set up by M.A. Yusuf Ali, was one of the direct beneficiaries of the ICTT highway. The Cochin Marina and the existing Bolghatty Palace hotel also benefitted from this connectivity. Regrettably, none of the enterprises such as DP World's IGTPL, LNG Terminal, the Grand Hyatt Hotel project, the CFS units or other enterprises that set up establishments at Vallarpadam, Puthuvypeen, and Bolgatty Islands demonstrated the willingness to employ persons from the displaced families, honouring the discharge of their corporate social responsibility. This is where the Government of Kerala should have intervened politically, ensuring that these newly established enterprises provided employment opportunities as agreed under the rehabilitation scheme. While some local inhabitants may have found employment, these did not come through the officially sanctioned rehabilitation programme.

Lessons from Vallarpadam Land Acquisition Experience

The Vallarpadam land acquisition experience offers several critical lessons, both positive and negative, that can guide future land acquisition projects.

One key issue that emerges is the need for government officials to enforce the law firmly yet sensitively. Equally important is strong political oversight of the process. The political leadership of the day must demonstrate sufficient understanding, compassion, and empathy towards those whose land is being acquired. Closer political involvement in executing compensation and resettlement efforts is essential—not only to reassure affected families and safeguard their rights but also to build trust and ensure a smoother, more humane implementation of the process.

Political oversight is essential to ensure that promises made to the affected individuals in the resettlement package are honoured. Wherever possible, rehabilitation should be located near the original settlements to minimise the disruption caused by displacement. This approach helps preserve existing livelihoods, social connections, and access to medical and educational facilities, thus reducing the overall impact of relocation. It is also necessary that local political leaders assess the suitability of resettlement land offered, ensuring that it is fit for habitation and equipped with basic facilities like electricity, water supply connections, and sanitation. Political leadership should not leave these to the government officials only, who may have limited discretion in these matters.

The time lag between planning and execution is another important factor. Public consultations as part of the Environmental Impact Assessment (EIA) for the project, including the Rehabilitation and Resettlement (R&R) plan, were conducted as early as 2001. However, land acquisition commenced only six to seven years later, by which time the ground realities had changed considerably. When projects are delayed by several years, it becomes crucial to revise or update the EIA. In hindsight, this was a significant oversight on our part.

The purpose of narrating this sequence of events is not to pass judgements or criticise any individual or institution but to highlight the lessons for the future.

It is heartening that the 2013 legislation on land acquisition, brought about by Prime Minister Manmohan Singh's government, has introduced a welcome shift towards fairness and transparency. The Right to Fair Compensation and Transparency in Land Acquisition, Rehabilitation, and Resettlement Act (RFCT-LARR), 2013 ensures market-linked compensation, comprehensive rehabilitation, and informed consent of affected families. This progressive framework addresses long-standing grievances, making land acquisition processes smoother and more just. Consequently, in recent years, land acquisition for major projects, such as national highways, has become more efficient and less contentious. This has facilitated rapid infrastructure development while ensuring that the rights of displaced people are protected, bringing a more inclusive and balanced approach.

Construction of Road Connectivity

In the decision made during the PMO meeting on 12 December 2005, the initial plan of establishing SPVs for the construction of road and rail connectivity was dropped. Instead, the responsibility of constructing the highway connectivity was entrusted to the NHAI, while the rail connectivity project would be executed by RVNL on behalf of the Ministry of Railways.

We were aware that the NHAI would be in a position to commence work only after the land was acquired and handed over to them. However, the land acquisition process experienced delays, far beyond what was anticipated. Consequently, when we succeeded in acquisition of even a small portion of the required land, we decided to hand it over to the NHAI and urged them to initiate construction work.

After several months of uncertainty, the NHAI finally launched the construction of the four-lane port connectivity road on 29 October 2007. I was very happy to inaugurate the construction project at a brief ceremony held at Kalamassery, attended by District Collector A.P.M. Muhammed Hanish, MP (Rajya Sabha)

Chandran Pillai, Deputy Mayor C.K. Manishankar, MLA K. Babu, and several other officials and dignitaries. As the road alignment passed through numerous riverine and backwater areas, the project included the construction of 12 bridges, with the Kothad-Moolampilly Bridge being the longest, spanning 760 metres. Although we moved forward with a brave face, it is worth noting that, at the start of construction, land acquisitions had only been completed for a 2-kilometre stretch of the road, which had been handed over to the NHAI and their contractors. The NHAI was also able to commence work on certain sections of land created through reclamation.

The Cochin Port Trust was entrusted with the task of reclaiming land for a 6.70-kilometre segment of the road through dredging in the backwaters and constructing embankments along the waterways. The creation of this stretch of land for a four-lane highway was itself a major undertaking, requiring extensive dredging and landfilling. Cochin Port, after conducting a tendering process, had awarded this dredging project to Jaisu Shipping, a dredging company. The company successfully completed the work, largely on schedule. Under the leadership of Chief Engineer J. Karthikeyan, Superintending Engineer P.M. Satheesh Kumar, and Executive Engineer Susamma Xavier, the port's civil engineering team successfully completed the demanding task of embankment construction and consolidation and handed over the reclaimed stretch to the NHAI by August 2009. Meanwhile, the disputes with FACT regarding compensations were resolved, allowing the NHAI to begin work on the FACT stretch as well.

Constructing a highway across a newly reclaimed stretch of land posed major technical challenges for the NHAI and its contractors, primarily due to the unstable nature of the soil, characterised by low bearing capacity, and high water content. Construction involved the application of various soil improvement techniques, such as soil stabilisation through vibro-compaction to densify the soil, the use of geotextiles for reinforcement, installation of stone columns, and in some stretches, soil replacement with stable fill in material. The NHAI was able to complete construction of one side of the highway connectivity and make it ready for operational use well in time before inauguration of the Vallarpadam project by Prime Minister Manmohan Singh in February, 2011, although some part of the second lane work was completed later.

The 17.2-kilometre-long, four-lane highway, designated as National Highway 966A, connects the Vallarpadam ICTT with National Highway 544 (NH544) at Kalamassery, intersecting National Highway 66 (NH66) at Cheranalloor. Starting from the second bridge of the Goshree Islands Development Authority (GIDA), the road passes through various Kochi suburbs, including Bolgatty-Mulavukad Islands, Moolampilly, Kothad, Cheranalloor, Manjummel, and FACT Gypsum Ground, before reaching Kalamassery. The road and rail links to the Vallarpadam port intersect at Mulavukad Island.

The four-lane Vallarpadam highway connectivity has not only fulfilled its original purpose of facilitating container evacuation but has also emerged as one of the most convenient arterial roads in Cochin, significantly de-congesting the city's road traffic. As it passes through regions of picturesque waterbodies and lagoons, it has become a popular attraction for local visitors and tourists alike. Over the years, numerous restaurants and picnic spots have sprung up along the route, adding to its appeal. This road has also become the principal approach route for other major development projects of Cochin Port in areas like Puthuvypeen, Vallarpadam, Mulavukad, and Bolgatty. As far as Cochin Port is concerned, it serves as the primary access point for its various energy ports, including the LNG terminal, BPCL-SPM and tank farms, the Multi-User Liquid Terminal (MULT), PBSEZs, and CFSs in the vicinity. A Ro-Ro[5] terminal was built, connecting this

5. A Ro-Ro (Roll-on/Roll-off) facility is a specialised terminal designed for handling vehicles, trucks, and trailers that can be driven directly onto and off a ship, ferry, or barge. This eliminates the need for cranes

highway, providing direct connectivity to the ICTT with the inland waterways. National Highway 966A also provides connectivity to the large hotels in the Bolgatty area, the Cochin Marina, and the new townships that have emerged near Mulavukad and the Marine Drive of Cochin, providing quick access to NH66, NH544, and the Cochin International Airport. Overall, this road project has had a positive impact on Cochin, enhancing travel convenience, improving transportation efficiency and boosting tourism in the city.

Rail Connectivity

The Rail Vikas Nigam Ltd (RVNL), a PSU under the Ministry of Railways, was entrusted with the responsibility of constructing the 9.3-kilometre railway line to the Vallarpadam terminal, which included the impressive 4.62-kilometre Vembanad Bridge, the longest railway viaduct bridge in India. The bridge traverses three small islands, including Idyakkara and Mulavukad, before reaching Vallarpadam, with the longest stretch of the bridge extending over the Vembanad Lake's backwaters. Constructing concrete structures within the backwater, where shallow water hindered barge-transportation of materials and concrete, turned out to be a major challenge for the RVNL and its contractor, Afcons Infrastructure. To address this, a temporary walkway and material transportation pathway were built across the island, allowing the placement of concrete tremie pipes. Concrete was then pumped from one end to the other, covering distances of up to 800 metres. This approach was employed for concreting for piling, pile caps, and various other structures like piers and pier caps. Another significant challenge involved transporting the 133 spans of pre-stressed concrete (PSC) girders, which were cast at the Vallarpadam end of the bridge,

---

or lifting equipment, making loading and unloading more efficient and cost-effective. Ro-Ro services are commonly used for transporting container-laden trucks, automobiles, heavy machinery, and other cargo on wheels, facilitating seamless movement across waterways and reducing road congestion.

to their respective span locations. To overcome this challenge, a pre-cast girder launcher, designed in Malaysia and fabricated in China, was used to transport and position the precast girders at their designated locations.

On 31 March 2010, a successful trial run marked a milestone in the completion of the railway line and its associated infrastructure. This rail link connecting the Vallarpadam ICTT with Edappally would cater exclusively to the transportation of goods containers to and from the terminal.

Despite interruptions caused by various *hartal*s and work stoppages, including persistent issues related to land acquisition, the construction of the railway bridge and the installation of railway tracks and overhead lines were completed well within the projected timelines, while strictly adhering to safety protocols and standards. The silent dedication and hard work of RVNL Project Director Keshav Chandran and his team, their grit, determination, and perseverance ensured the successful and timely completion of this critical infrastructure project. This accomplishment was highly appreciated by the port authorities, government agencies and the Ministry of Railways. It was a mega project with numerous technical complexities, challenges posed by nature as well as resistance movements and hartals. Yet, the project was completed within the allocated timeframe, with minimal cost escalation.

Underutilisation of Rail Connectivity

While Cochin Port fulfilled its contractual obligations with DP World by providing an exclusive railway line, lately there have been concerns regarding its severe underutilisation. This can be attributed partly to the container port's own relative under-performance, which has only reached 83.5 per cent of its projected capacity of 1 million TEUs in the first phase. Reportedly, there is also a general reluctance among transporters to use railways as an alternative to haulage by trucks, especially over short distances. It must be mentioned here that the decision to relocate the container terminal from Willingdon Island to Vallarpadam was partly influenced by the Indian Navy's requirement to relocate the railway overhead power lines that were in close proximity to the naval airport runway, posing an aviation hazard. Also, the height of the container port's cranes used in the existing Willingdon Island container terminal had posed safety concerns for the Indian Navy's air traffic. With the migration of the container port to Vallarpadam, the associated safety concerns have been addressed. However, the issue of the railway line remaining underutilised continues to persist.

Considering that the Government of India invested approximately Rs 373 crores in building this rail connectivity asset, it is imperative to address the underutilisation issue. There are also related questions regarding the container port's performance that has fallen short of its projected capacity. It is important to make collaborative efforts with stakeholders, such as shipping logistics providers and transporters, to promote rail transport for container goods.

An out-of-the-box idea to address the underutilisation of the ICTT rail connectivity could be to explore its partial repurposing for shared use with Kochi Metro. This could be achieved by laying additional rails to fit the gauge of the Kochi Metro, allowing concurrent use of the asset by the railways and Kochi Metro. Although this suggestion may sound unconventional, such an integration could maximize the asset's utility by connecting Vallarpadam, Vypeen, and nearby suburbs on the western coast, thereby improving urban mobility and reducing road traffic congestion in an area which has tremendous commercial and tourism potential. The feasibility of this shared use should be studied, considering the high financial and environmental costs at which the ICTT rail connectivity was constructed.

The Dredging Project

Cochin Port, situated within the sheltered waters of the Vembanad backwater system close to its confluence with the Arabian

Sea, grapples with silt accumulation in its navigation channels and basins, almost throughout the year. Six rivers—Periyar, Muvattupuzha, Pampa, Manimala, Meenachil, and Achankovil—discharge into the Vembanad backwaters, depositing substantial sediment loads to the estuarine system. This sedimentation is further compounded by the phenomenon of littoral drift in the region near the mouth of the estuary.

Scientists attribute the continuous buildup of silt and mud to a complex interplay of a combination of factors, including soil erosion in the catchment areas, wave and tide dynamics, coastal erosion, littoral drift, and the shifting of mudbanks. Studies have shown that the siltation observed within Cochin Port primarily arises from the incessant influx of muddy waters originating in the Arabian Sea. This is due to the churning of the seabed by wave action, which transports sediment into the backwaters during high tides. Much of the sediment is deposited in the channels during the ebbing phase of the tide. Additionally, the persistent scouring processes occurring along the seacoast—particularly pronounced during the monsoon season—as well as the relentless redistribution of shifting sediment accumulations or mudbanks, driven by littoral currents, further compound the phenomenon of continuous siltation of port's basins and channels.

The problem of continuous siltation, which intensifies during the monsoon months, necessitates regular maintenance dredging throughout the year to maintain the required depth in the port's channels and basins as well as to ensure safe navigation and the smooth operation of maritime traffic. However, dredging comes at a substantial cost. To cover the expenses associated with maintenance dredging and other operational costs, it is necessary to pass on the burden of these costs to the port's customers. While this is a common practice across the world, it can lead to higher shipping and logistics costs for businesses and industries that rely on the port's services. Nevertheless, this is a necessary trade-off to sustain the port's functionality and ensure the safety and reliability of maritime operations.

Balancing these financial considerations with the need for ongoing maintenance is a complex task that port authorities and stakeholders must navigate to sustain the operational efficiency of the port with due bearing on the total door-to-door transport cost. Most importantly, the proper maintenance of Cochin Port channels is a requirement today, not only for the port's conventional shipping operations but also for the ICTT, the LNG port, the MULTs as well as for the Indian Navy, the Coast Guard, the Lakshadweep terminals and the Cochin Shipyard. In this sense, Cochin Port truly serves as a common user facility.

Deepening of Basins and Navigation Channels

The contract between Cochin Port and DP World placed a binding responsibility on the port to carry out capital dredging operations to deepen the navigational channels and basins to maintain a draught of 14.5 metres. Taking into account the minimum clearance maintained between the keel of the ship and the seabed to avoid grounding, the port channels and turning circles are required to maintain a depth of 16 to 17 metres. It is worth noting here that a similar draught was necessary for the upcoming LNG port development project as well. Given the considerable cost associated with capital dredging, which was beyond the port's financial capabilities, Cochin Port once again turned to the Central government for public funding.

One major obstacle emerged from an earlier decision of the interministerial meeting at the Prime Minister's Office in December 2005, where it was decided that the port would be responsible for arranging its own funding for the dredging project. In the meantime, the port's Civil Engineering Department had undertaken a comprehensive study and prepared a Detailed Project Report (DPR) for the capital dredging work. As directed by the Ministry of Shipping, additional financial analysis and structuring were conducted and reviewed by professional financial institutions and consultants. Multiple revalidation studies were conducted before the proposal moved forward to the Planning

Commission's Project Appraisal Management Department, the Public Investment Board (PIB), and the Cabinet Committee on Economic Affairs. After numerous rounds of correspondence, meetings with various ministries, and persistent efforts by the Ministry of Shipping, the much-needed funds were finally approved. Of course, this approval became possible only through the crucial support of the PMO.

Engineering Challenges and Environmental Impact Management

The environmental, operational, and engineering challenges were many. First, the sediment type and soil density in the area posed difficulties due to the dense and cohesive nature of the mud. This contained high silt and clay, requiring specialised dredging techniques because it resettled quickly, impacting both dredging efficiency and environmental sustainability. Given that Willingdon Island, Vallarpadam Island, and surrounding facilities, stood on reclaimed land, the stability of these structures was paramount. Reclaimed land can be prone to shifting, subsidence, and settling, especially when dredging causes pressure changes in adjacent areas. The goal was to deepen the navigation channels, berth frontage, basins, and turning circles to accommodate a draught of 14.5 metres, requiring deepening up to 16 metres. Achieving this target and sustaining this depth would be a challenge, especially since mud and silt tend to accumulate quickly apart from collapsing underwater soil formations in the vicinity. Environmental considerations were also paramount. The dredging operations risked disturbing marine ecosystems, and their mitigation and management required extensive environmental planning and monitoring of dredging activities. The management of dredged material presented major logistical and environmental challenges, as disposal sites had to be carefully chosen to prevent coastal erosion, ecological damage, and contamination.

Right from the project planning stage, the port teams independently undertook the necessary scientific studies, supported by external experts. These included detailed physical and mathematical model studies aimed at optimising the channel and approach dimensions, conducted at the Central Water and Power Research Station (CWPRS), Pune. Special mention must be made of the invaluable contributions of scientists from the National Institute of Oceanography (NIO), Cochin, whose expertise in coastal dynamics, sediment transport, and marine ecosystems was crucial to the environmental studies for the dredging project. The NIO scientists conducted baseline surveys and assessed impacts on water quality, marine biodiversity, and seabed morphology, thereby evaluating the potential ecological consequences of dredging and recommending effective mitigation measures. Their studies were vital for preparing the Environmental Impact Assessment (EIA) and securing regulatory clearances. These recommendations were formally approved by the High-Level Committee of the Ministry of Environment, and were meticulously implemented by Cochin Port.

Capital Dredging Operations

For Cochin Port and the man-made Willingdon Island, which itself was born out of a similar process, the world of dredging is no novelty. For the capital dredging work, Cochin Port had engaged the services of Jaisu Shipping, a Gujarat-based company that won the contract in the competitive tendering process. The capital dredging operations began in December 2008, employing diverse types of dredging equipment, including trailing suction hopper dredgers, cutter suction dredgers, grab dredgers, bucket dredgers, backhoe dredgers, and other specialised machinery. The scale of the project was immense, involving round-the-clock operations and the removal of vast volumes of sediment from the channels and basins. This material was transported to pre-designated offshore locations, strictly in compliance with the environmental clearance stipulations. While the dredging project went well in the initial days, it was beset with disruptions and disputes towards the end of the project.

The first vessel to dock at the newly built ICTT berth was *ASL Sentosa*, towing a dumb barge carrying six Rubber Tyred Gantry Cranes (RTGC), on 15 May 2010. This was a celebratory event for both the Cochin Port officials and the representatives of DP World. Unable to contain his excitement, IGTPL General Manager Suresh Joseph personally took a boat to the anchorage area to escort the vessel to Vallarpadam. Some of us from Cochin Port, together with the SEZ Development Commissioner C.J. Mathew and Customs Commissioner Donald Ingty, eagerly awaited the vessel's arrival at the berth, each one of us equally charged up to receive the historic first vessel to anchor at the ICTT and partake in the happiness and the *laddoo*s that were distributed.

Phase 1A of the ICTT project was designed to include 15 RTGCs (yard cranes), of which four were to be transferred from the existing RGCT at Cochin Port, while the remaining 11 were to be imported from Abu Dhabi. Also, the new terminal was to be equipped with six highly sophisticated ship-to-shore (STS) cranes. Of these, two were to be relocated from RGCT, while the remaining four were to be imported from Zhenhua Heavy Industries Company (ZPMC) in China.

While *ASL Sentosa* had previously managed to dock at Vallarpadam without issue, we experienced several anxious days when *Zhen Hua 10*, the Chinese vessel transporting the ship-to-shore cranes, was unable to berth at the newly constructed basin due to insufficient draught. After an unsuccessful attempt on 23 June 2010, the vessel had to be moved to the anchorage. Jaisu Shipping, the dredging company, made continuous efforts to achieve the required depths, but success eluded us for several days. Strangely, while hydrographic chart measurements indicated that the basin depths were adequate, the vessel was still unable to dock alongside the berth despite repeated attempts. The dredging company attributed the issue to the presence of construction debris in one area on the basin floor, which they claimed their dredgers could not remove. Weeks were spent clearing this hard material, and the dredging company even brought what they said was excavated debris to us by barge for inspection. They subsequently requested additional time to complete the dredging, which led to disputes between the port and the contractor.

Eventually, *Zhen Hua 10* was able to berth, and the cranes were transferred to the ICTT deck. However, delays in deepening the basin and the prolonged berthing constraints led to considerable anxiety and frustration among all stakeholders.

The capital dredging project was marked by numerous disputes, claims, and counterclaims between the contracting parties, with contested claims of alterations in the project scope, unanticipated seabed conditions, and disagreements over the contractual terms and compensations. To complicate matters, a different dredging company was engaged by DP World for their berth-front excavations which had deployed its dredgers in the same general area where the container terminal's basin dredging work was in progress. The dredging work in both these areas was equally critical for the timely completion of the project, but a fierce dispute erupted between the two dredging companies, with one alleging that the presence of the other's dredgers in the vicinity was disrupting their operations and posing a risk of potential accidents. The port's dredging company, Jaisu Shipping, claimed that the steel-stay ropes of their bucket dredger needed to be secured at all the four corners, necessitating an uninterrupted work space for their operations.

At one point, tensions escalated to a breaking point when the dredging company abruptly withdrew one of its crucial dredgers from Vallarpadam. After a stormy night, the main workhorse of their fleet had mysteriously vanished. It was later discovered that the company had quietly sailed the dredger off to Mumbai Port for use in another ongoing contract! This one whimsical move caused some serious delays in our already time-sensitive dredging schedule.

Thanks to the timely intervention of Shipping Secretary K. Mohandas, and with the consent of the Mumbai Port Chairman, the bucket dredger was recalled and returned to Cochin, where we were racing against a deadline, with the ICTT inauguration already scheduled. However, the dredger's sudden withdrawal had created significant backlogs and disrupted progress. Once returned, Jaisu Shipping resumed dredging work in the basin and the turning circle area, albeit with multiple extensions beyond the agreed timeframe. In spite of the bickering and ongoing disputes, most of the capital dredging—covering the channel, basin, turning circle, and berth frontage—was completed in time for the ICTT inauguration, establishing Vallarpadam's navigational capabilities as a deep-water port capable of accommodating a wide range of container vessels.

We all finally heaved a sigh of relief when the first container ship docked at Vallarpadam terminal to mark the formal inauguration of the ICTT by the Prime Minister on 11 February 2011. However, as a substantial portion of the dredging work remained incomplete under the contract terms, disputes with the dredging company continued and eventually led to prolonged litigation. Paul Antony, who succeeded me as the Chairman in February 2011, diligently pursued the remaining dredging work, which was later completed, enabling larger mainline vessels to dock at the ICTT.

Those Behind the Vallarpadam Vision

Many persons played a crucial role in shaping the vision of the Vallarpadam ICTT. The commitment and foresight of Prime Minister Manmohan Singh, along with the proactive involvement of his Principal Secretary, T.K.A. Nair, and the strong support from the PMO, were instrumental in securing timely approvals and essential financial backing for the project. Principal Secretary T.K.A. Nair assiduously followed up, ensuring that the project reached its fruition. Whenever we noticed that a project element was going off track or getting delayed, I would knock at the doors of the Principal Secretary and request him to hold a coordination meeting. During these five years, Nair convened nearly two dozen high-level meetings with departmental secretaries and senior officers from multiple Central ministries, state government departments, and PSUs, both in his South Block office and at Cochin Port. Similarly, the then Shipping Minister T.R. Baalu too supervised the project very closely and held numerous coordination meetings to review progress of this project. The contributions of Shipping Minister T.R. Baalu, a hard taskmaster, were invaluable.

Thanks to the relentless efforts of my predecessor Chairman Jacob Thomas and his team, the entire tendering and contract finalisation process was carried out with much foresight. As a dream project of the state, Kerala's political leadership both in the UDF and LDF played crucial roles in making this vision come true. The project received enthusiastic support from Members of Parliament, MLAs, other elected representatives and political leaders across party lines. The contributions and the leadership of Chief Ministers Oommen Chandy and V.S. Achuthanandan and their cabinet colleagues were most important, especially at some of the crucial junctures of the project development. Without the help of these leaders, we wouldn't have succeeded in resolving the innumerable roadblocks and protests that erupted at different stages and in various parts of the city in relation to matters of environmental clearance, land acquisition, and rehabilitation. The project was closely monitored by successive Shipping Secretaries D.T. Joseph, A.K. Mahapatra, A.P.V.N. Sarma, and K. Mohandas. While every secretary in the Shipping Ministry and their teams played key roles, the tenure of Shipping Secretary K. Mohandas was particularly crucial. He was responsible for resolving many critical issues towards the last two years of the project construction, when a number of crises erupted. Secretary Mohandas's steadfast support and guidance were instrumental in overcoming some of the most difficult challenges.

The role and teamwork of DP World, the project's concessionaire, deserve special mention. To begin with, Dubai Port Authority's (DPA's) first international venture outside the UAE, led by Chairman Sultan Ahmed Bin Sulayem and CEO Mohammad Sharaf, was to bid for the Cochin Port Trust Concession. This initiative, with Regional Head Ganesh Raj playing a key role in building the business case and leading negotiations, led to the transformation of DPA into Dubai Port International, and subsequently DP World. Under Ganesh Raj's leadership, DP

World became a leading container port terminal operator in the subcontinent, leading to significant growth and expansion in the region. On the ground, Suresh Joseph and his team skilfully navigated the terminal construction and its logistical complexities and coordinated effectively among various stakeholders. After Suresh Joseph stepped down in 2010, Krishna Das came in, diligently ensuring the terminal's operational readiness on schedule.

The road and rail connectivity to Vallarpadam were crucial components of the integrated port project and each of these was a major infrastructure project in itself. The dedicated work of the NHAI and the RVNL and their controlling ministries was instrumental in completing these projects within the set time limits despite extremely tight schedules and significant local challenges. Here again, whenever bottlenecks appeared to delay the road project, I sought the intervention of the secretary and chairpersons of the NHAI, and they always extended their timely assistance. Special appreciation is due to NHAI Project Director C.T. Abraham and RVNL Project Chief Keshav Chandran and their teams, whose leadership and commitment ensured the on-time completion of these vital infrastructure projects.

The timely construction of the ICTT and its supporting projects stands as a remarkable testament to the power of teamwork. At every stage, the Cochin Port Trust Board worked with the port administration, providing the crucial governance oversight and guidance, enabling, supporting and holding hands. There were crises galore, when the guidance and support of the Board members, both individually and collectively, became critical. Also at play was the indefatigable spirit of Cochin Port's officers and staff in toiling persistently, day in and day out, in realising this major project without any significant project delays or cost escalations. This was a remarkable achievement in times when project delays are common, especially in mega infrastructure projects. The overall leadership of the ICTT project was provided by Chief Engineer J. Karthikeyan and his dynamic team.

Cabotage Law: The Albatross around Vallarpadam's Neck

Cabotage laws[6] are intended to protect a nation's shipping industry from foreign competition and encourage growth of domestic shipping. Across the world, many maritime nations impose cabotage restrictions to protect their national shipping. For example, the US allows only the ships built, owned, registered, and manned by Americans to carry out coastal trading within the US. Cabotage laws serve as regulatory barriers that restrict the movement of foreign-owned vessels within a country's coastal waters. Cabotage restrictions in force since Vallarpadam ICTT's launch in 2011 undermined its early advantages and hampered its early growth by preventing foreign vessels from moving transshipment cargo between Indian ports, limiting its competitiveness. Their relaxation in 2018 allowed direct mainline vessel calls. While transshipment volumes remain modest, Vallarpadam now handles direct services to Europe, the Far East, the Middle East, and Southeast Asia, contributing to India's EXIM cargo movement.

The Indian Cabotage Law, part of the Merchant Shipping Act, 1958, was designed to prevent foreign-owned vessels from transporting goods between Indian ports. The law aims to safeguard the country's domestic shipping industry. While India with its vast coastline and burgeoning maritime trade is poised to become a global maritime trade power, the continued existence

---

6. Cabotage law refers to regulations that restrict the transport of goods or passengers between two points within the same country to domestically registered vessels or carriers. This law is primarily intended to protect a nation's shipping industry from foreign competition, ensuring economic benefits and national security. The concept of cabotage originated in France in the early 16th century, with the term derived from the French word cabotage, meaning coastal navigation. Over time, similar laws were adopted by maritime nations, including the United States (Jones Act, 1920), India, and several European and Asian countries to regulate domestic shipping and aviation sectors.

of cabotage restrictions and regulations has posed an impediment to realising this potential. The inherent problem lies in India's minuscule shipping capacity, which constitutes a mere fraction of the global tonnage. Consequently, India's cabotage restrictions significantly narrow the options available to transport goods between Indian ports, resulting in fewer choices and considerably higher costs for the shipping industry.

Cabotage Law is Hindering India's Commercial Interests

The primary objective behind the construction and development of Cochin's Vallarpadam ICTT was to attract at least part of the transshipment volumes to Cochin and reduce India's dependency on foreign transshipment. However, despite its modern infrastructure and capabilities, Vallarpadam still struggles to achieve its full potential due to the lingering impact of cabotage laws. While some mainline vessels have started calling at Vallarpadam, several mainline shipping lines continue to bypass Indian ports, making it difficult for Vallarpadam to attract a critical mass of international shipping services.

Impact of Cabotage Law Restrictions on Indian Transshipment Business

Cabotage law restrictions have long posed a barrier to India's aspirations of developing successful transshipment hubs. Currently, nearly 70 per cent of India's transshipment containers are routed through foreign ports like Colombo, Singapore, Jebel Ali, and Port Klang. For instance, when a mother vessel arrives at an Indian transshipment port and offloads containers destined for other Indian ports, those containers must be transported onward by Indian-flagged feeder vessels only. With the limited capacity of the Indian shipping industry, this creates high demand and low supply of coastal vessels, driving up costs and causing delays.

As a result, major shipping lines find it more convenient to conduct transshipment operations in India's neighbouring countries, where they are not encumbered by cabotage law restrictions. This long-standing regulatory disadvantage has discouraged global shipping lines from selecting Indian ports for transshipment, leading to a loss of business, higher logistics costs, and diminished competitiveness for Indian ports. The Vallarpadam ICTT suffered this disadvantage since its inception.

Even during the early stages of developing the Vallarpadam ICTT, Cochin Port engaged in a series of consultations with trade and business bodies to understand the conditions necessary for the terminal to thrive. One of the most critical insights that emerged was that world-class infrastructure alone would not be enough to attract mainline vessels to call at Cochin. Shipping companies prioritise ports that offer cost-efficiency, operational ease, and minimal procedural hurdles. They are particularly discouraged by complex legal formalities, especially those associated with cabotage restrictions. This becomes even more significant when nearby alternative ports such as Colombo, Jebel Ali, and Singapore offer a more seamless and business-friendly operating environment.

Anticipating this complication, Cochin Port had written to the Ministry of Shipping requesting the Government of India to lift the cabotage restrictions completely, without which we were aware that the ICTT could not attract any significant transshipment business. Several discussions were held and we also requested the department-related Parliamentary Standing Committee on the Ministry of Shipping to lift these restrictive laws. The committee, chaired those days by Sitaram Yechury, MP, held two hearings where we presented our case. While the government as well as the Parliamentary Committee were sympathetic, in the face of heavy resistance from certain interested lobbies, our request achieved only partial success, resulting in partial lifting of certain restrictions while simultaneously inserting various new provisos to the existing rules. As the container transshipment industry finds it much simpler to do business in neighbouring countries with no cabotage restrictions, the issue has persisted since.

For any Indian transshipment port to survive, the importance of a complete lifting of cabotage restrictions cannot be overstated. It is easy to see how the application of cabotage law results in the loss of millions of dollars to the Indian export-import trade every year. These huge economic losses contradict the intended purpose of protecting the Indian shipping industry through a flat-footed application of the cabotage law. Completely doing away with cabotage law has become a strategic necessity which could result in several far-reaching benefits. Cost reduction is the most important. Allowing direct and unencumbered transshipment of Indian containers between Indian ports would significantly reduce shipping costs, making Indian exports more competitive in the global market.

Another crucial consideration is time efficiency. By eliminating detours via foreign transshipment hubs, India can reduce transit times, helping businesses to meet tighter delivery schedules and enhance overall trade efficiency. Most importantly, increased transshipment traffic at Indian ports offers a substantial boost in revenue, both for port authorities and the government, while also enhancing the ports' global competitiveness. This growth has the potential to generate widespread employment opportunities across the logistics ecosystem—from port workers to supply chain professionals. As global trade dynamics evolve, India must position itself as a preferred maritime gateway for international cargo.

Resistance to lifting the cabotage law in favour of the Vallarpadam ICTT was driven by various vested interests, which effectively undermined India's efforts to attract transshipment business from ports in neighbouring countries. The Indian National Shipowners' Association (INSA), for instance, led a campaign against relaxing cabotage regulations, arguing that allowing foreign vessels to operate along the Indian coast would harm domestic shipping companies. This opposition significantly constrained the ICTT's potential to evolve into a transshipment hub from the outset. It also illustrated how narrow interests can obstruct policy measures designed to strengthen national maritime infrastructure and competitiveness. Despite the evident benefits of easing cabotage restrictions, such as strengthening India's export-import trade and reducing dependence on foreign transshipment hubs, this resistance resulted in prejudiced decisions that impeded progress. In effect, , these actions curtailed the trade and economic gains India could have secured by allowing more efficient routing of its container traffic. This experience underlines the urgent need for bold, decisive policymaking that prioritises long-term national interests over narrow sectoral considerations.

At the same time, robust support for the domestic shipping is essential to building a resilient and self-reliant maritime sector. India must adopt innovative and non-conventional strategies to incentivise this industry, such as tax benefits, preferential or dedicated berthing, and discounts on vessel-related charges and wharfage, particularly or coastal shipping. Promoting coastal shipping through regular services between domestic ports can significantly ease road congestion and reduce vehicular pollution. A strong ecosystem for Indian carriers can be developed through appropriate policy interventions aimed at strengthening coastal trade and enhancing the competitiveness of domestic shipping.

From its very inception, cabotage laws have been an albatross around the neck of the Vallarpadam ICTT. As long as these restrictions remain, no Indian transshipment port can truly take flight. In the context of maritime industry dynamics, partial or conditional relaxations do not help reach an escape velocity. Thankfully, the emergence of influential private operators in India's port sector in recent times is expected to bring more pressure on the government that could augur well for a more liberalised regulatory framework, benefiting the overall industry. Despite the Shipping Ministry's relaxation of cabotage laws to encourage coastal movement of EXIM containers, announced in 2012 and 2018, Indian transshipment ports have yet to fully attract the container transshipment industry. Established ports like Colombo, Singapore, and Dubai offer unrestricted operations without any complexities involving cabotage, apart from competitive costs, efficient turnaround times, and reliable services that many Indian ports have yet to match. My conversations with shipping professionals reveal that unless cabotage laws are entirely annulled or withdrawn, the perception of regulatory complexities may continue to deter transshipment operators from most Indian ports.

A cost-benefit analysis would clearly reveal that the drawbacks of India's cabotage law regime outweigh the benefits. It has demonstrated questionable effectiveness since its inception. Despite the protection, Indian domestic shipping has struggled to grow, while the policy has inflicted immense harm by driving away transshipment business to neighbouring country ports. The recent relaxation in cabotage laws is a welcome move. However, any restrictive eligibility criteria involving transshipment volumes or other considerations may impede fair competition among Indian ports. Such limitations could unfairly benefit a few larger ports while disadvantaging others. Therefore, there is merit in advocating for a complete annulment of cabotage restrictions.

Concerns of Security

One of the reasons cited against relaxing cabotage rules is the heightened container security vulnerabilities associated with transshipment. Even without transshipments, cargo containers pose major security risks that can be exploited by enemy states and non-state actors. Transshipments further exacerbate these vulnerabilities. As containers move through complex and extensive global supply chains, the opportunities for smuggling weapons, explosives, or hazardous materials, including radioactive materials, rise. The primary security concerns in the container transshipment industry stem from the convergence and dispersion of containers from various countries at transshipment ports.

X-ray inspection of cargo containers is a time-consuming process, typically taking 10 to 15 minutes per container. This means that, on average, fewer than 100 containers can be inspected per day per unit. However, most ports handle thousands of containers daily, making it practically impossible to inspect each one through X-ray scanning. As a result, only a small fraction of containers are inspected, based on a risk management approach. The sheer volume of containers, combined with the numerous handoffs between different transport modes and operators, makes comprehensive monitoring difficult. This complexity amplifies the risk of security vulnerabilities, such as undetected tampering with container seals. Furthermore, as containers pass through multiple international ports and jurisdictions, they mix with those from various countries and often undergo minimal scrutiny. This makes them an attractive means for illicit activities and creating exploitable gaps in security. It underscores the significant challenges faced by customs and port authorities in ensuring container security while also maintaining the smooth and efficient flow of cargo.

Such gaps pose serious national security threats, as hostile actors could use cargo containers to infiltrate critical infrastructure, disrupt supply chains, or even stage coordinated attacks on a large scale. Advanced surveillance technologies and stronger international cooperation are essential to mitigate these risks, but ensuring airtight security across the entire logistics network remains a daunting challenge.

While gateway container terminals mostly handle direct import and export traffic, transshipment ports face unique challenges due to their role as intermediary hubs. Non-transshipment terminals typically deal with containers from the host country, simplifying inspection and monitoring. In contrast, transshipment ports handle containers in transit, often on tight schedules with multiple international stakeholders. It must be noted that the lifecycle of a container in transit can involve both transshipment and direct shipping phases. These complexities make it impractical to even carry out dependable risk assessments, thus elevating the potential for security breaches.

But then, container security vulnerabilities are not unique to India. Every country, especially those handling huge volumes of cargo containers through their ports, faces these challenges.

To effectively enhance container security, maritime powers have adopted both tactical and strategic measures.

Tactically, ports worldwide have implemented stringent access control measures, advanced screening technologies like X-ray and gamma-ray scanners to detect illicit contents in containers, and conduct regular security audits to ensure that only authorised personnel handle cargo. Further, electronic tracking systems such as Global Positioning Systems (GPS) and Radio Frequency Identification (RFID) are employed to monitor container movements and maintain their integrity.

Strategically, countries adopt international security standards, such as the International Ship and Port Facility Security (ISPS) Code, to harmonise security practices. They also strengthen international cooperation and information sharing with global customs and maritime agencies to pre-empt and counter potential threats. Furthermore, most ports globally are investing in cybersecurity measures to protect critical data and systems from cyberattacks. PPPs have been utilised to bolster these efforts by pooling resources and expertise.

Collectively, these measures have significantly reduced the risk of illicit activities and enhanced the overall security of container port operations around the world.

It is crucial for our country to implement such measures that safeguard our national interests and security. However, the effectiveness and relevance of restrictions like cabotage laws should be evaluated based on their proportionality and impact on trade. Globally, there is limited evidence to suggest that cabotage restrictions significantly improve security. While such policies can enhance security to a certain extent by controlling foreign vessel operations, they often limit competition, raise shipping costs, and increase inefficiencies. Therefore, while we must strengthen our container security regime, we must also balance policy concerns with pragmatic economic considerations to ensure that these measures do not unduly hinder the country's trade interests. Obviously, applying cabotage rules indiscriminately under the pretext of security concerns would amount to throwing the baby out with the bathwater.

ICTT's Business Performance

The business performance of the Vallarpadam ICTT has fallen short of initial expectations. Although the terminal was envisioned to serve as a premier transshipment hub, it has yet to attract the anticipated volume of mainline container vessels. During the year 2024-25, the terminal achieved a throughput of 8.35 lakh TEUs, as against the projected target of one million TEUs in the first phase.

The suboptimal business performance of the Vallarpadam ICTT can be attributed to a combination of factors, particularly the limited industrialisation in Kerala, which has resulted in low cargo generation from its hinterland. In its initial years, the terminal's growth as a transshipment hub was further hampered by restrictive cabotage laws that prohibited foreign vessels from carrying transshipment cargo between Indian ports. Although these restrictions were later partially relaxed, the delay cost the terminal valuable momentum. Further, the global trend of increasing ship sizes poses a challenge, as Vallarpadam's draught restrictions prevent the berthing of the largest mother vessels of the day. This significantly limits its appeal as a transshipment hub. However, the terminal does have significant potential to attract medium-sized mainline vessels and direct sailing services.

Many industry stakeholders believe that the port-related charges at Cochin are much higher compared to regional competitors like Colombo and Singapore. It is suggested that the IGTPL should adopt more strategic pricing for its services. The shipping industry also opines that the IGTPL should expedite the construction of the second phase to accommodate more container vessels simultaneously. However, there is a dilemma concerning the necessity for further deepening the channels to handle larger vessels. Officers in the port authority argue that investments in this regard should only be made if there is assured business from vessel arrivals. In effect, this presents a classic "chicken and egg" situation.

It is encouraging, however, that the Cochin Port Authority and DP World are actively engaged in discussions on the next phase of development for the terminal, along with strategies to expand the ICTT's capacity.

Realising the Vallarpadam Dream

A port itself does not generate cargo, but merely facilitates the movement of goods that are produced and consumed by industries or businesses in its hinterland. The prosperity and industrialisation of the hinterland are crucial to sustaining and growing the volume of cargo passing through a port. When the hinterland develops, industries expand, and trade increases, creating more demand for efficient port services. This can lead to a virtuous cycle where a well-functioning port attracts more industries to the region, providing them with access to global markets while industrial growth, in turn, boosts the port's throughput.

For such a cycle to thrive, it is essential to invest in complementary infrastructure, such as transportation networks, industrial parks, and logistics hubs. Ports can also play a role by offering value-added services, such as warehousing, cold storage, and customs facilitation, making them more attractive to industries. Ultimately, the port and its hinterland grow in tandem, fostering regional economic growth and integration into the country's trade networks. The future of Vallarpadam will thus depend on how Kerala makes use of these opportunities to develop its industry and commerce across the state.

Nevertheless, Vallarpadam's role as a gateway port remains intact, providing connectivity and logistical services within India's maritime network. Operational since 2011, it has a well-established presence in the maritime industry. Vallarpadam has a state-of-the-art cargo handling infrastructure and equipment tailored to efficiently handle transshipment cargo, customs, and other regulatory approval facilities in place, and streamlined cargo handling processes, giving it a competitive edge. Over the years, the port has cultivated an extensive network of shipping lines, logistics providers, and stakeholders facilitating smooth cargo movements.

Recently, concerns have been raised in some quarters about the long-term relevance of the Vallarpadam ICTT, primarily due to its 14.5-metre draught. However, it is important to note that Jawaharlal Nehru Port (JNPT), India's largest container port, at Navi Mumbai also operates with a similar draught, yet continues to thrive. This underscores the fact that draught alone does not determine a port's viability or competitiveness. Attracting shipping lines depends significantly on factors such as efficient hinterland connectivity, cost-effective operations, and reliable, competitive services. Globally, many successful ports with comparable draughts handle large volumes by leveraging strong feeder networks, advanced port infrastructure, and streamlined cargo handling systems.

Despite its draught restrictions, direct-sailing mainline vessels continue to service the ICTT. The ability of a port to efficiently connect containers to direct shipping lines without delays, coupled with overall door-to-door costs, determines the growth or fall in its business volumes. Thus, container shipping business has been witnessing unprecedented churning in many ways, which highlights why it is important for ports to evolve according to the changing dimensions and needs of the industry. There is no one-size-fits-all approach or a single, long-term business model for success in the container ports industry.

However, the future success of Vallarpadam will hinge upon its ability to deliver quick, efficient, and convenient services at reasonable costs. The arrival of deep-draught ports like Vizhinjam is likely to hugely increase competition, further impacting Vallarpadam's business prospects, unless it quickly adapts to changing market dynamics, intelligently navigating regional and cultural complexities. The true test will be how future port managers navigate the complexities and dynamics of demand and supply. These factors collectively highlight the need for strategic planning and policy support to maintain Vallarpadam's relevance in the maritime industry.

Comparing Vallarpadam and Vizhinjam Ports

The now-operational Vizhinjam Port, situated on the deep southwestern coast of India, holds immense strategic importance. Its deep draught allows it to accommodate the world's largest container ships, while its proximity to major international shipping lanes positions it as a prime hub for container transshipment. Vizhinjam has the potential to capture a significant share of the transshipment cargo currently routed through ports such as Colombo, Singapore, and Dubai.

While direct comparisons may not be fair, some salient features can be highlighted. Once fully operational, the Vizhinjam International Seaport (VISP) near Thiruvananthapuram is poised to become a major transshipment hub, leveraging its strategic location near international shipping routes. This port is expected to accommodate some of the world's largest container ships, with capacities of up to 24,000 TEUs. Its location makes it an ideal hub for transshipment activities, reducing India's reliance on foreign transshipment ports like Colombo, Singapore, and Dubai. The biggest advantage of Vizhinjam is that it is a deep-water port with minimum requirement of dredging that would make it a cost-effective port for large container vessels. While Vizhinjam may also attract some gateway cargo, its true promise lies in becoming a pivotal trade hub, primarily as a transshipment port. The construction of Vizhinjam Port, which began in 2015, initially faced delays due to multiple challenges. However, the completion of its first phase marks a major step forward. Although road connectivity is still incomplete, the state government has recently granted in-principle approval for a dedicated rail link. Despite these infrastructural gaps, the port has already begun receiving some of the world's largest container vessels, demonstrating its promise as a key transshipment hub. On 2 May 2025, Prime Minister Narendra Modi formally dedicated Vizhinjam Seaport to the nation, marking a significant milestone in India's maritime development.

It is worth noting here that the total investments in first phase of the Vizhinjam Port, as per recent disclosures by the company, stands at approximately Rs 8,867 crores. Of this, 63 per cent is funded by the state government, 9 per cent by the Central government as Viability Gap Funding in the form of an interest-free repayable loan, and the remaining 27 per cent is invested by the Adani Ports Limited. This means that the state government is committed to make an initial investment of Rs 5,595 crores while the Central government brings in Rs 818 crores, apart from the private investor Adani's investment of Rs 2,454 crores. The private investment is likely to rise, with the next phases of construction. According to press reports, the state government has also recently approved the DPR for a rail connectivity at an approximate public expenditure of Rs 1,482 crores, bringing the total public expenditure to Rs 7,795 crores. As against this, the public investments in Vallarpadam has been far smaller, involving Rs 914 crores for the national highway connectivity, Rs 373 crores for rail connectivity and Rs 323 crores for the capital dredging, together amounting to a total of Rs 1,610 crores. The entire cost of construction and development of the Vallarpadam Container Terminal was met by the concessionaire, DP World. It must also be mentioned here that the ICTT's road and rail connectivity as well as the deepened channels have been developed by Cochin Port as shared common user facilities to be used not only by the ICTT, but also other installations like the LNG terminal, PBSEZs, and a slew of energy terminals at Puthuvypeen. The Cochin Port navigation channel is also a common user facility, shared with the Indian Navy, the Coast Guard and the Cochin Shipyard.

The Concession Agreements for Vallarpadam and Vizhinjam Ports differ significantly in revenue-sharing models and strategic timelines. The Vallarpadam Concession Agreement is valid for 30 years, while the Vizhinjam concession, originally set for 40 years, has been extended by an additional five years and will now run until 2060. Vallarpadam, operated by DP World, follows a revenue-sharing model where 33.3 per cent of the operator's revenue is paid to the concessioning authority, the Cochin Port Trust, providing a steady and substantial income from day one. In contrast, Vizhinjam Port, managed by Adani Vizhinjam Ports Pvt Ltd (AVPPL), has a 15-year post-COD (Commercial Operation Date) period during which no revenue is shared with the concessioning authority, the Kerala government, allowing the operator to first recoup its investment. According to publicly available information, the Kerala government will start receiving 1 per cent of the port's revenue from the 16th year after the deemed COD, set for December 2034. This share will increase by 1 per cent annually, ultimately reaching 40 per cent by the end of the concession period in 2060. Under this arrangement, the state faces a prolonged delay before receiving meaningful returns from the project.

Both the Vallarpadam and Vizhinjam terminals have an initial estimated capacity of 1 million TEUs each, in the first phase. Vizhinjam already has announced plans to complete its construction of additional berths to enable handling of 3 million TEUs by the year 2028. On the other hand, the Vallarpadam ICTT is yet to reach its 1 million TEU capacity. In 2024-2025, Vallarpadam's total throughput reached 8.35 lakh TEUs. The terminal has a long way to go.

India Needs More Vallarpadams and Vizhinjams

For India, with its rapidly expanding export-import trade, the establishment of a deep-draught transshipment terminal capable of handling the largest container ships of the day is a strategic imperative. Vizhinjam, with its natural deep draught and proximity to key trunk maritime routes, is ideally positioned to meet this need. Both Vizhinjam and Vallarpadam should be viewed as crucial economic assets, each offering distinct strengths and business prospects within the maritime and logistics sector. While some degree of competition between the two is inevitable, it is essential to recognise that they cater to different market segments. Vizhinjam has the potential to attract transshipment volumes that currently flow through Colombo, Singapore, and Dubai, positioning it as a major hub in the regional maritime transshipment trade network. In contrast, Vallarpadam will continue to operate as a gateway terminal. With some direct mainline vessels and robust coastal services, it is well-suited to meet the export-import trade requirements of southern India's hinterland, particularly for cargo originating from or destined for the region. This complementary dynamic between Vizhinjam and Vallarpadam will enhance the overall capacity and efficiency of India's port infrastructure, enabling the country to better accommodate diverse shipping and cargo handling demands.

India must significantly expand its port capacity to keep pace with its rapid economic growth. Enhancing port infrastructure is essential for streamlining supply chains and bolstering its global trade competitiveness. It is important that both Vallarpadam and Vizhinjam realise their full potential quickly so that India's export-import containers are not dependent on transshipment in neighbouring countries. Encouraging a healthy competition between the two is likely to benefit both the country's economy in general and the shipping industry in particular. The competition may also motivate DP World, the operator of Vallarpadam, to make more efforts to attract cargo by offering more cost-effective services and higher efficiency. There has been a perception within the trade in Cochin that DP World has not done enough to reduce tariffs to attract cargo. It is also required to lengthen and expand the ICTT berthing infrastructure as part of its next phase of expansion.

Needless to say, a healthy competition between ports is essential to prevent monopoly situations and to ensure competitive pricing of services. To promote this across both the public and private sectors, government policies should focus on creating a level playing field. Such a competitiveness would reward efficiency and punish inefficiencies. Government policies should aim at optimising the use of each port by identifying their unique niches and operational strengths. Encouraging collaboration among ports, rather than preferential treatments or unhealthy competition, will ultimately enhance India's overall maritime trade capacity.

The success of Cochin, Vizhinjam and other container ports in the country will be contingent on their ability to leverage their unique strengths, resulting in relatively less total cost for door-to-door transport of containers. As India's container logistics sector continues to evolve, both ports hold promising prospects. What is important for both facilities is to compete in terms of efficiencies, cost effectiveness and reliability of services. Those that falter or fail to meet the standards will be mercilessly erased out of business anyway.

India is the fastest-growing major economy in the world and is rapidly emerging as a global economic powerhouse. However, the country needs to cover a very long distance in terms of port capacity, shipping tonnage and cargo throughput. To put things in perspective, China recorded a staggering 330 million TEUs in container throughput in 2024, whereas India's container throughput during the corresponding period remained approximately 20 million TEUs. As the "factory of the world", exporting products globally, China has made matching investments in world-class port infrastructure, including deep draughts, advanced automation, high-capacity cargo handling cranes, and seamless multimodal connectivity via rail, road, and inland waterways. India's port capacity in comparison is nowhere near China's. In terms of cargo throughput, we are still a tiny speck on the global stage!

At the same time, India must also adopt an aggressive strategy to rapidly expand its shipbuilding industry and drastically increase its national tonnage capacity. In stark contrast to China, which now constructs over 70 per cent of the world's merchant ships by gross tonnage and has become the largest ship-owning nation globally, India lags far behind, with only a marginal presence in terms of gross tonnage and limited performance in both shipbuilding and fleet ownership. To close this gap, India must implement proactive policies and streamline regulatory procedures to attract more vessels to register under the Indian flag.

As the nation continues to make strides in its export-import activities, expanding its shipping logistics and container handling capacity is of paramount importance. The growth of India's economy is closely linked to its ability to provide reliable and efficient shipping infrastructure. Upgrading and expanding container ports and transshipment hubs, implementing advanced technologies, and developing robust intermodal transport systems are crucial steps to support this growth. This means that the country will need many more container ports and transshipment centres. India still has a lot of ground to cover and much work ahead before it can even come close to these goals.

5

THE COCHIN LNG TERMINAL

A Potential Game Changer of India's Energy Landscape

This chapter describes how Cochin Port and the joint sector company Petronet LNG Limited (PLL) worked together to overcome a plethora of teething troubles, complexities, resistance, and political challenges to establish the Cochin LNG[1] terminal and regasification plant. The construction and development of this mega project, located in an environmentally sensitive area, faced numerous challenges that required our teams to plan meticulously and work tirelessly, skilfully navigating various engineering challenges and political minefields along the way. Under a Licence Agreement between Petronet LNG Ltd (PLL) and Cochin Port, the preliminary preparatory work for the LNG terminal and regasification plant began in 2006, followed by the start of construction in 2007. Construction of the terminal and

1. LNG, or Liquefied Natural Gas, is natural gas that has been cooled to a liquid state at approximately -162°C (-260°F) for ease of storage and transportation. In its liquid form, LNG occupies about 1/600th the volume of natural gas in its gaseous state, making it efficient for export and transportation by specialised tanker ships. It is considered a cleaner alternative to other fossil fuels, producing lower emissions of carbon dioxide and air pollutants.

regasification plant were completed by 2012 and commissioned in the year 2013. In January 2014, Prime Minister Manmohan Singh formally dedicated this state-of-the-art LNG port terminal and regasification plant facility to the nation.

To complement the LNG terminal, the Gas Authority of India Limited (presently GAIL (India) Ltd) was assigned the responsibility of developing an extensive pipeline network to supply gas to consumption points in Kerala, Tamil Nadu, and Karnataka, while also integrating it with the National Gas Grid. The LNG terminal and regasification plant were established at an approximate cost of Rs 4,200 crores, and the pipeline project was projected to cost Rs 5,909 crores. Along with supporting infrastructure, these initiatives represented one of the largest industrial investments in Kerala to date, with a combined expenditure exceeding Rs 10,000 crores. However, despite initial progress, GAIL has yet to complete the entire pipeline network, even 12 years after the LNG facility at Cochin was commissioned. The delay has impacted the full operational potential of the terminal. More about this in subsequent sections of this chapter.

The Context

India, like many other countries, has been striving to diversify its energy sources through the adoption of cleaner and more sustainable options. In the late 1990s, the Government of India recognised the growing need for efficient energy sources to support the nation's expanding economy and reduce dependence on traditional fossil fuels. With India's industrial and urban sectors demanding reliable energy, LNG emerged as a strategic solution to diversify the country's energy portfolio. The government envisioned the development of two LNG terminals—one at Dahej in Gujarat and another at Cochin in Kerala—as part of a broader plan to enhance energy security and promote industrial growth. The rationale for establishing the two terminals lay in their strategic locations. The aim was for the Dahej terminal to cater to the energy-intensive industries and urban centres in western and northern India, while the Cochin terminal was envisioned to serve the industrial requirements and urban centres of southern India—the states of Kerala, Tamil Nadu, and Karnataka. This initiative was propelled by access to global LNG markets, enabling imports through modern, specialised port terminals to be built in India, to offset the shortfall in domestic natural gas production.

The primary vision of the Government of India in developing these two LNG terminals has been to provide an alternative energy source to traditional fossil fuels, such as coal and oil. LNG usage has definite environmental benefits, as natural gas has lower emissions than other fossil fuels and can help India meet its climate change goals. The use of natural gas thus helps reduce air pollution and improve air quality. LNG also promises to provide clean and reliable piped gas supplies to homes as well as industries, big and small. Across the world, LNG has been gaining popularity as a fuel for electricity generation and transportation, as it has the potential to replace diesel for powering trucks and ships. Moreover, the use of LNG can bring about significant job creation and private sector growth, particularly through small and medium enterprises (SMEs), drive value addition and manufacturing, and boost the demand for goods and services as well as exports.

As India's economy continues to grow, her energy demands are expected to rise significantly. Recognising the importance of natural gas—not only as an energy source but also as a key component for fertilisers and petrochemicals—it became clear that popularising LNG as a preferred fuel option could bring substantial benefits to the country.

India's Forays into LNG Business

India's ventures into the LNG industry began with an agreement signed between the Indian and Qatari governments in the late 1990s. This historic document outlined the supply of 7.5 million metric tonnes per annum (MMTPA) of LNG to India over a span of 25 years. Under this commitment, 5 MMTPA of LNG was earmarked for the proposed Dahej LNG terminal in Gujarat, while 2.5 MMTPA was allocated to the proposed Cochin LNG terminal.

It was formally signed in the presence of V.K. Ramamurthy, India's Minister of Petroleum and Natural Gas, and Yousef Hussain Kamal Al Emadi, the Qatari Minister of Finance, Economy, and Commerce. Subsequently, in 1999, Qatar's RasGas and India's PLL further solidified their partnership by entering into a binding contract, based on their existing long-term LNG Sale and Purchase Agreement (SPA). This step laid the foundation for the subsequent development of India's LNG import and regasification industry.

Meanwhile, in July 1997, the Government of India established Petronet LNG Limited (PLL) as a joint venture company (JVC),[2] with a 50 per cent shareholding jointly held among four major public sector oil and gas companies: Oil and Natural Gas Corporation (ONGC), Indian Oil Corporation Limited (IOCL), GAIL and BPCL.

What is LNG?

LNG is a highly versatile form of natural gas that has been converted into a liquid state to facilitate its transportation and storage. This conversion involves a cryogenic process in which the gas is cooled to an extremely low temperature of minus 162 degrees Celsius, causing it to condense into a liquid. The transformation into LNG reduces the gas's volume to just 1/600th of its original gaseous state, enabling cost-effective long-distance transportation using specialised vessels called LNG carriers. These carriers play a vital role in delivering LNG to markets across the globe. One of the key advantages of LNG is its ability to produce significantly lower emissions of pollutants like carbon dioxide (CO_2) and sulphur dioxide (SO_2), making it an environmentally friendly fuel source. It also contains minimal ash content and particulate matter, making it

2. According to the Articles of Association of Petronet LNG Ltd (PLL), at any given point of time, not more than 50 per cent of the company's share capital shall be held, whether directly or indirectly, by the government, including any government company and Public Sector Undertaking (PSU). The remaining 50 per cent equity was to be held by the public, strategic partners, and financial institutions.

a cleaner option. Furthermore, LNG has higher methane and energy content as well as a stable composition, making it an efficient energy alternative for residential and commercial consumers.

While the production of LNG requires energy and generates greenhouse gases, its overall carbon emissions are considerably lower than those of traditional fuels. LNG could thus be a key catalyst for promoting a more sustainable energy future, providing an affordable, low-carbon solution for consumers worldwide. Experts predict that LNG (as mentioned earlier) has the potential to replace diesel as the primary fuel for trucks and ships in the future, further helping to reduce emissions in these sectors.

Cochin Port's Early Ventures into LNG

Cochin Port's tryst with LNG began in November 1997 when GAIL approached the port administration with a proposal to set up a captive LNG import facility at Cochin. The port chairman, C. Babu Rajeev, and his team welcomed the proposal and conveyed an "in principle" approval to allocate 50 acres of land for the project in the Puthuvypeen area, after obtaining the approval of the Port Trust Board. The Board, while allowing the lease of land for a period of 30 years, had asked GAIL to quickly prepare a Detailed Project Report (DPR). Following this, Cochin Port moved the Shipping Ministry for formal approval of the project.

Immediately after its incorporation, the PLL carried out comprehensive feasibility studies for both the Dahej and Cochin projects, confirming the commercial viability of both. By December, 1998, the PLL submitted the Detailed Feasibility Report (DFR) to Cochin Port, prepared by a consortium led by Mitsubishi Heavy Industries Ltd of Japan. The DFR included mainly the technical aspects of the proposed LNG receiving terminal and marine facilities, design data, and safety protection systems apart from the economic evaluation and financial analysis. Cochin Port also obtained all preliminary statutory clearances for the project from the Kerala Coastal Zone Management Authority (KCRZMA) office, Pollution Control Board, State Fisheries Department,

Airports Authority of India and the naval authorities. PLL worked closely with Cochin Port teams, following up on the proposal to establish an LNG import and regasification terminal in the Puthuvypeen area of the port. By then, the PLL had completed the essential techno-economic study and obtained key statutory and environmental approvals, including environmental clearances in June 2003.

While the PLL proceeded with the construction and commissioning of their LNG terminal in Gujarat's Dahej, there was a noticeable lack of enthusiasm on their part to take up the Cochin terminal project. Although the government intended to establish both terminals simultaneously, the PLL argued that market conditions were not "conducive" for implementing the Cochin project alongside the Dahej one. This explanation seemed facile, as it did not seem to apply to the Dahej terminal, which began commercial operations in January 2004, while the Cochin project still remained on paper.

The successful implementation of the Dahej terminal was a significant milestone for the PLL as well as for India's LNG industry, being the first LNG terminal to be built in India.[3] However, the delay in the implementation of the Cochin project meant that India missed out on a crucial opportunity to expand its LNG infrastructure to cater to the growing demand for natural gas in the southern part of the country.

---

3. The Dahej LNG terminal was established on a 48-hectare plot of land allocated by the Government of Gujarat. Petronet LNG Ltd. (PLL) entered into a Memorandum of Understanding (MoU) with the Gujarat Maritime Board (GMB) for the development of the terminal and the associated regassification plants as well as for its subsequent expansion projects. The PLL implemented the first-phase terminal and the project on a build-operate-transfer (BOT) basis under a 30-year concession, which ends in December 2035 when the port will be transferred to the Gujarat Maritime Board. The PLL will own the regasification facility for 90 years.

All this while, Kerala Chief Minister Oommen Chandy was continuously exerting pressure on the Central government to implement the Cochin LNG terminal. My predecessor, Jacob Thomas, and the Cochin Port project team followed up at every stage and went ahead with the preparatory work. It was in the early part of 2005 that the PLL came back to the Port Trust with a proposal to revive the project. The port management responded quickly and on 27 May 2005, the Port Trust Board decided to allocate 32.36 hectares of seafront land at Puthuvypeen for the purpose. In a review meeting held at Cochin four months later, in September 2005, the PLL assured Kerala Chief Minister Oommen Chandy that the project work would begin soon and that it would be commissioned by December, 2009. Meanwhile, it opened a site office in Cochin and appointed the former chairman of Cochin Port, Jacob Thomas, as the project director. However, the PLL did not take over the land allotted by Cochin Port for the construction of the terminal even several months after the allotment letters were issued.

I first learnt about the proposed LNG terminal and regasification plant while on a routine field visit sometime in October 2005, a few days after I joined the port. We were inspecting the land usage plan and the land parcels earmarked for different projects in the Puthuvypeen region. It was during this visit that I was shown an expansive parcel of land facing the Arabian Sea that had already been set aside for the LNG terminal. Since I had previously read about the successful commissioning of the Dahej LNG project in Gujarat and knew that both projects were originally conceived simultaneously, I was curious to find out why the Cochin project was yet to take off. I began to study the files and convened a series of meetings to explore the details of the proposal and to determine ways to move the project forward.

By then, it was evident that some nudging was necessary to coax the PLL to kick the project forward. While the Government of India's vision was to develop both the Cochin and Dahej LNG terminals simultaneously, the Cochin project was clearly on the back-burner, while the Dahej project had already become operational. I approached Union Shipping Secretary D.T. Joseph, and requested him to speak with the petroleum secretary, who also chaired the PLL Board. Following their conversation, I was directed to meet with the PLL Chief Executive Officer (CEO) and Managing Director (MD), P. Dasgupta. Subsequently, I made several trips to the PLL's World Trade Centre headquarters in New Delhi, where I met Dasgupta and other members of the senior PLL leadership. In a short time, Dasgupta and I developed a strong bond. The members of his senior leadership team, with whom I had the opportunity to interact, were all friendly, competent, and bright people, consistently exuding enthusiasm. I visited officers in the Ministry of Petroleum and Natural Gas, where I also came across batchmates and colleagues from my parent cadre, Assam-Meghalaya. While verbal assurances poured in, there were no signs of kick-starting the project and I was getting impatient!

In the meantime, I began to make informal inquiries to understand the reasons for PLL's apparent loss of interest in the Cochin LNG project, which was getting somewhat worrisome. The PLL MD Dasgupta kept assuring me that my worries were misplaced and that interest in the Cochin project remained strong. However, in our interactions with the PLL and Petroleum Ministry teams, I faced specific queries regarding the industrial relations situation at Cochin Port. Specifically, I was told that teams of officers of the Petroleum Ministry, the PLL and its promoter PSUs during their visits to Cochin Port for the preparatory work, had frequently witnessed multiple instances of flash strikes and work stoppages. These episodes, although not directed against the PLL at that point of time, may have triggered their adverse perceptions about the industrial climate. The narrative went somewhat like this: As a fledgling organisation, the PLL did not want to enter an area where they feared a volatile industrial climate of frequent work stoppages and consequent unpredictability in implementation of the project. On my part, I assured all those concerned that these perceptions may have been exaggerated, and that Cochin Port trade unions were genuinely keen on a quick realisation of the project.

Apart from following up with officials of the PLL and Petroleum Ministry, I called on Defence Minister A.K. Antony as well as Union Minister of Overseas Indian Affairs, Vayalar Ravi, who also happened to head some of the most powerful trade unions of Cochin Port. A word from the political leadership might help speed up things. I briefed both the ministers about the inordinate delay in commencement of the project and they agreed to follow up with the Minister for Petroleum and Natural Gas. Later, the PLL MD Dasgupta called me and assured that, having successfully established the Dahej plant, the PLL was now ready and willing to take up the Cochin project. In fact, he mentioned that the PLL Board had already approved the Cochin LNG terminal, allaying our fears of delays.

The PMO's Push

As mentioned earlier, one strategy that I consistently followed was keeping T.K.A. Nair, the Principal Secretary to the Prime Minister, briefed. He was deeply committed to developmental projects across the country and showed a keen interest in all the major infrastructure work undertaken by Cochin Port. He frequently convened review meetings, involving the state government and Central ministries, to ensure seamless coordination and the smooth progress of these ventures. His dedication and commitment were a constant source of confidence and inspiration for the Cochin Port team. Shortly after joining Cochin Port, I took the first opportunity to call on the Principal Secretary to brief him about the status of the large projects on the port's agenda. Among other requests, I sought his intervention to begin work on implementation of the LNG project without further delay. Following this, he convened a meeting at the PMO on 29 October 2005, when he reviewed the progress of the Vallarpadam ICTT and a few other projects. It was at this meeting that PLL MD Dasgupta gave a firm assurance that the Cochin LNG terminal would be taken up without any further delay.

The Crucial First Steps

Moving forward, the first step would be defining the legal and commercial relationship between Cochin Port and the PLL and signing a comprehensive Licence/Concession Agreement. First of all, the earmarked land had to be formally handed over to the PLL. However, a complication arose due to the PLL's joint venture status. While public sector oil companies, namely GAIL, the BPCL, the ONGC, and Indian Oil Corporation Limited (IOCL), collectively owned 50 per cent of the company's shares, the remaining half was held by public shareholders and financial institutions, which implied that the PLL did not qualify as a PSU. The Ministry of Shipping's land policy of 8 March 2004 permitted the allotment of land to PSU companies without a tendering process. However, concerns were voiced that allocating land to a non-government entity without such a competitive process might be subject to scrutiny or questioned at a later stage.

To resolve these questions, Cochin Port approached the Ministry of Shipping while discussions continued between the port and the PLL. Before proceeding further, we would need approval of the Shipping Ministry. The incumbent Shipping Secretary D.T. Joseph, a key figure in the development of the Indian ports, made it possible. A highly respected and visionary IAS officer, Joseph had a deep understanding of the policies and possibilities in the shipping sector. Despite his vast knowledge, he remained humble and approachable, always willing to guide and mentor. As someone new to the shipping and port sector, I looked up to him for guidance. He showed an amazing clarity about the development trajectory that the Indian port sector should follow and was always willing to take risks in public interest. He would caution us about potential landmines and would patiently teach us how to navigate crucial documentations in a timely and correct manner. What I found particularly impressive about D.T. Joseph was his ability to balance vision with practicality, while also being grounded enough to recognise the challenges and limitations we could face. His guidance was invaluable in helping me develop a deeper understanding of the sector and to navigate complex issues.

All the issues concerning the Cochin LNG project were thoroughly discussed by the Shipping Secretary and his team during a meeting convened on 23 January 2006. It was pointed out that the existing guidelines to be followed by major port trusts for private sector participation permitted the allotment of land and waterfront for 100 per cent captive facilities without recourse to a tender. This required that the industries were port-specific and the proposal was approved by the administrative ministries. Private sector participation was also permitted under provisions of the Major Port Trusts Act, 1963. Port-specific industries are those that require 100 per cent captive berths and back-up areas for the import of raw material and the export of finished products. The PLL proposal clearly came under these provisions and the meeting decided to proceed with the LNG terminal and regasification project of Cochin Port. Both the PLL and Cochin Port were asked to formalise the arrangement through a detailed Licence Agreement, clearly laying down their respective rights and obligations, and spelling out the terms on which the facilities would be operated. The draft of a Licence Agreement for the establishment of a captive LNG terminal was to be negotiated, finalised, and approved by the Port Trust Board and submitted to the Ministry for the government's approval.

Armed with this clear mandate, Cochin Port began working in earnest, with the PLL team fully on board as well. While awaiting official approval from the Ministry, ongoing discussions between Cochin Port and the PLL continued to make progress. According to the mutual understanding that emerged, the PLL would take full responsibility for the construction and development of the LNG port terminal, including the construction of breakwaters, the establishment of the regasification plant, and all other associated facilities. The PLL would also bear the expenses for capital dredging, which would be necessary to create a dedicated basin for LNG vessel berthing. It was also agreed that the PLL would contribute to the cost of maintenance dredging for the primary navigational and approach channels, based on an appropriate formula while calculating future tariffs.

After the Port Trust Board approved the general decisions regarding the course of action, the port proceeded to transfer the first parcel of the designated land area of 32.3611 hectares (about 78 acres) to the PLL, subject to the completion of certain formalities. This transfer took place at a simple ceremony held at Cochin Port on 6 February 2006.

The Elusive Concession Agreement

At this stage, the teams from Cochin Port and the PLL began to negotiate, aiming to determine the commercial and legal terms of the Concession Agreement. However, this intricate process ran into several hurdles, as both parties had disagreements, divergences, and stalemates on various matters. Between PLL MD Dasgupta and me, we focused on the critical issues at hand and were able to reach a common ground on most matters that would be mutually advantageous or agreeable to both sides. However, a few contentious issues remained, which continued to cast uncertainty over the entire project. As a result of the lingering disputes, the finalisation of the Concession Agreement remained elusive for an extended period of time.

Rewards of Risk-Taking

As the negotiations between Cochin Port and the PLL progressed, it became increasingly clear that reaching an agreement on certain aspects of the terms as well as obtaining the necessary government approvals for the Concession Agreement would be a long, time-consuming process. Eventually, the Agreement would require clearances from the Shipping Ministry, the Planning Commission, and the Finance Ministry before it would be moved for the

Cabinet's approval. Considering all this, both Cochin Port and the PLL felt that the preparatory construction work should begin without waiting for the finalisation of the Concession Agreement. Both parties had built up a certain level of trust and when I requested PLL MD Dasgupta to commence preparatory work for the project implementation, he was more than willing to do so. Following our verbal understanding, the PLL commenced land development and construction of the boundary wall around the proposed terminal site. Very soon, it initiated the tendering process for selecting the Engineering, Procurement, and Construction (EPC) contractor and the project management consultant, setting the plan in motion. After several months of preparatory work, we realised that the Licence Agreement was getting inordinately delayed and the PLL had been making substantial expenditures based on the hope that the contract would soon be signed.

Looking back, we were to discover that commencing preparatory construction work without waiting for the required approvals would ultimately help in completing the entire construction work without significant time or cost overruns. However, it was an immense risk to take, both on the part of Cochin Port and the PLL. Although the obstacles and delays encountered during the negotiation process were substantial and unforeseen, we had taken the plunge in good faith. As I recount the following events, it will be evident that the protracted negotiations and the different iterations of the Concession/Licence Agreement continued for nearly three years before we could finalise and sign the documents. Throughout this winding process, the PLL continued to carry out some of the key stages of the project development in good faith. By the time the Licence Agreement was eventually signed in March 2009, significant progress in the construction of most facilities had already been accomplished. This ensured that the project remained on schedule, resulting in the timely completion of work despite a three-year delay in finalising the Licence Agreement.

This leads us to the question of balancing risk-taking and risk-avoidance while handling development projects. Undoubtedly, taking some calculated risks can avoid unnecessary delays. An excessively risk-averse approach can hinder project implementation and impede progress. At the same time, a reckless approach can compromise project objectives and its sustainability. Reckless risk-taking has the potential to land public officials in trouble. Ultimately, finding the right balance between risk-avoidance and risk-taking is like walking a tightrope, and the key lies in finding the crucial balance within the context of each project.

The Purpose of a Licence Agreement

While embarking on a large-scale infrastructure project, it is important to establish a comprehensive agreement that defines the rights and responsibilities of each partner concerning the utilisation of the port's public assets. Under normal circumstances, the first step would have been the signing of an agreement to outline the project's scope as well as the commercial and legal framework for cooperation. Such a foundational agreement would cover various essential aspects relating to the port's maritime assets and facilities, the duration of the licence, any limitations or restrictions on usage, and regulations concerning the transfer of the licence. These provisions ensure that the project operates within well-defined boundaries and safeguard the interests of the parties involved. From the commercial angle, the agreement would incorporate a detailed payment structure that governs the PLL's use of Cochin Port's public assets. Such a structure would include elements such as land rents, royalty payments, wharfage charges for imported or exported LNG, vessel-related fees, and other financial benefits allocated to the port. By establishing transparent financial terms, the agreement ensures fair conditions for asset utilisation and distribution of benefits between the involved parties.

Above all, the proposed Licence Agreement would serve as a vital legal document that ensures the smooth operation of the project, providing clarity and guidance to both parties, minimising potential misunderstandings and conflicts. Expected to set up mechanisms for dispute resolution, it would include provisions for terminating the agreement in the event of non-compliance by either party along with corresponding compensation arrangements. These dispute resolution mechanisms are essential for maintaining a harmonious and productive relationship throughout the project's lifespan. Thus, a well-crafted agreement would play an indispensable role in defining the rights, obligations, and operational guidelines, acting as a foundation for the partnership.

The Initial Draft

The preparation of a Licence Agreement for a mega LNG terminal within an existing major port owned by the Central government presented several challenges. Unlike the PLL's previous venture in Dahej which operated according to the policies of the Gujarat State Maritime Board, there were no pre-existing templates of a Licence Agreement or a Concession Agreement to serve as a reference.

Nevertheless, we requested the PLL to provide us with copies of their Dahej documents, including the Detailed Project Report (DPR) as well as a draft Licence Agreement for the Cochin project. The PLL promptly shared the documents related to the Dahej terminal and also engaged a London-based international consultant to prepare several draft documents, such as separate Lease and Possession Agreements for the LNG port and LNG regasification facility, along with an LNG Port User Agreement. Primarily prepared within an international framework, these documents had major cultural differences when compared to our context.

The port's civil engineering and legal teams reviewed the templates submitted by the PLL, and identified multiple clauses that contravened numerous existing Central government policies, and may not have served Cochin Port's interests. Although the PLL understandably desired a swift resolution, the port was unable to accept their draft, not even as a working document. The Cochin Port team, therefore, set out to develop its own draft document that would serve as a starting point for further negotiations. Thus, it became clear that a customised Licence Agreement needed to be created specifically for the Cochin LNG terminal, in compliance with the policies of the Central government. As a pioneer in this endeavour, Cochin Port was required to forge a new, uncharted course. This meant that the drafting process had to start from scratch, considering the specific requirements and complexities of the project.

The Model Concession Agreement

The Model Concession Agreement (MCA) was already in the air, and its different iterations had already been used in diverse sectors such as the national highways, power plants, and various other infrastructure projects. The MCA had already gained recognition for its usefulness in creating standardised agreements although it was yet to be formally adapted for the port sector. A.K. Bhalla, the Joint Secretary in the Shipping Ministry, and Director Punya Srivastava had worked on this and suggested that we make use of the draft which was still not complete.

As suggested by officials from the Shipping Ministry, I met with Gajendra Haldea, the original proponent of the MCA, at his office in the Planning Commission. Haldea's contributions to the development sector were well known, and the MCA had become a standardised template for defining the terms and conditions of private sector participation in infrastructure projects in India, particularly in PPP collaborations. The MCA aimed to establish a uniform framework for various sectors, including transportation, power, and water supply, addressing essential aspects such as project structuring, risk distribution, performance standards, and dispute resolution mechanisms. However, we soon realised that the LNG project may not strictly fit into the draft MCA framework. Haldea suggested that Cochin Port develop a modified version of the MCA, tailored specifically to the LNG project. He recommended that we carefully list and explain the required departures from the standard MCA to present to the relevant authorities. He offered to assist and guide us in this endeavour.

Modifying the MCA to Fit a Captive Project

After obtaining a copy of the draft MCA from the Shipping Ministry officials, the Cochin Port's project team began work on writing a draft of the LNG Project Licence Agreement, largely, as mentioned earlier, based on the framework outlined in the MCA document. We needed to customise it to suit the LNG project, which would be a captive facility, not a common user one. Typically, the MCA would be applicable for common user facilities where the concessionaire is an SPV set up by the successful bidder and not for a captive facility by a listed company. In this case, the project would involve huge investments by the captive user. Many clauses of the MCA would not be applicable to the proposed agreement and at the same time, there would be no provisions in the existing MCA to meet certain specific requirements of a project to build a captive LNG port facility and regasification plant. There would be deviations from the broad principles contained in the MCA. It would also be necessary to insert provisions to seek approval of the concessioning authority to deal with situations in which the shareholding pattern of the concessionaire's changes during the exclusivity period. Being a captive project, the agreement would ultimately necessitate obtaining an exemption from the Public-Private Partnership Appraisal Committee (PPP-AC) process. Finally, the approval of the Cabinet Committee on Economic Affairs (CCEA) would be required for the departures from existing government policies.

The Civil Engineering Department of the port had some of the brightest of engineers, known for their professional calibre and dedication. Using the MCA template, the team, led by Chief Engineer J. Karthikeyan and Senior Project Engineer E. Rema, prepared the first draft within a few days. Subsequently, I sat with the entire management team to discuss and finalise the document before beginning specific negotiations with the PLL. The management team had developed a culture of free discussions, encouraging all members to openly express their views. The core team included Deputy Chairman Captain Subhash Kumar, Financial Advisor G. Krishnakumar (who was later succeeded by K.G. Nath), Chief Engineer J. Karthikeyan, Deputy Conservator Captain Paul N. Joseph, Harbour Master Captain Joseph J. Alapatt, Chief Mechanical Engineer Niteen Borwankar, Secretary Cyril George, and Deputy Secretary Unnikrishnan Nair. This dedicated group meticulously reviewed the entire draft document clause by clause. After several rounds of detailed and lively discussions, Cochin Port was able to share the first draft of the agreement with the PLL team by October 2006.

The first draft flagged several outstanding issues that needed tackling, many of which were beyond the powers of the port's management or the Port Trust Board, requiring the Government of India's approval.

PLL's Shareholding

A key challenge arose from the PLL's unique shareholding structure, with 50 per cent of its shares held by its core promoters, the four public sector oil majors, while the remaining shares were owned by the public and financial institutions. Despite the petroleum secretary serving as the ex-officio chairman of the PLL, the legal status of the PLL was that of a private sector entity. The instant proposal involved granting the PLL the licence to build and operate an LNG terminal and regasification plant on a nomination basis, without going through a competitive tendering process, and this created all the complexity in the deal. While the Shipping Ministry's policy allowed private sector participation through nomination for establishment of captive facilities, the PLL sought various additional concessions that would have been typically available only to PSUs.

A related complication arose when Cochin Port requested that the PLL provide an assurance that the existing shareholdings of its core promoters would not be further diluted, during the exclusivity period of the project. However, the PLL was in no position to give a non-disposal undertaking, regarding the shares held by its core promoters, as it could not guarantee that those shares would remain unchanged throughout the exclusivity period.

Another area that led to intense negotiations and frequently derailed our discussions on many occasions was the PLL's insistence on an indemnification guarantee through a "liquidated damages" clause, which the port was unwilling to accept. Once again, the PLL insisted on including such a clause, citing that it was required to meet their lenders' stipulations. Fortunately, Shipping Secretary A.K. Mahapatra intervened, emphasising that the PLL was already being granted concessional rights on a preferential basis, as this was a project of national importance. He pointed out that if any issues arose regarding the fulfilment of obligations in the future, the PLL could always seek redressal from the Government of India. Eventually, the PLL agreed to drop the indemnification clause.

Obtaining the Approvals

The Port Trust Board diligently discussed every aspect of the draft Licence Agreement and evaluated the various departures from the MCA. The Board appreciated the rationale and legitimacy of the PLL's request for an extended tenure of the licence. Securing affordable financing for the project would serve the long-term interests of the port. Thus, the Port Trust Board unanimously recommended that the Government of India grant a special exemption on the duration of the concession, considering the project's national significance and potential regional economic impact.

After obtaining the Board's approval, it was necessary to bring in the Shipping Ministry. Shipping Secretary A.K. Mahapatra as well as Shipping Minister T.R. Baalu appreciated the Port Trust Board's recommendation to allow an extended lease plan in relaxation of existing policies. Their advice was that if a departure from the existing land policy was considered absolutely essential, the matter, with due justifications, should be included in the note for consideration of the CCEA. Apart from the policy on land tenure rules, there would be several other relaxations or departures from the MCA format, but the CCEA could be approached for a waiver of those provisions.

In the subsequent days, the Shipping Ministry prepared the cabinet notes and circulated them to the participating ministries for their scrutiny and evaluation. I followed up by making multiple trips to meet senior officers in the Planning Commission as well as the Petroleum and Finance Ministries. While most sections of the proposed Licence Agreement sailed through, there were objections, particularly concerning the clause related to relaxing the 30-year land lease tenure policy. Consequently, the proposal was returned to us without placing it before the CCEA. This, of course, led to some disappointment.

Tenure of the Licence Agreement

The most knotty part of the negotiations with the PLL revolved around the duration of the Licence Agreement. Ordinarily, ports have the authority to grant a maximum land lease tenure of 30 years, which, in turn, limits the length of Concession Agreements they can enter into. Drawing on the example of Dahej, the PLL negotiators initially sought a 99-year tenure for the land on which the regasification plant would be built. However, after being apprised of policy constraints, they withdrew this demand. They still requested a reasonable tenure to ensure the project's competitiveness.

The issue of the length of the licence period became a focal point in several rounds of discussions and deliberations. The PLL argued that since the normal operational lifespan of the LNG terminal and regasification plant is approximately 50 years, the port should consider granting a similar tenure to make the project cost-effective. Given the substantial investment of over US$ 1 billion required for the entire project, including the port terminal, regasification plant, and the pipeline network, the PLL argued that a 30-year lease would be insufficient. They raised concerns about the future of the LNG terminal, regasification plant, and other specialised assets after the 30-year lease expired, as this would undermine the project's financial viability.

The PLL's position was that a longer lease tenure would help instil investor confidence in the project's long-term viability, enabling more affordable financing. They rightly pointed out that higher investment costs would lead to higher LNG prices, which could make the fuel unaffordable for consumers.

The PLL also pointed out that the Shipping Ministry's land policy for major ports allowed for the relaxation of the 30-year tenure rule under certain circumstances, permitting leases of up to a maximum period of 99 years, subject to prior approval from the Ministry of Shipping. Consequently, during a meeting held by the Shipping Secretary on 4 June 2007, it was decided that given the high-scale investments required for the project, the PLL's revised request for a 40-year tenure could be recommended to the CCEA for approval. In the meantime, the Shipping Secretary chaired several meetings to resolve this and other outstanding issues.

The PLL's need for a reasonable length of tenure needed to be addressed. However, successive iterations of our proposals suggesting different solutions to provide confidence to the PLL were turned down by the Finance Ministry, which remained unrelenting on the 30-year tenure rule. While the PLL had a justifiable argument, the port was obligated to adhere to government policy. Negotiations with the PLL continued, with port authorities working to persuade the PLL to accept the 30-year tenure rule.

On 14 September 2007, Principal Secretary T.K.A. Nair convened a coordination meeting, where I was asked to brief the participants about the major issues that stood in the way of approval of the Licence Agreement. The meeting was attended by Shipping Secretary A.K. Mahapatra, Petroleum Secretary M.S. Srinivasan, and several key officials from the PMO, including R. Gopalakrishnan, Vini Mahajan, and Ashish Gupta. Besides Joint Secretary Arvind Mayaram representing the Department of Economic Affairs, the meeting was also attended by the managing directors of PLL, National Thermal Power Corporation (NTPC), and Fertilizers and Chemicals of Travancore (FACT).[4]

R. Gopalakrishnan, who sadly is no longer with us, played a vital role as a primary point of contact for me, not only within the PMO, but also across various ministries of the Government of India. He would diligently follow up on numerous projects on behalf of Cochin Port. Sanjay Baru, who served as Manmohan Singh's media advisor, aptly described him as someone who combined the commitment of a social activist, the discipline of a civil servant, and the creativity of a wordsmith. His untimely passing was a matter of profound grief.

Several significant decisions were taken in this meeting to address important issues. A different approach to deal with the duration of the licence was suggested, ensuring that the tenure of the Licence Agreement should cover at least 25 clear years from the commencement of the LNG supply. Secondly, it was agreed that upon expiration of the agreement, the PLL would have the option to continue utilising the facility through a right of first refusal (ROFR) on mutually agreed terms. Further, a formula was reached to address the issue of non-dilution of shareholdings of the core promoters of the PLL, through which the combined shareholding of the core promoters should not fall below 26 per cent of the issued and subscribed share capital of the PLL, during the exclusivity period. Lastly, Cochin Port was asked to provide a commitment to the PLL regarding timely completion of capital dredging, assuring it that the required channel depths for handling LNG vessels would be maintained. The importance of this was emphasised, considering that funds had already been allocated for capital dredging from the Central government budgetary resources for the ongoing ICTT project.

4. FACT and the NTPC were initially expected to be major consumers of LNG from the Cochin terminal. However, their interest declined over time due to factors such as changes in energy pricing, delays in infrastructure readiness, shifts in fuel sourcing strategies, and the substantial investments required to modify existing machinery to switch from naphtha to LNG.

Following this, Cochin Port's project team completed the necessary modifications in the draft Concession Agreement, and after several rounds of consultations with the PLL, we were able to send the revised documents to the Shipping Ministry. Regarding the project tenure, the revised document outlined a 30-year tenure from the date of award of the concession, or a 25-year tenure from the date of commencement of LNG supply, whichever occurred later. It also stipulated that the PLL would be entitled to the continued use of the LNG terminal and facilities under a first right of refusal on mutually agreed terms and on a chargeable basis. However, this would only apply if the facilities were still under their operation at that time.

After due scrutiny by the Shipping Ministry, the modified documents were circulated among the concerned ministries for the interministerial consultations. Once again, I resumed my visits to officers in the Planning Commission and various ministries to follow up. Senior officers in these ministries, including those in the Finance Ministry, endorsed our proposal and I returned to Cochin with a sense of optimism. However, we were in for a jolt, when for the fourth time, the proposal was once again returned by the Finance Ministry, resulting in missing the CCEA meeting yet again.

With this, we had a crisis staring at us, bringing the project to the brink of a stalemate, and casting a shadow over its entire future. We found ourselves in a precarious situation because the PLL had already invested significant amounts of money in the project construction in progress, relying on our verbal assurances that the Licence Agreement would be finalised, approved, and signed soon. Both parties were eager to avoid delays in the project and worked in good faith. Most importantly, the PLL had already awarded the EPC contract and appointed contractors for various other works and services, following global tendering processes. Construction activities at the site were in full swing. All statutory clearances had already been obtained. And here we were, stuck without the foundational Concession/Licence Agreement, and even unable to decide on the project tenure! Meanwhile, these developments got leaked out to the press, and some newspapers came out with predictions of a project failure and even some conspiracy theories.

PLL MD Dasgupta expressed his grave concern, stating that any further delay in the approval of the agreement would significantly jeopardise the financing of the project. By then, the PLL had already submitted bids for a gas-tie up with Exxon and made alternate arrangements to secure a firm commitment regarding the gas supply to the Cochin LNG terminal. This development triggered considerable anxiety among port officials about the potential consequences of this rejection. At the time, we already had our hands full with numerous other large-scale projects that were under way, such as the Vallarpadam ICTT, road and rail connectivity projects, and dredging work for deepening of the navigation channels. Each one had time-bound deadlines. The port was also in the midst of implementing a crucial, organisation-wide SAP-based ERP, requiring constant monitoring, along with several other smaller infrastructure projects demanding continuous attention. To make matters worse, we were grappling with recurring work stoppages, strikes, and multiple labour disputes, both in the port and at the container terminal. Multiple agitations were also occurring in different parts of the city against the land acquisition for connectivity projects. Our teams were stretched to their limits. Meanwhile, since the PLL had been carrying out all the work thus far based on a verbal understanding, its MD Dasgupta requested us to provide a written document from the port, asking them to proceed with the construction work in anticipation of the Licence Agreement's finalisation. I promptly signed a document to address this request.

Amidst this backdrop of mounting uncertainties, the port team became increasingly apprehensive about the future of the LNG project. Finalising an agreement acceptable to both Cochin Port and the PLL within the government policy framework became urgent, yet the path forward remained somewhat hazy. Faced with this deadlock, I sought guidance from Shipping Secretary A.P.V.N. Sarma and Shipping Minister T.R. Baalu. Both the Secretary and the Minister shared their concerns and instructed us to prepare revised documentation. I worked closely with Rakesh Srivastava, Joint Secretary in the Shipping Ministry, and his team through several rounds of reading and revising of the documents, taking into account and addressing all objections raised by the Finance Ministry. Follow-up meetings were held at Cochin Port between the project team and the PLL representatives to refine and finalise the document. An understanding was arrived at, after detailed deliberations at the port level and at meetings in the Department of Shipping attended by representatives of the Ministry of Petroleum and Natural Gas, and the Department of Economic Affairs, besides representatives of Cochin Port and the PLL. This was once again followed by the interministerial consultations through circulation of the draft to the Departments of Economic Affairs (DEA), Expenditure (DoE), and Department of Fertilisers, Ministries of Petroleum, Power, and Law and Justice.

All this time, the support from the PMO remained steadfast. On 14 November 2008, Principal Secretary T.K.A. Nair convened another significant meeting which was attended by Petroleum Secretary R.S. Pandey, Shipping Ministry Joint Secretary Rakesh Srivastava, and representatives from the PLL. He expressed his deep dissatisfaction over the continued delay in finalising the foundational agreement with the PLL and asked all concerned to expedite the process. He set firm timelines for the follow-up process as well. Within days, the Shipping Ministry was able to circulate the updated Cabinet note to the participating ministries.

Toil Amidst Festivities

It was December 2008, and Willingdon Island was abuzz with excitement as it hosted the prestigious Volvo Ocean Race—an internationally acclaimed, round-the-world sailing competition. The atmosphere was electric, with sporting events, business meetings, cultural programmes, and social gatherings filling the days and evenings. With hundreds of international participants and a daily footfall of over a lakh domestic visitors attending the events, the entire Willingdon Island was illuminated, and the atmosphere was filled with a festive spirit. The 15-day festivities attracted a steady stream of celebrities, cinema and sports stars, members of the diplomatic community representing different countries, business tycoons from across the world, and state and Central ministers.

Amidst the celebratory atmosphere, Chief Engineer J. Karthikeyan, FA & CAO K.G. Nath, Secretary Cyril George, and other HoDs—along with their respective teams from nearly every division of the port—were focused on an important mission. They were tasked with redrafting the modified Licence Agreement for the LNG project, incorporating all the changes agreed upon, based on the final comments received from the participating ministries. Time was of the essence, and the pressure was on.

Every night, while the cultural and social events were in progress in the Volvo Race Village only a few hundred metres away, we would gather at the chairman's office to redraft the Licence Agreement, meticulously reviewing the document clause by clause, and line by line. We were required to complete the work within a specified time frame to catch the next CCEA meeting, ensuring that the revised agreement captured all the crucial details and reflected the final positions agreed upon during the interministerial consultations. Despite the distractions and festivities around them, Cochin Port officers, both men and women, remained focused on their task, dedicating their evenings to this process carefully, while the atmosphere outside pulsated with joyous activity. It was truly inspiring to witness the sense of purpose, dedication, determination, motivation, and teamwork of these officers.

Once the redrafting of the agreement was completed in line with the agreed terms, we presented a copy to the PLL for their approval and then submitted it to the Port Trust Board. A few days later, the Shipping Ministry once again prepared the Cabinet notes and circulated them to the relevant ministries and departments. This led to several rounds of consultations between the Ministries of Shipping, Finance, Petroleum and Natural Gas, and the Planning

Commission, during which the proposals for various deviations from the MCA were examined threadbare.

We breathed a sigh of relief when Finance Minister P. Chidambaram finally approved the proposed scheme and forwarded it for CCEA approval.

On 6 March 2009, we received a formal communication from the Government of India, conveying the much-awaited cabinet approval, clearing the way for Cochin Port and the PLL to sign the Licence Agreement. It was a moment of immense relief, as the final approval of the document had overcome numerous hurdles to reach this important milestone. The agreement, to be signed between Cochin Port and the PLL, was to consist of two parts. The first was a Licence Agreement for the development of the captive LNG port terminal and associated waterfront facilities in conformity with the policy for private sector participation in major ports. The second was a land lease agreement for setting up of the LNG regasification facility on the land allotted to the PLL by the port on a nomination basis, under the land policy of the Department of Shipping. While preparatory work for the LNG project commenced around March 2006, constructions began in 2007. However, the formal Licence Agreement could only be signed on 12 March 2009, by which time construction had already progressed and gathered considerable momentum. This proactive approach by both the PLL and the port to begin work in anticipation of signing the Licence Agreement enabled the project to be completed largely within the anticipated timeframe and budget.

Saving $100 Million on Breakwaters?

One crucial step at the planning stage of construction of port terminals is to conduct various scientific studies to evaluate the influence of wave dynamics on ship berthing. The outcomes of such studies would be instrumental in establishing environmental parameters, optimising terminal development, and addressing operational performance requirements. An earlier study, carried out by the Pune-based Central Water and Power Research Station

(CWPRS), had recommended the construction of breakwaters to ensure the safe berthing of LNG tankers at the proposed terminal. In a significant move, the PLL suggested a fresh round of marine studies and appointed the UK firm, HR Wallingford, for the purpose. The most dramatic outcome of this study has been the conclusion that the proposed access channel and turning area sufficiently dissipated wave energy, rendering the construction of breakwaters unnecessary. In fact, the study concluded that such a construction would provide only marginal benefits for the LNG berth. Considering the exorbitant cost of breakwater construction, this discovery resulted in enormous monetary savings for the project. The firm claimed that through their study, the PLL has been able to save nearly $100 million on the project cost!

This claim may have been exaggerated, but undoubtedly, there were substantial savings in money, time, and environmental capital. And this was only part of the story. Subsequently, HR Wallingford conducted additional marine studies and identified another key factor impacting the approach channel. In addition to the primary issue of mud infill, they observed a significant littoral drift of sand moving from north to south along the coastline. To mitigate this, they recommended the construction of a bund on the northern side of the LNG basin to counteract the predominant north-to-south sand drift. It was anticipated that this bund would improve the shoreline. However, upon the completion of the 135-metre-long northern spur bund in 2012, heavy siltation occurred on the northern side, with sand covering approximately 70 to 80 per cent of its length. Further studies by the CWPRS have apparently suggested extending the northern spur bund to mitigate the heavy siltation in the basin, which might reduce the need for dredging. While the phenomenon of littoral drift adds to the woes of siltation in the navigation channels, it has also benefited Cochin Port through the continuous formation of substantial chunks of precious additional land on the Puthuvypeen beach, towards the northern aspect of the LNG port. However, in the context of ongoing coastal protection efforts and the persistent challenges posed by scouring and littoral drift, continuous scientific monitoring of wave dynamics, sediment transport, and shoreline changes is essential to ensure that these interventions do not adversely affect the neighbouring beaches along the northern and southern stretches of the coastline.

Project Implementation

The construction of the Cochin LNG terminal was a complex and challenging project due to the difficult site conditions of the naturally formed land facing the Arabian Sea. In its existing state, the land was not sufficiently stable to support the enormous weight of the LNG storage tanks and their contents. Soil investigation conducted by the EPC contractor confirmed the need for extensive piling work, as the soft soil had a low bearing capacity. Considering that the fully filled storage tanks could weigh up to 50,000 metric tonnes, extensive piling work was essential to provide the necessary foundation support and ensure the stability of the tanks.

LNG containment tanks are engineered to store liquefied natural gas at extremely low temperatures (around minus162 degrees Celsius). To maintain these temperatures and ensure the safety and integrity of the tanks, advanced engineering and technology were employed in the construction of the tanks and the roof lid. The foundation work involved driving concrete piles deep into the ground until they reached a hard strata capable of supporting the massive load. With approximately 1,400 to 1,500 personnel engaged during the initial phase, the project quickly gathered momentum. Following the completion of piling work, construction of the LNG storage tanks began, using precast concrete panels made of high-strength concrete capable of withstanding the enormous weight of the tanks and their contents.

One of the most captivating and thrilling experiences during the construction of the Cochin LNG terminal was participating in the process of "raising the roof lid" of the LNG storage tank. The roof lid is a crucial component of the full containment tank design, and is capable of providing the right levels of structural support, effectively containing any potential leaks. The lid-raising procedure is a remarkable process that culminates in the formation of the roof lid, ensuring both the integrity of the structure and its ability to contain any leaks.

Along with District Collector M. Beena, Customs Commissioner Donald Ingty, Additional Commissioner Rema Mathew, and SEZ Commissioner C.J. Mathew, I had the rare opportunity to witness the spectacular procedure of installing the roof lid of one of the LNG storage tanks. The process used a technique in which the inner dome was pre-assembled at ground level and then lifted into place using advanced, remotely-controlled jacking systems. Once the inner dome was secured, an outer concrete layer would be added on top, providing additional reinforcement and insulation. The Japanese engineers and scientists who accomplished this feat had employed high-precision software and equipment. They explained that this method significantly reduced the need for scaffolding and the overall construction time. Operating LNG containment tanks requires specialised knowledge, skills, and equipment due to LNG's cryogenic properties and safety concerns. This underscores the necessity for trained professionals who strictly adhere to established safety protocols and regulations.

As we were perched atop the enormous structure of the tank, the scale and complexity of the project began to unfold before us. The height—55 metres (180 feet)—and enormity of the LNG storage tanks, combined with the meticulous precision of the lid-raising operation, displayed a remarkable feat of engineering and human ingenuity. Imagine watching a massive steel roof, weighing hundreds of tonnes, slowly lifted into position, using nothing but low-pressure air. The lid rose in perfect balance, a breathtaking display of physics, design and expert control. From the vantage point, we could fully appreciate the fusion of cutting-edge technology and skilled craftsmanship that culminated in the safe and successful completion of this critical phase in LNG infrastructure development. To make sure that the tanks were built to the highest quality standards, a team of engineers and quality control experts closely monitored the entire construction process. Their oversight ensured that the tanks met all design specifications and were strong enough to withstand the harsh marine environment. A process of rigorous testing would also be followed to guarantee their safety and reliability.

Although the port was not directly responsible for the day-to-day construction activities of the LNG terminal, the entire process was so captivating that I frequently visited the site to observe the work in progress. It was always a valuable learning experience to interact with the engineers, scientists, and workers there. Interestingly, a large number of construction workers hailed from Assam, and the opportunity to converse with them in Assamese added an extra layer of excitement for me! I may point out here that in Kerala today, a significant population of migrant workers, predominantly hailing from north and northeast India, plays a vital yet often overlooked role in the state's economic activity. Their silent but hard work has been instrumental in driving infrastructure development and supporting various sectors of the economy. It is important to recognise their invaluable contribution in building Cochin Port's infrastructure.

A Road to Port-Based Special Economic Zone

As part of the agreement with the PLL, Cochin Port was obligated to provide direct road connectivity to the LNG site from the existing Goshree Island Development Authority (GIDA) roads. The PLL and Cochin Port were to share the cost of building this road connectivity under a specified formula. In line with Cochin Port's broader development vision, the entire Puthuvypeen region was to be transformed into a Port-Based Special Economic Zone (PBSEZ) to promote value addition and exports. The proposed PBSEZ was envisioned to host key infrastructure projects, including the LNG terminal and regasification plant, BPCL Kochi Refinery's SPM and associated shore tank farms, along with several other energy-based industries in the pipeline. Similar to the nearby Vallarpadam

PBSEZ, the Puthuvypeen PBSEZ would be a dedicated geographic zone facilitating seamless imports and exports after value addition. It would offer various incentives to resident businesses, such as reliable infrastructure, duty-free procurements, tax benefits, and other measures designed to streamline operations and enhance the ease of doing business.

Thanks to the indefatigable efforts of C.J. Mathew, the then Cochin SEZ Development Commissioner, who was also a member of the Cochin Port Trust Board, government notifications declaring the Puthuvypeen and the Vallarpadam areas as PBSEZs were expedited and obtained well in time. However, the existing approach roads to these facilities were narrow and meandered through village settlements. The construction of the PLL's LNG terminal urgently required an all-weather, reliable, and modern road to facilitate the transportation of construction material to the worksite.

Cochin Port had already begun construction of a suitable road approach to the Puthuvypeen PBSEZ. The engineering drawings, environmental planning, and other preparatory work for the proposed road connectivity project to the upcoming SEZ area were ready. Given the urgency, the civil engineering team led by Chief Engineer J. Karthikeyan launched an all-out effort to expedite the project. The project faced challenges as the alignment passed through densely built-up settlements at one end and marshy, low-lying land at the other. There was also a tidal backwater channel that had to be bridged. Land acquisition and rehabilitation became a sensitive political issue. However, with the support of the district administration, elected representatives, and local political leaders, an amicable solution was reached. Affected families were resettled nearby with generous compensation packages, well before work began. Meanwhile, Cochin Port built a crucial bridge across the backwater body and raised the marshy land using an enormous 2,28,201 cubic metres of land filling. The timely completion of the SEZ road connectivity was a key milestone in the development of the LNG terminal and Puthuvypeen PBSEZ.

The Project's Progress

Initially estimated to be completed by the end of 2011, the project completion target was later revised to 2012. This was partly because of the raising of the project capacity from its initial 2.5 million metric tonnes per annum (MMTPA) to 5 MMTPA, based on a reassessment of the demand potential for LNG in south India, with the capability to increase to 10 MMTPA.

By early 2011, even as I was preparing to relinquish charge as chairman of Cochin Port, it was a matter of deep satisfaction for me that a state-of-the-art LNG port terminal was nearing its completion. The LNG terminal area had been turned into a PBSEZ, and Cochin Port had already completed the road to the area. By this time, construction of the regasification plant and its allied civil works for the terminal had been in progress, being constructed by the CTCI of Taiwan, while the civil contract for the regasification plant was being done by Simplex Infrastructures Limited. Meanwhile, the PLL had also appointed Whessoe Oil and Gas of the UK as project management consultants (PMC). The PMC consultant was responsible for supervising design planning, construction supervision, and project stage inspection. Afcons India Limited, responsible for the construction of marine facilities, were making progress in the capital dredging project to deepen the LNG basin and the berthing area to 18 metres depth. Cochin Port was already providing a depth of 16.70 metres to 17.40 metres in the approach channel as part of the developments for the ICTT at Vallarpadam. This depth of channel development was seen as adequate for the navigation of the LNG carriers also.

By this time, the IHI Corporation of Japan had completed construction of the two vital LNG storage tanks. Built using pre-stressed concrete, the inner surfaces of the tank were coated with 9 per cent nickel. To ensure the highest safety standards, the tanks featured a double-wall structure with a one-metre gap between the inner and outer walls and filled with "perlite", a substance prepared from volcanic ash, that, when heated, acquires the insulating properties similar to glass wool. The tank walls were constructed with 800mm of concrete for insulation, designed to withstand the extreme cryogenic temperatures required for LNG storage.

Throughout the construction phase, a dedicated team of the PLL officials, their consultants, engineers, and contractors, together with some 2,000 workers tirelessly worked around the clock. The site was constantly buzzing with activity, as the workers and construction equipment were in continuous motion. The PLL's work required meticulous planning, coordination, and synchronised action to ensure steady progress, adherence to safety standards and avoidance of project delays. According to the PLL's project implementation team, the project faced challenges at several levels, especially because of the character of soil in the entire project site. The soil was marine clay with very little load-bearing capacity, so each storage tank had to be built on nearly 600 piles, while the entire project itself was supported by approximately 3,500 concrete piles, many of them reaching a depth of 80 to 85 metres!

The Cochin LNG Terminal features world-class marine infrastructure capable of berthing LNG tankers ranging from 65,000 to 216,000 cubic metres in capacity. This includes the capability to berth Q-Flex LNG carriers, which are among the largest in the world. A dedicated LNG jetty and approach trestle connect the berth to the shore, enabling efficient unloading operations. The terminal is equipped with two advanced onshore storage tanks, each with a capacity of 1,55,000 cubic metres, along with a stainless steel insulated pipeline system for transferring LNG to the storage tanks, and a state-of-the-art regasification facility. The unloading system consists of three arms connecting the ship's manifold to the pipeline.

Supporting infrastructure includes control rooms near the jetty, an electric substation, fire and radio offices, administrative blocks, and health centres. The marine setup comprises a central platform, five breasting dolphins with super cone fenders, and mooring dolphins. To ensure smooth vessel handling, the PLL also procured two powerful, specialised tugs. The entire facility meets international standards for safety and operational efficiency.

Teamwork

As I write this book, the entire LNG terminal and regasification plant stand testimony to teamwork and collaboration. Apart from the PLL's own dedicated officers and workers, the entire district and state administration, teams of Cochin Port as well as various other limbs of the Central and state governments supported the implementation of the project and its timely completion. During the construction stage, engineers, technicians, contractors, and support staff worked in close coordination across multiple disciplines. Despite the complexity and scale of the project, tight deadlines, and challenging site conditions, their collective commitment ensured the success of the project. Each team brought specialised expertise—from marine works to mechanical, electrical, and safety systems—contributing to the project's success, setting a benchmark in infrastructure development.

While senior PLL executives managed construction on-site in Cochin, Senior Vice President Pushp Khetrapal served as the key liaison with port authorities. He ensured smooth coordination, resolved critical issues, and maintained steady communication with stakeholders in Cochin, playing a vital role in keeping the project on track during its most challenging phases.

How Does Cochin Port Benefit?

The introduction of the PLL's LNG terminal was set to bring a significant economic boost to Cochin Port, yielding direct financial benefits and a substantial increase in revenue streams. These benefits include rents from the 33.40 hectares (82.5 acres)[5] of land and adjoining waterfront facilities covering an area of 43.5 hectares (107.5 acres) leased to the PLL for the LNG terminal along with vessel-related charges from LNG carriers that dock at the terminal, and wharfage fees based on tonnage. Once

5. The PLL was initially allotted 32.36 hectares of land. With a subsequent additional allotment of 1.04 hectares, the total land area allotted increased to 33.40 hectares.

fully operational, the LNG terminal and associated facilities are expected to bring substantial streams of revenue for the port. These earnings will support infrastructure development, maintenance, and modernisation, ensuring a sustainable revenue stream for its future operations.

Waterfront Royalty

It was after protracted negotiations, that Cochin Port and the PLL reached an agreement on the waterfront royalty rates payable by the PLL to Cochin Port, which would become a significant source of revenue for the port. Right from the start of the negotiations, Cochin Port insisted that the PLL should pay the same rates as they were already paying to the Gujarat government at Dahej, a proposition that the PLL resisted. They argued that the competitiveness and business prospects in Dahej and Cochin were not comparable. Despite this, the port's firm stance led to a mutually agreed-upon waterfront royalty rate, set at Rs 103.68 per tonne, with a base date of 1 April 2010, and provisions for a 20 per cent escalation every three years. It was anticipated that the waterfront royalty on LNG imports would become one of the largest sources of income for Cochin Port in the future. However, while the PLL eventually agreed to these terms, which had to be incorporated in the Licence Agreement, this marked the beginning of some tension and the cooling of relationships.

The Uncertainties Surrounding the Pipeline Network

Looking back more than a decade after the completion of the state-of-the-art LNG terminal and the regasification plant at an immense cost, it is difficult to come to terms with such protracted delays in laying the vital pipeline network for gas distribution to consumption points through the National Gas Grid. This raises many critical questions. First, how do we reconcile the huge underutilisation of this crucial national asset over such a long period? How do we account for the immense gap in resource optimisation, which has led to continuing economic and opportunity losses? It is surprising that there has been very little political attention or public discussion on this topic.

A functional and reliable pipeline network is integral to the success of any LNG terminal. Without the means to transport regasified LNG to its intended destinations, and without the necessary last-mile connections to residential, commercial, and industrial consumers, an LNG project does not meet its purpose. From the early stages of planning the LNG terminal, GAIL had envisioned and planned the Kochi-Koottanad-Bengaluru-Mangaluru (KKBM) pipeline network, aiming to link the Cochin LNG terminal with various consumption centres throughout the region.

The Petroleum and Natural Gas Regulatory Board (PNGRB) had mandated GAIL to complete the laying work and commissioning of the pipeline latest by March 2013. This itself was a revised target date. The ambitious 1104-kilometre KKBM pipeline, traversing approximately 938 kilometres through the states of Kerala (510 kilometres), Karnataka (299 kilometres), and Tamil Nadu (129 kilometres), in addition to various spur lines, was designed to serve as the main lifeline for the Cochin LNG terminal, with the ultimate goal of connecting to the National Gas Grid. During the construction phase of the LNG terminal, several project review meetings were held by the Principal Secretary to the Prime Minister with the Petroleum Secretary, and the CMD of GAIL, both at Cochin Port and in the PMO. The pipeline project achieved significant progress during those early days of implementation, completing the 43-kilometre-long first phase. Unfortunately, after the initial pressure on the executing agency waned, the GAIL pipeline project seems to have lost its momentum, leading to inexcusable delays.

GAIL's LNG pipeline project faced an array of challenges, delaying the full utilisation of the entire LNG project beyond all expectations. The project faced various impediments, including widespread protests and resistance from local inhabitants in different stretches along the pipeline alignment. Even as the construction work dragged on slowly and remained stagnant for years, the PNGRB continued to grant repeated extensions for the project's completion.

What went wrong? Did the project receive the critical political support from the state governments of Kerala, Tamil Nadu, and Karnataka? Was there a failure on the part of these states in creating an enabling environment for the project, in expediting the approval processes, facilitating land acquisitions, and providing the necessary resources and infrastructure for the pipeline construction? Could the objections raised by local people have been so insurmountable? Was there adequate political and administrative support to the project from the Central government to resolve those issues? Was any accountability fixed?

Interestingly, the Cochin LNG terminal was formally inaugurated by Prime Minister Manmohan Singh in January 2014, even though the principal part of the pipeline, which was due for simultaneous commissioning, had not yet been constructed. Eight years later, in 2021, Prime Minister Narendra Modi inaugurated another part of the project, this time in the Mangalore segment of the pipeline. However, the utilisation of the Cochin LNG terminal continues to face serious limitations and constraints. The most critical stretch of the pipeline, connecting Coimbatore, Salem, and Bangalore, and ultimately linking to the National Gas Grid, still remains incomplete.

An honest look at the history of this pipeline project will reveal a pattern of apathy from our political leaders, policymakers, the joint sector bureaucracies, the regulatory bodies and the public. Remarkably, this lack of accountability has gone largely unquestioned—neither the media nor the citizens have found it necessary to discuss it or seek answers!

City Gas Distribution is Still a Pipe Dream

One of the key values of the Cochin LNG project was its potential to transform the everyday life of citizens by providing a city gas distribution network for urban areas in Kerala, Tamil Nadu, and

Karnataka. City gas distribution of RLNG (regasified LNG) offers multiple advantages over conventional LPG cylinders. It ensures a steady and reliable supply of natural gas directly to households via a pipeline network, eliminating the need for storage, handling, and frequent cylinder refills. Moreover, RLNG is a cleaner-burning fuel, generating fewer emissions and pollutants, thus making it a more environmentally sustainable option. Over time, it proves to be more cost-effective due to lower logistics and distribution expenses, providing households with a safer, more convenient, and eco-friendly energy solution compared to traditional LPG cylinders.

The use of RLNG for domestic applications through city gas distribution networks presents a big business potential for Cochin and other cities in South India, drawing on the experiences of successful models like Dahej in India and other international LNG terminals. The Dahej LNG terminal has demonstrated the feasibility of integrating RLNG into city gas grids in many large cities. The expansion of city gas networks in regions connected to Dahej has significantly reduced dependence on traditional fuels like LPG and kerosene, leading to improved air quality and reduced carbon footprints. With the Cochin LNG terminal's strategic location, there is an opportunity to replicate this model and extend city gas distribution to major urban centres and industrial clusters in South India.

However, the efforts in implementing the LNG-based city gas distribution have been equally underwhelming, even within the city of Cochin. Led by a joint sector company, it aimed to transport RLNG from the Cochin LNG terminal to households in Cochin through pipelines. However, the project has encountered numerous obstacles, including regulatory challenges and logistical bottlenecks. Land acquisition for laying gas pipelines remains a political hot potato in Kerala, posing a major barrier. Similarly, city administrators are generally hesitant to allow digging up the already narrow city roads, which has been a factor delaying the laying of city gas pipelines.

Transporting LNG by Road

Although commercially less viable, transporting LNG through trucks has been in vogue, especially in regions where physical pipelines do not reach the consumption points. This scheme allows for flexible transportation of LNG to remote areas, industrial zones, or smaller consumption points where laying pipelines is not economically feasible. Thus, while trucking LNG can be more expensive than pipeline transportation over long distances, it provides the flexibility to reach off-grid locations and serves as a practical interim solution until an adequate pipeline infrastructure is developed. The process is governed by stringent safety protocols, involving handling by trained personnel, and adherence to guidelines from regulatory authorities.

At the Cochin LNG terminal, some initiatives have been made to distribute LNG through trucking to expand its market. The terminal has set up truck-loading facilities for moving LNG into cryogenic tanker trucks, enabling the distribution of LNG directly to consumers who are not connected by pipelines. The focus has been on supplying LNG to industrial units in Kerala and neighbouring states, particularly industries which can use LNG as a cleaner fuel alternative. Initiatives were undertaken to collaborate with local distributors and city gas supply companies. While trucking LNG from the Cochin LNG terminal has shown some promise, its long-term viability depends on factors such as the cost of LNG, demand stability, and investments in infrastructure.

Cochin LNG Terminal and its Unrealised Potential

More than a decade after its commissioning, the immense potential of the Cochin LNG terminal to catalyse the industrial and economic development of Kerala and other south Indian states has remained largely untapped. Considering the remarkable successes in Dahej, Gujarat, and other examples worldwide, India's southern states must take proactive steps to harness the vast potential of this

LNG terminal for driving forward regional industrialisation and economic growth. The terminal has the potential to play a central role in developing the region by providing clean and affordable natural gas for domestic and industrial usage including power generation, fertilisers, petrochemicals, and other industries. The opportunities and possibilities are immense.

The availability of gas supplies from the Cochin LNG terminal has the potential to bring about transformative changes in the region's industrialisation. Utilising LNG as a clean fuel for domestic use can replace traditional biomass fuels, resulting in improved indoor air quality, reduced health risks, and enhanced quality of life for households. Moreover, a reliable and cost-effective supply of gas can support the growth of small and medium enterprises, foster entrepreneurship, and create employment opportunities. The construction of the pipeline to southern Kerala and Tamil Nadu districts was expected to ensure the availability of gas and democratise its access across the southern regions of the country. At the time of its conceptualisation, it was envisaged that the downstream industries in the region such as the FACT fertiliser unit, Kochi Refinery, NTPC Kayamkulam, power plants in Mangalore, foundry and textile units in the Salem–Coimbatore area would benefit from using LNG as an energy source, compared to other expensive feedstock such as naphtha, thereby reducing the cost of production.

With its central role as an energy hub, the Cochin LNG terminal has the potential to build and nurture shared economic zones and industrial corridors that augment integration and boost industrial output across southern India. It can also provide reliable clean energy for MSMEs, for sectors such as textiles, food processing, pharmaceuticals, metal industries, paper mills, automotives, hospitality and electronics.

The terminal can further fuel and bring about industrial growth by supplying feedstock and supporting the development of a downstream ecosystem for industries like plastics, synthetic fibres, and rubber. This could stimulate the formation of industrial clusters, where sectors benefit from one another's resource proximity and synergy, as demonstrated in Dahej. LNG can also support heavy manufacturing industries, such as cement, glass, paper, and metal processing, which rely on cost-effective energy sources. Such industrial growth also opens up export opportunities, particularly in chemicals, fertilisers, and engineering products.

It is worth noting that LNG supports greener industrialisation by providing a cleaner burning fuel compared to coal and oil, enabling industries to reduce emissions and align with global environmental standards. This is attractive to investors, as it offers existing industries a chance to lower their carbon footprint, opening up new markets for green and sustainable products. The LNG facility also can drive the development of ancillary services like logistics, warehousing, and transport networks, which further connects Kerala with other south Indian states, creating a robust industrial corridor.

Other hugely impactful areas where Kerala could emerge as a leader are agribusiness and organic farming, promoting specialty crops and value addition, fisheries and marine products. Some of the largest exports from Cochin Port are agricultural and marine products. These sectors offer significant opportunities to augment Kerala's food security, expand its export potential, and generate employment opportunities. Surprisingly, there have been limited efforts to harness the readily available and cost-effective cold energy generated during the LNG regasification process. Thus, we have an ironic situation in which agricultural and marine products are going to waste for want of adequate cold storage capacity, while the cold energy generated during LNG regasification remains untapped and is also wasted.

An often overlooked opportunity lies in energy-related academic research. Universities and institutions in Kerala, such as the Cochin University of Science and Technology, should pursue research and innovation in areas like energy technology, cleaner fuels, and industrial efficiency. With its strong base of scientists, researchers, and an educated workforce, Kerala has the potential to become an innovation hub, attracting partnerships and investments in energy research. A collaboration between the LNG terminal and local universities could foster specialised programmes in energy management, chemical engineering, and industrial technology, building a skilled talent pool to support future growth.

It is unfortunate that years after the commissioning of the Cochin LNG port and regasification plant, its utilisation remains disappointingly low, with few new industries taking advantage of the easy availability of LNG. This situation calls for serious introspection by Kerala's political leaders, industrialists, entrepreneurs, and government officials to understand the reasons behind the state's failure to fully exploit this clean fuel source, what the impediments could be and what, if any, may have gone wrong.

The missed opportunities in Kerala stand in stark contrast to the success of the Dahej LNG terminal, which spurred a massive wave of industrialisation in its hinterland in Gujarat and other states in North India. If Kerala had effectively harnessed even a fraction of these opportunities, it could have stimulated significant industrial development and job creation. It is high time that Kerala reassessed its strategies, addressed the roadblocks, and implemented effective measures to maximise the economic potential of its LNG infrastructure.

It is important to note that the PLL and GAIL have collectively invested over a billion dollars in this project, including the terminal, the regasification plant, and the pipelines constructed so far. The country can ill-afford to allow this substantial investment to remain stagnant without sufficient returns. More about this in Chapter 8.

6

CELEBRATING COCHIN

The chairman's office, located on the sixth floor of the iconic administrative building, offers breathtaking views of the majestic Vembanad backwaters as they merge with the Arabian Sea. Right before you lies an intricate network of meandering water channels, rivers, rivulets, and lagoons, weaving around vast clusters of picturesque islands. The office perks include crimson sunsets and mesmerising displays of colours that paint the evening sky. As the sun descends, the skies burst into a kaleidoscope of hues, casting a spell over the backwaters and lagoons, which, in turn, reflect the riotous colours of the western sky—a show not to be missed, creating a surreal experience. The ebbing evening tides and the labyrinth of rivers and rivulets quietly converge with the sea, blurring the lines between reality and fantasy. During the monsoon months, thick sheets of black clouds approach menacingly from the seas, lashing against the glass of the French window with incredible intensity before bursting into torrential rains—an experience to savour, an awe-inspiring spectacle to cherish.

Just a few metres from the building, the Ernakulam and Mattancherry shipping channels come alive, as vessels of various sizes, shapes, and nationalities glide past, carrying passengers, cargo containers, petroleum, and other merchandise. When colossal cruise ships approach, with thousands of passengers lining their decks and waving at those on the shore, it feels as though a floating city is passing by. Then there are quaint fishing vessels, passenger boats, and junkers crisscrossing the tranquil waterways, ferrying people and vehicles through a world where time itself appears to remain still. In the distance, the ever-changing skyline of Cochin's Marine Drive incessantly rises, a city in perpetual growth.

Fishing and Fisheries Harbour

Silhouetted against the horizon, the iconic Chinese fishing nets, or *cheena valas*, sway gracefully over Cochin's coastal landscape. These historic structures, integral to Cochin's scenic charm, are believed to have been introduced centuries ago by Chinese traders. However, some historians trace their origin to Portuguese traders, who brought them from Macau. The Portuguese influence is evident in the terminology of the nets' parts, which are distinctly Portuguese rather than Chinese. These nets stand as living relics, connecting the present to a bygone era.

Watching the operation of these nets is captivating. Their cantilever design is a blend of balance and teamwork, involving a group of six fishermen. One of them lowers the net into the water, using his weight on the main beam, aided by counterweights made of stones tied to ropes. After a brief submersion, the net is hoisted up in a flurry of coordinated activities—a perfect demonstration of gravitational physics. Visitors are invited to participate, to try their hands at operating these giant nets under the guidance of skilled fishermen. The activity is often accompanied by traditional songs, adding to the celebratory atmosphere.

For the fishermen, the nets are a source of livelihood; for visitors, they offer more than just a photo op. They provide an adventure, a cultural immersion, and a connection to Cochin's vibrant history—a unique opportunity to create lasting memories and partake in the spirit of the city's heritage.

On the opposite side of the Mattancherry navigation channel, in the Thoppumpady area, stands the bustling Cochin Fisheries Harbour. This facility is an integral part of Cochin Port and serves as a vital lifeline for the city's fishing community, which includes both artisanal fishermen and those engaged in deep-sea fishing and trawling. Artisanal fishermen are small-scale fishers who use traditional, often low-tech methods to catch fish, mostly operating non-mechanised or motorised craft in coastal or inland waters, employing techniques such as handlines, nets, small boats, or even fishing by hand, which have been passed down through generations. Both men and women play key roles in this sector, contributing to activities like unloading, sorting, and icing the catch as well as engaging in traditional fish curing and drying methods. In contrast, deep-sea fishing boat workers venture far from the shore, pursuing specific targets of fish species in deeper ocean waters.

The life of a fisherman here, like those elsewhere, is physically demanding, with most commencing their day at around 3 a.m. Their routine involves preparing boat and equipment, assessing the weather, and embarking on journeys to various fishing spots, some of which are quite distant from the shore. The act of hauling in the catch is physically strenuous. Fishing remains deeply rooted in Cochin's age-old practices although modern technology and communication systems have started to make inroads. For generations, the fishermen of Cochin have lived in harmony with the sea, aided by their intimate knowledge of its currents, winds, and stars guiding their daily expeditions. With a deep-rooted connection to the sea, they venture out in the wee hours, their precise departure times determined by the chosen fishing destination. Every aspect of their journey—weather conditions, cloud patterns, and water currents—is meticulously observed. The presence and behaviour of seagulls and other birds offer vital clues. It is interesting to watch how intuition and experience often outmatch even the most sophisticated GPS systems and Google maps.

The colourful deep-sea fishing boats of the Cochin Fisheries Harbour attract the attention of locals and visitors alike. Each boat, painted in a dazzling array of colours, is a work of art, reflecting the individuality and pride of its owner. The bright hues and intricate designs often have deep cultural significance. The aesthetics of these boats is not only visually striking but also serves a practical purpose, making the vessels easily identifiable from a distance as they stand out in the vast expanse of the sea. Very often, the motifs embody the fishermen's hopes and beliefs. The decorations often include religious symbols, mythological figures, and auspicious motifs, intended to bring good fortune and protection during the perilous journeys at sea. This tradition of decorating fishing boats is passed down through generations. Frequently, on festive occasions like Onam, Eid, or Christmas, the fishing boats sail in vibrant processions, attracting thousands of tourists and locals who line up on the shores to watch and cheer them.

The Cochin Fisheries Harbour is an integral arm of Cochin Port. Its strategic location and existing infrastructure make it indispensable not only to the local fishing community but also to businesses engaged in seafood processing and export. The harbour's significance is evident from the frequency of high-level official visits and the strong interest shown by international markets, particularly countries with which India has established marine product export ties, regarding the facilities available on-site. However, to fully realise its potential and align with international standards, the harbour requires substantial investment in modernisation. Key areas for improvement include upgrading hygiene standards and enhancing infrastructure such as cold storage units, fish-handling zones, and auction facilities.

To move forward, a carefully crafted master plan was deemed essential. While the modernisation plan could be carried out in phases, the initial focus would be on developing state-of-the-art cold chain facilities, advanced waste management systems, and ensuring adherence to global hygiene standards. Unplanned construction must be avoided at all costs. Partnering with international seafood export companies and pursuing PPPs can provide the necessary funding and expertise for these upgrades. Moreover, tapping into government grants aimed at expanding fisheries and exploring foreign investment opportunities could significantly accelerate modernisation efforts. Needless to say, this will make the Cochin Fisheries Harbour a world-class facility and boost its contribution to Cochin's economic growth.

India is among the world's top five fish-exporting countries, contributing eight per cent to global fish production. Kerala, especially Cochin, plays a vital role in this sector, exporting marine products such as shrimp, cuttlefish, squid, and other highly sought-after varieties to international markets. However, the supply is often insufficient to keep up with the global appetite, which is driven by increasing demand in markets like the United States, the European Union, Japan, and Southeast Asia. In terms of statistics, India exported around 1.78 million tonnes of seafood worth over US$7 billion in the fiscal year 2023-24, with Kerala contributing a sizable portion of these exports, particularly through ports like Cochin. However, the state faces challenges such as overfishing, inadequate cold storage facilities, and outdated infrastructure, which limit its ability to fully capitalise on the growing demand. To meet the rising domestic and international appetite for seafood, Kerala needs to scale up sustainable fishing practices, renovate its harbours, and increase the production capacity to enhance the quality and volume of exports.

Connecting Lakshadweep

Cochin Port serves as an important maritime gateway for the Lakshadweep Islands, facilitating the movement of goods and people between these clusters of islands and mainland India. This connection is vital for the islands' economic sustenance and daily life, as it ensures the supply of essential commodities, construction materials, and consumer goods, which are not locally produced. Cochin Port is the primary hub for the shipping services that connect Lakshadweep to the rest of India. The port has been operating regular ferry services and cargo shipments, which are pivotal for the transportation of passengers, agricultural products, and local handicrafts. Cochin Port also plays a key role in the distribution of petroleum products and other supplies to the islands, all necessary for their energy needs and infrastructure development. The islanders are dependent on the mainland for advanced medical treatment and educational facilities as well.

One major problem faced by the Lakshadweep passengers had been the lack of a dedicated passenger terminal for Lakshadweep ships at Cochin Port. Passengers often got stranded at various places when ships were suddenly cancelled or delayed due to the monsoon or weather-related reasons. Sometimes they were even forced to wait in front of the office of the Lakshadweep administration or somewhere in the city when ships got delayed. This problem was regularly the subject of discussions whenever I met the Lakshadweep MP and also when the administrator came over to meet me. To address the issue of a dedicated terminal for Lakshadweep passengers, Cochin Port and the Lakshadweep administration collaborated to build a new terminal on the Mattancherry channel. This terminal, with 300 metres of quay length and 12 metres width, can berth three vessels at a time and was built with funding from the Central government. It included facilities for security checks, passenger waiting zones, and other related amenities. The construction of the terminal that began in 2009 was completed by early 2012 during the tenure of my successor, Paul Antony, bringing considerable relief to the people of the islands.

Lakshadweep, with its pristine beaches and unspoiled natural beauty, holds immense potential as a premier tourism destination. However, the current infrastructure, particularly in terms of accommodation, is insufficient to meet the surging demand from tourists who travel by air or passenger ships. This accommodation shortage is a significant drawback, limiting the islands' ability to cater to a higher volume of visitors.

To address this issue, introducing cruise ships that operate between Cochin Port and the Lakshadweep Islands could be a game-changing solution. Cruise tourism offers a sustainable approach to boost tourist numbers without overwhelming the islands' delicate ecosystem. By using cruise ships as floating accommodations, the strain on the existing limited infrastructure on the islands would be alleviated, and would prove to be a comfortable and convenient option for tourists. Cruise services could offer various packages, including island-hopping itineraries, water sports, diving excursions, and cultural experiences, tailored to different tourist preferences. Special themed cruises focusing on wellness, adventure, or ecotourism could be vital for attracting a diverse range of travellers. The ships could also host onboard events such as local cultural performances and cuisine tastings, allowing tourists to experience Lakshadweep's unique heritage without compromising the islands' carrying capacity.

Kochi International Marina

Marinas are modern berthing facilities for ocean-going yachts, with specialised waterfront features designed to moor, service, and accommodate boats and yachts. They offer amenities and services such as fuelling, maintenance, and security, making them central hubs for boat enthusiasts, adventure sailors, and those engaged in recreational boating. In many parts of the world, thriving marinas have sprung up near large cities, eliminating the need to separately develop additional facilities like hotel accommodation as well as repair, servicing, or bunkering facilities. Cochin meets all these requirements and this has been the reason why hordes of luxury yachts gravitate to Cochin's Bolgatty channel every year.

Developing a world-class marina at Cochin Port was an exciting prospect, which was considered one of the port's most readily achievable infrastructure goals. The main promise of the Cochin Port Marina project lies in its potential to invigorate and support Kerala's vibrant tourism industry and the local economy. However, Cochin Port's aspirations for marina development remained in the conceptual stage for several years, partly due to the absence of road connectivity to Bolgatty Island. The newly developed Goshree bridges gave a fresh impetus to this ambition. At the same time, there were important considerations of national security, immigration, customs, and navigational safety that made it crucial to have these operations brought under strict regulatory control.

The initial vision was that the proposed marina would be jointly developed by Cochin Port and the Kerala Tourism Development Corporation (KTDC). Such a partnership would hold several strategic advantages. Cochin Port would bring its expertise in maritime infrastructure, ensuring technical excellence and compliance with maritime safety standards. The KTDC, in turn, bring its strengths in tourism promotion and management, leveraging its capacity to attract visitors through a variety of offerings. Moreover, Cochin Port already had systems in place for receiving and accommodating foreign-flagged vessels and international visitors, including customs and immigration facilities operating on-site. However, the proposed joint venture between the port and the KTDC for the marina's construction and shared operation did not materialise due to a series of unforeseen developments.

The initial challenge lay in identifying the ideal location, considering factors such as waterfront suitability, appropriate water depths, and the availability of land for constructing the necessary infrastructure. In 2003, the KTDC and its subsidiary, Tourism Resorts Kerala Ltd (TRKL), had approached the port, expressing their interest to establish an international marina at Bolgatty, utilising the adjacent waters on the eastern side of the island. While this request received the port's approval, subsequent site visits and discussions led to the emergence of various alternative proposals.

Meanwhile, the Port Trust Board had approved the reclamation of approximately 10 hectares of land on Bolgatty Island's western side, which was nearing its completion. TRKL expressed its interest to secure a portion of this newly reclaimed land for the marina project. However, technical studies revealed that the western waterfront of Bolgatty was shallow and prone to continuous siltation. This meant that the development of a marina on the western waterfront would necessitate extensive dredging, rendering the project financially unviable. Thus, the TRKL was advised to revert to their original proposal of establishing the marina on the eastern waterfront of Bolgatty, where the natural water flow would provide the necessary draught for yacht operations.

The immediate reason for the port's withdrawal from the joint project proposal arose when the TRKL communicated its intention to collaborate with a Malaysian entity for the marina project. This proposed partnership with a foreign entity introduced regulatory complexities, making it difficult for the Port Trust to associate with a foreign partner or to provide land to TRKL at a concessional rate, as initially planned. While allocating land at a concessional rate to the Kerala government, the KTDC or its wholly owned subsidiary TRKL posed no issues, the involvement of a multinational partner would necessitate a competitive tendering process.

Bharat Bhushan, the Additional Chief Secretary overseeing tourism affairs, agreed to visit and explore various alternatives. After joint site visits and subsequent deliberations, it was decided that Cochin Port would not partner with the state government on the marina project due to the reasons outlined. Instead, the TRKL would undertake the construction and execution of the project on the eastern side of Bolgatty. An essential requirement of an international marina is proximity to a hotel, providing yacht travellers with convenient lodging and dining options. The magnificent Bolgatty Palace and Island Resort of the KTDC added value to this location by offering such amenities. However, a major challenge remained: Bolgatty Island did not have a road connectivity, with access only possible by boat. Even after the newly built Goshree bridges connected the island to the mainland, the existing land approach to the hotel was a narrow passageway, winding through some very congested, residential settlements.

This issue was suitably resolved when the Port Trust offered to support the marina project by providing 1.1 hectares of land free of cost to the KTDC/TRKL in order to construct a two-lane approach road from the Goshree road to Bolgatty, offering a direct and wide access to both the existing public sector Bolgatty Palace

Hotel as well as the proposed marina. Of course, this offer by the port was not entirely altruistic. The proposed approach road would also provide connectivity and add value to the Port Trust's land that was under reclamation on the western bank of Bolgatty Island. While the development of a direct two-lane road became a game changer for the existing Bolgatty Palace Hotel and the marina project, it would also significantly enhance the attractiveness of the port's own land under reclamation to prospective investors. The Port Trust Board promptly approved these proposals, considering the public value that they would bring.

Eventually, road connectivity and the marina project were executed by the KTDC and the TRKL, with design and development led by various multinational firms. Ownership and management of the marina were vested with the KTDC. On 24 April 2010, the marina was officially inaugurated by Defence Minister A.K. Antony, with Kerala's Minister for Home and Tourism, Kodiyeri Balakrishnan, also in attendance. The event was well-attended by public representatives, officials, and local citizens. The establishment of the Kochi International Marina was the realisation of a long-held dream for Kerala's tourism sector. However, like all tourism infrastructure, the development of the marina should not be viewed as a one-time achievement. Ongoing promotional efforts, focusing on demand generation alongside periodic infrastructure upgrades, will be essential. Its future growth and success will require continuous dedication, passion, and forward-thinking vision from future generations.

Financial Crunch and Redevelopment of Bolgatty

The construction of the road to Bolgatty Island led to significant redevelopment of the island, marking a milestone in the rejuvenation of the existing public sector KTDC Hotel and the establishment of the Kochi International Marina. This magnificent island, once accessible only by boat, saw a substantial increase in land value due to the direct road access. One highlight of the island's redevelopment was the establishment of a large hotel-cum-convention centre on a 26-acre plot of land on Bolgatty's western waterfront.

Cochin Port owns several prime land parcels scattered across the city. Although these chunks of land are not directly suited for shipping activities, government policies allowed them to be leased for commercial purposes, such as offices, hotels, or tourism-related ventures. Facing a financial crisis in 2009, the port had sought to lease some of these properties, but the existing 30-year lease limit deterred serious investors. To address this, the Ministry of Shipping allowed a one-time renewal option at prevailing market rates beyond the initial 30 years. Armed with the new policy, the port once again invited tenders for lease of these land parcels, which included this newly reclaimed 10.6 hectares (approximately 26 acres) of land on Bolgatty. However, potential investors remained hesitant to commit large investments, as they considered the lease period a limiting factor, even with the new policy allowing one renewal after the initial 30 years at prevailing market rates. The feedback from potential investors was that the freshly reclaimed land with its soft muddy soil would require expensive land consolidations, which therefore dampened investor interest.

Repeated tendering efforts to attract developers were initially unsuccessful. Apart from wide publicity through advertisements, the port wrote to several national and international hotel chains, inviting them to submit their tenders for this prime land. Top executives of many prominent Indian hotel chains and many business tycoons personally visited the site to explore the opportunity. These included Sant Singh Chatwal, the New York-based Indian American hotelier, and R.K. Krishna Kumar, Director, Tata Sons and former head of the Indian Hotels, as well as owners and CEOs of other well-known hotel chains. While the multiple pre-tender meetings were well attended by interested investors, the initial responses to successive tendering efforts either drew a blank or were at best lukewarm. Real estate developers did not evince interest as the lease was only for a period of 30 years, with a one-time renewal option for another 30 years at prevailing market rates and no ownership transfer was permitted. A final round of tendering eventually resulted in awarding the lease to M. A. Yusuff Ali, the UAE-based NRI businessman. This leasing decision was questioned by some persons, leading to protracted litigations, possibly engineered by competing business interests.

Meanwhile, the port's financial crisis deepened, particularly after the Ministry of Shipping announced a pay revision for port workers in 2010, retrospectively effective from January 2007. Cochin Port, like other major ports, had to shoulder the entire financial burden without Central government support. Despite financial constraints, the port managed to implement the revised salary structure and other benefits, but did not have the resources to pay the arrears as they involved a substantial amount. Faced with the mounting pressures from trade unions demanding the payment of arrears, the port sought a government loan, but eventually secured a Rs 100-crore loan from the Mumbai Port. The positive approach of Mumbai Port Chairman Rahul Asthana and the intervention of Shipping Secretary K. Mohandas expedited this process.

While the 100-crore loan came to us quickly, I was determined to repay it before I handed over charge in the coming months, considering its high interest burdens. The leasing of the Bolgatty land would be crucial for this. However, considering the strong backlash from certain interests, and to avoid any future complications, we decided to proceed cautiously and placed the matter before the Port Trust Board once again for its reconsideration. The Port Trust Board re-examined the entire process, keeping the Shipping Ministry informed of all aspects. The litigation finally reached the Kerala High Court. The port team had ensured complete transparency and fairness in the entire tendering process, diligently documenting all steps followed along with the reasons. This culture of openness and meticulous record-keeping proved valuable, as the Division Bench of the Kerala High Court upheld the Cochin Port Trust Board's decision. The land was formally handed over to Yusuff Ali, who went on to develop the expansive Grand Hyatt Kochi Bolgatty, a hotel-cum-convention centre. This strategic decision by the port not only helped it overcome its immediate financial crisis but also resulted in putting the land, which was otherwise lying fallow, to productive use, adding to the city's economic activity and generating employment for many. Today, Bolgatty Island stands as one of the city's prominent landmarks, making it a major attraction for both international and domestic tourists, as well as business travellers.

Building Ro-Ro Infrastructure

The Bolgatty redevelopment also included the construction of a Roll-on, Roll-off (Ro-Ro) terminal, primarily to transport container-laden lorries through Ro-Ro services between Willingdon Island and the newly built ICTT at Vallarpadam. This was made possible with a grant from the Inland Water Transport Department of the Government of India. The vision behind the building of the Ro-Ro terminal was also to leverage Kerala's vast network of water bodies for efficient inland waterway transportation, especially to the upcoming ICTT. This could activate many inland ports in Kerala like the Kottayam inland water port and others, and also to service coir-products manufacturing centres in Alappuzha district, thus reducing road congestion as well as the costs of cargo movement. The Government of India has formulated an ambitious vision for developing Kerala's waterways. Despite this plan, the transportation of containers via these waterways has not fully taken off, primarily due to challenges in infrastructure at these interior ports and the underutilisation of available water routes arising from other competing requirements. In many countries, inland waterways are effectively used to transport containers and bulk cargo, significantly reducing road traffic and lowering transportation costs.

Kerala's inland water transportation has not fully realised its potential despite the state's vast network of waterways. Several challenges have hindered its development. Poor infrastructure, such as inadequate jetties and poorly maintained navigation channels, is a major issue. Encroachments along waterways further restrict access and navigation. One major problem is that fishermen often lay nets across navigation routes, obstructing vessels. The lack of coordinated investment in modernising watercraft and the inadequate efforts to align various agencies involved in water transport have contributed to the lack of use of this eco-friendly and cost-effective mode of transportation.

These are not insurmountable challenges. Fishing activities can be regulated and fishermen, who may get adversely impacted, can be offered alternative employment or other more attractive sources of livelihood. A clear vision and focused work could transform Kerala's waterways into vibrant corridors for both tourism and goods transport. Thousands of tourists travel daily between Cochin and Kumarakom, Alleppey, and other destinations. If the waterways are fully opened up, more tourists would take the scenic water route to savour Kerala's pristine natural beauty. Moreover, the waterways could host waterborne marketplaces, akin to those in Venice and Bangkok, creating a unique allure and boosting the local economy.

The Cochin Stopover of the 2008 Volvo Ocean Race

The Volvo Ocean Race, the premier ocean marathon, is considered one of the most exhilarating and hazardous nautical sporting events. It involves sailing and crisscrossing the globe, touching pre-selected ports of call in key economic and cultural hotspots of the world. Sailors participating in this race push their limits, navigating through tumultuous and dangerous waters, often at breakneck speeds. Competing in this race requires an intense competitive spirit, grit, and physical courage. Described as the "Formula One" of ocean racing, this event takes place once every three years, with each edition spanning over nine to ten months and featuring stopovers at selected ports of call across the globe.

The chance to host the prestigious Volvo Ocean Race Stopover came unexpectedly—an opportunity we couldn't afford to miss. Despite our teams being stretched to their limits with critical projects and deadlines, we decided to seize this rare chance. We knew it could have tremendous benefits, so we expected it would bring heightened visibility, financial gains, and a tourism boost to both the state and the country.

When such a possibility knocks, should one let it slip away? At a time when the team was fully engrossed and racing against time on existing projects, was it wise to venture into something as different as bidding for an international sporting event? We decided it was. Amid our daily challenges and the ongoing tests of our team's endurance and resolve, the Cochin Port team boldly moved forward with a bid to host the Volvo Ocean Race Stopover. In December 2007, when the race officials visited my office, I sensed a tremendous opportunity. Bringing a global event of this scale to India for the first time could be transformative. India had never hosted this race before, and during our discussions, it became clear that the organisers were equally enthusiastic about bringing the Volvo Ocean Race to Indian shores.

At the same time, organising a major international event like the Volvo Ocean Race Stopover would require substantial resources, meticulous planning and flawless execution, including logistics, security, and hospitality arrangements. It would require building specialised infrastructure and the entire expenditure would need to be met by the port itself through advertisements and sponsorships. It would involve huge marketing and promotion efforts in the midst of a looming global financial crisis, not to speak of considerable risks. But then the entire port team was full of enthusiasm, and we understood that without taking risks, nothing could ever be achieved!

Cochin Port's hosting of the prestigious Volvo Ocean Race in December 2008 was met with great excitement and anticipation.

And when the event did unfold, it turned out to be an unforgettable experience that left a lasting impression on the recent history of Cochin Port. The selection of the picturesque port city and the state of Kerala as the venue for this sporting extravaganza provided a momentous opportunity for Cochin Port and Kerala to showcase as a leading international tourism destination while also demonstrating the country's capabilities on a global platform.

The race teams spend close to 40 weeks living and working on board a 72-foot carbon fibre vessel, one of the most advanced boats on the planet, designed to withstand the harshest weather conditions, including thunderstorms, icebergs, and 40-foot waves. These boats are seen as a marvel of engineering, with the ability to endure winds of up to 60 miles per hour and cyclones as well as the treacherous waters of the Southern Ocean spanning nearly 8,000 nautical miles around Antarctica. The teams are required to be self-sufficient, carrying all their supplies, including food, water, and spare parts, for the entire duration of the race.

Interestingly, the boats are required to sail by relying solely on wind power and human effort to propel themselves through the seas. Although the boats are equipped with engines, the Volvo Ocean Race rules do not allow the use of engines during the race, except for life-threatening emergency situations. To ensure that the rules are followed, each boat is equipped with a satellite tracking system that monitors its position, speed, and direction. The race officials use this system to keep track of the boats and make sure they are following the prescribed race course. The boats are inspected before and during the race by a team of race officials who check for any unauthorised modifications or equipment that could be used to power the boat, such as hidden engines or fuel tanks. Moreover, the race has a protest system in place that allows competitors to raise concerns if they suspect another team of breaking the rules. If a boat is found to have used its engine during the race, it could be penalised or even disqualified from the entire race.

Clinching the Deal

Consenting to host the event and to bid for it was a tricky decision. Before formally pitching for it, the port teams held several rounds of internal discussions, involving an informal feasibility study, listing out the pros and cons to assess the risks and benefits of hosting such an event. There was a general consensus that the benefits would outweigh the risks and challenges. The event could not only enhance the reputation and profile of the port but would also bring significant economic and tourism benefits to the region.

During the series of discussions with the Volvo Ocean Race CEO and his team, we conveyed our "in principle" intent to host the stopover, but there were several uncertainties, and therefore, we were unable to confirm our participation immediately. First, we would require the permission of the Government of India to host the event, and second, we would need to bring in the Kerala government and the state's Tourism Department on board as a partner. The Volvo Ocean Race team's offer was that the occasion would attract several thousands of foreign tourists to the city apart from hordes of domestic tourists. There were possibilities of getting some advertising revenues. It was easy to recognise the value that the event could bring and we were ready to grasp the chance and go ahead.

Then came the catch. The hosting port would be required to pay five million euros for what the organisers said was the entry fee. The port, in turn, would be able to raise revenues through sponsorship rights, they claimed. For a cash-strapped port like ours, there was no question of making any payment to secure a sporting event and I told the negotiators in no uncertain terms that we were not interested in "buying" the stopover rights. During the interactions, it was clear to us that the organisers of the Volvo Ocean Race were keen to have an Indian stopover if they were to choose the route under discussion. Coming from Cape Town and on the way to Singapore, Cochin would be the nearest and the most ideal port in India where the boats could be anchored without having to take a long detour. I could sense that with some hard bargaining, we could clinch the stopover without having to pay the entry fee. Finally, after extensive evaluations by the race officials and many rounds of negotiations that went on for a few months, Cochin was chosen for the India stopover of the Volvo Ocean Race for the first time. As a special gesture, the port would be exempted from paying the hosting fee.

Signing the Agreement

Before approaching the Government of India for permission, it was important to bring the Kerala government on board. The dynamic and energetic Tourism Secretary of Kerala, V. Venu, instantly recognised the huge tourism potential of the event and, after due consultations with his superiors assured all support and partnership with the port. With the Kerala government on board, obtaining the green signal from the Shipping Ministry would be the next crucial step. But the Ministries of Home Affairs and External Affairs too had to agree. Shipping Secretary A.K. Mahapatra's positive approach and helpful nature had endeared all the officers in the port sector and he promised to process our request quickly. However, in spite of his best efforts to persuade the relevant ministries, there were inordinate bureaucratic delays, bringing uncertainty to the entire project.

At a certain point, obtaining the Central government's permission before the scheduled signing of the agreement between Cochin Port, the Kerala Tourism Department, and the Volvo Ocean Race looked doubtful. We were under pressure from the race organisers to finalise the deal quickly, but were unable to sign the agreement without the formal permission from the Central government. Faced with the unpredictability and delays, I requested Venu that the Tourism Department should execute the agreement with Volvo Ocean Race. Following this, Venu made all arrangements to execute a revised bipartite agreement and the stage was set for the signing ceremony. Fortunately, Shipping Secretary A.K. Mahapatra's persistent efforts in overcoming bureaucratic obstacles finally did bear fruit, and the government of India's authorisation reached us just hours before the signing ceremony. Happily, we were able to rework and sign the three-party agreement, and the Cochin stopover of the Volvo Ocean Race was formally announced. Kerala's Minister for Home and Tourism, Kodiyeri Balakrishnan, witnessed the signing ceremony.

The 2008–09 race route was altered from previous years to include stopovers in India and China for the first time. Setting out from Alicante in Spain in October 2008, this edition of the race was to cover 39,000 nautical miles (72,000 kilometres) stopping over at Cape Town (South Africa), Cochin, Singapore, Qingdao (China), Rio de Janeiro (Brazil), Boston (the US), Galway (Ireland), Gothenburg and Stockholm (both in Sweden), before finally winding up at St Petersburg (Russia). The choice of Cochin Port was seen as a major recognition of our importance on the world stage and our strategic location.

After the agreement was signed, the port was required to create the offshore and onshore infrastructure, including berthing facilities as well as a "race village" to accommodate the visiting teams and their entourages. The "race village" would include temporary residential facilities for the teams, a full boat shop, and repair facilities with professional sailmakers to provide equal shore support to all the teams. Besides these, there had to be an area for cultural shows, exhibitions, and markets or malls for shopping. The cultural and exhibition areas of the race village would be open to the general public, including foreign tourists. The participating teams would include national teams from Russia and Spain, along with teams sponsored by multinational corporate houses like Ericsson (Sweden) and Puma (Germany).

Racing Towards the Ocean Race

The Boat Train Pier (BTP) was deemed the perfect location for the race boats to be received and docked. However, to complicate matters, a major construction project was already underway to widen and lengthen the existing BTP berth by reconstructing the

North Coal Berth, but according to the existing plans, the work would take another year to complete and would not be ready before the race events began. At the same time, a widened and lengthened BTP would be long enough to receive the arriving teams and accommodate the surge of crowds that were expected. Further, the adjacent area was considered ideal for construction of the "race village" as well as erecting facilities for cultural programmes and exhibition stalls.

Chief Engineer J. Karthikeyan, Executive Engineer A.G. Sathyan and their team took on this task head on and began working towards expediting and completing the project well ahead of the event. Over the next seven months, they worked tirelessly alongside the contractors—day and night—taking every possible measure to ensure timely completion without compromising on safety or quality standards. However, meeting the deadline seemed daunting. Despite the formidable circumstances, the team displayed admirable commitment to set up the infrastructure, which got completed just a few days before the event. With meticulous planning and execution, they ultimately managed to achieve the target, overcoming the umpteen obstacles along the way. Their determination and hard work were truly inspiring.

Although Cochin Port had anticipated significant amounts of sponsorship and advertisement revenues, challenges began to pile up. The feared global financial crisis was already upon the entire business world and we were not able to raise as many sponsorships and advertising funds as anticipated. Business houses were apprehensive and reluctant to invest in advertising. This proved to be a huge dampener. However, we were fortunate enough to secure a small number of sponsorships, just enough to carry us through. Even the large business houses that had initially pledged support eventually backed out.

Meanwhile, with financial support from the Union Ministry of Tourism, the port launched an extensive beautification campaign. This effort focused on upgrading roads, public infrastructure, and tourism-friendly accommodations that would serve as the "race village" headquarters and control centre. Adjacent roads were redeveloped with pedestrian walkways and other tourism amenities. The enhanced infrastructure proved essential for hosting various race-related facilities. Cochin Port ultimately established a stunning "race village", fully equipped with standard amenities for boat maintenance, team accommodations, exhibition areas, media centres, communication hubs, control rooms, and other critical support systems. Simultaneously, an impressive floating berth was erected adjacent to the BTP to accommodate all participating competition boats.

Security

For a mega international sporting event of the magnitude of the Volvo Ocean Race, painstaking security planning was crucial. Cochin Port had drawn up a comprehensive security strategy for the Ocean Race, in close collaboration with the Central Industrial Security Force (CISF) unit and the Cochin City Police. Police Commissioner Manoj Abraham and CISF Senior Commandant D. Shyamala carefully coordinated security preparations, with the city police responsible for general area security and the CISF overseeing protected port zones and the "race village".

Less than a week before the boats were due to arrive at Cochin, the city of Mumbai came under a devastating terror attack that claimed the lives of more than 140 people, sending shockwaves across the world. Even as the attack was being played out on television screens throughout the world, I was receiving anxious phone calls from the Volvo Ocean Race organisers at London, questioning if it would be safe for the race to come to India. I provided the callers with firm assurances that Cochin was a secure city, and that we had implemented a robust security plan for the 15-day event. Moreover, since Cochin was more than 600 nautical miles away from Mumbai, it was unlikely to be affected by the attack, which was being effectively tackled by the Mumbai police and other Central security and armed forces. Despite our confidence in the security plan, we did not want to leave anything to chance. I reached out to Police Commissioner Manoj Abraham once again and conveyed the concerns of the race organisers. He confidently reassured me of the city's robust and comprehensive security arrangements. CISF Senior Commandant D. Shyamala and Deputy Commandant V.G. Markam rechecked the entire security plan, reinforcing vulnerable areas and briefing all personnel. In the run-up to the event and throughout the 15-day race, these officers remained actively focused, patrolling the port and waterfront, ensuring that security stayed dependable and was safeguarding the event successfully.

The Festivities

The India stopover of the Volvo Ocean Race in 2008 was transformed into a vibrant extravaganza, leaving unforgettable memories with both the participants and the local community. Each participating boat's arrival was a highly anticipated event, and a festive atmosphere enveloped the surroundings. The port welcomed a diverse crowd, including local residents, sailing enthusiasts, domestic and international tourists, all eager to greet the boats and their crews. As each competing vessel sailed into the harbour, it was met with fervent cheers and applause from ecstatic onlookers. Each leg of the Volvo Ocean Race had a winner. For the leg from Cape Town to Kochi, Team Ericsson emerged victorious. Many people had closely followed the race and were thrilled to see the boats up close and meet the courageous crews. The presence of international sports media further heightened the excitement, delivering real-time updates and race details to global audiences, raising interest and enthusiasm.

The stopovers are designed to offer an opportunity for the competing crews to rest and prepare for the next leg of the race. The 15-day-long stopover of the Volvo Ocean Race created a joyful ambience, with the "race village" registering an impressive footfall of nearly one lakh visitors every day. The entire Willingdon Island was transformed into a carnival-like celebration, drawing in people from all parts of Cochin, the state of Kerala, different regions of India, and from various countries around the world, providing an opportunity for people to witness the cultural events and celebrate the spirit of sailing and adventure. The race village showcased unforgettable cultural events, featuring performances by some of the most renowned artists in music, dance, and traditional Indian art forms, such as Kathakali and other classical and folk dances. The performances showcased the rich cultural heritage of India and left a lasting impression on the visitors, especially the international audience. The careful planning and coordination of the cultural events presented by so many celebrated artistes in the country was another area where the Cochin Port officers displayed their organisational skills.

However, the true heart of the celebration lay in the interactions between the daring sailors and the local community. The "race village" served as a mingling spot where visitors could engage with the crew members, and listen to stories of their remarkable journeys. They could also gain insights into the incredible determination required to circumnavigate the globe. Schoolchildren, in particular, were enraptured by these seafaring adventurers, their faces lighting up with elation as they explored the race village, interacted with the crews, and learned about navigation and ocean conservation. The India stopover of the Volvo Ocean Race in 2008 was not just about sailing; it was a celebration of human achievement, cultural diversity, and the enduring spirit of adventure. It fostered a sense of community and pride in partaking in such a prestigious event. The festivities showcased the port's potential as a vibrant maritime centre, inspiring future generations to embrace the thrill of the open sea.

Finally, after 15 days of festivities, the Volvo Ocean Race left Cochin for the next stopover destination of Singapore on 18 December 2008. Cochin Port choreographed a grand and memorable send-off for the race participants. Union Minister of Tourism Ambika Soni, Kerala Home and Tourism Minister Kodiyeri Balakrishnan, Leader of Opposition Oommen Chandy, Kerala's Sports Minister M. Vijaya Kumar, and several other dignitaries, senior political leaders, local citizens and government officials were present.

The preparation for the Volvo Ocean Race had showcased an outstanding demonstration of teamwork by the entire port's staff, leading to its remarkable success. Secretary Cyril George had remained in charge of the overall arrangements, assisted by Public Relations Officer Jijo Thomas. The entire infrastructure requirements were built by the Civil Engineering Department led by Chief Engineer J. Karthikeyan and the Marine Department led by Deputy Conservator Captain Paul N. Joseph and Harbour Master Captain Joseph J. Alapatt. Financial Advisor K.G. Nath and his deputies, B. Bhagyanath and K. Poothapandi, controlled the finances, diligently accounting for all sponsorship revenues and expenditure. Joint director Unnikrishnan Nair, assisted by Jijo Thomas, spearheaded a dynamic communication campaign that effectively broadcast the event's message both statewide and nationally. It was truly heartening to witness every department, officer, and worker of the port come together as one cohesive team in preparing for the event. The occasion garnered enthusiastic support from all trade unions of the port, with several officers and staff members expressing a strong sense of pride and motivation in being a part of this dedicated team.

An Ode to the Port Workers

While the contributions of various teams from the port, government, and sectoral partners in successfully hosting the Volvo Ocean Race have been rightly applauded, it is equally important to acknowledge the quiet dedication of the humble port workers. Amidst the excitement and attention surrounding the event, they continued to perform their routine duties with diligence, ensuring that the port's daily operations remained uninterrupted and fully functional.

The anonymous port worker is the unseen force behind the smooth operation of the port. Day and night, the port workers handle a wide range of demanding tasks with dedication and precision. They load and unload cargo, operate complex machinery, manage tugboats to help anchor colossal ships, man the mooring boats, and operate dredgers to keep channels navigable. In the vessel traffic control room, they monitor and guide ship movements in the seas as well as inside port waters, working closely with port pilots to manoeuvre giant vessels through navigation channels. Their efforts form the backbone of the entire port ecosystem, so that the port operates like a well-oiled machine. Their roles are diverse and physically demanding, involving a range of skills and responsibilities that are crucial to the maritime and logistics operations in the port. Maintaining the civil, electrical, mechanical, and marine facilities of the port and making these services available on a round-the-clock basis involves the dedication of hundreds of officers and staff who work tirelessly 24/7.

The day-to-day duties of port workers often involve intense physical labour. Dock labour, for example, involves the primary responsibility for loading and unloading cargo from ships to the shore and from the shore to ships. This involves operating heavy, sophisticated machinery and mammoth cranes to move containers and bulk cargo items onto and off vessels for hours together. These workers have to be adept at handling these machines safely and efficiently, often in small spaces and under tight deadlines. For shipping and cargo operations, time is money and every task has to be accomplished safely, efficiently, and within schedules, where every second counts.

Marine operations are always accident-prone. Highly skilled pilots navigate ships through the port's channels while tugboat operators assist with docking and undocking, and mooring crews secure ships at the docks. These roles require precise coordination and a deep understanding of maritime procedures to prevent accidents and ensure safety. Environmental conservation is another critical role in the daily port operations. Workers monitor and manage pollution levels, implement anti-oil spill measures, and oversee the treatment and disposal of ballast water discharged by ships. These activities are vital for maintaining the ecological health of the surrounding marine areas. Environmental preservation, safety, security, and emergency preparedness are non-negotiable—requiring fierce concentration and precision.

In addition to the physical labour, there are highly technical and specialised roles within the port. For instance, container handling requires precision in operating gantry cranes to lift containers from vessels and place them onto transport vehicles or into designated spots in the storage yard. Workers must manage the weight and balance of containers to prevent accidents while maintaining efficiency in handling them. The transportation and stacking of containers within the yard follow strict guidelines to optimise space and facilitate easy access for future moves, requiring careful coordination and attention to detail. Throughout the day, accurate tracking and documentation are maintained to update the terminal's inventory system as containers are moved, ensuring all paperwork complies with shipping regulations. Continuous attention to safety is paramount; workers adhere to safety guidelines, use personal protective equipment, and participate in regular safety drills.

Port workers perform their duties under tough and hazardous conditions, braving adverse weather, extended hours, and the inherent dangers associated with operating heavy machinery and large vessels. In the midst of these challenges, they are dedicated to their roles, fully aware that their work enables the continuous movement of operations. Though rarely acknowledged, they are the true unsung heroes who keep the port running smoothly every day.

7

LOOKING AHEAD

The Port and the Possibilities

I look back on our five years and four months of teamwork in Cochin with a deep sense of satisfaction, knowing that the time was spent meaningfully. Throughout this period, the port's team focused on three key priorities. The first was to set our own house in order—streamlining systems and processes, rooting out harmful and toxic practices, eliminating illegal extortions, improving labour booking systems, and successfully implementing comprehensive labour reforms.

The second major initiative was the implementation of an enterprise-wide SAP-based ERP system. This was no small feat, as the implementation was driven by our own in-house officers and staff, with support and guidance from the system integrator, Tata Consultancy Services (TCS). The ERP system has since replaced legacy manual operational and administrative systems—a first in India's port sector and a rare success for a large government organisation in a highly unionised setting. The entire Cochin Port team worked passionately to make this transformation possible.

The third focus was on the implementation of a slew of large infrastructure projects. From their conceptual stages, the Cochin Port team, together with our partner organisations, worked jointly and diligently through every phase to complete and commission these projects—including the Vallarpadam ICTT and its highway and rail connectivity links, and the deepening of navigation channels. Earlier, the BPCL Kochi Refinery's Single Point Mooring (SPM) system, along with its associated onshore facilities at Cochin Port, was commissioned in December 2007. This strategic infrastructure allowed the refinery to receive crude oil through Very Large Crude Carriers (VLCCs), boosting operational efficiency and reducing freight costs. While construction of the LNG port terminal and regasification plant was completed in 2012, it was officially commissioned in 2013.

These new infrastructure additions have significantly strengthened the cargo-handling capacity, streamlined processes, and enhanced data integration, making Cochin Port more efficient and competitive. Overall, these advancements have positioned the organisation on a path towards sustained growth and profitability.

While the transition to ERP-driven operations was smooth, and our staff adapted well to new workflows, the increased automation resulted in a reduction of some manual jobs while simultaneously creating new opportunities in other areas. Technology and automation are fundamental realities of today's world, and their influence is only expected to grow in the future. While tools like ERP systems and automation are essential for driving efficiency and competitiveness in large organisations, they also present the challenge of job displacement, which must be proactively addressed by creating new employment opportunities. The true success of these large infrastructure projects will be achieved when they stimulate growth in secondary and downstream industries such as logistics, warehousing, manufacturing, and processing, which can generate new avenues for employment in the port's hinterland and beyond.

A Future Vision for Cochin Port's Diversification

Cochin Port has reached a stage where it would benefit from diversifying its operations beyond traditional bulk and break-bulk cargo-based port activities. Diversification will help build resilience and foster growth beyond customary shipping and cargo operations, creating stable, alternative revenue streams. The availability of surplus land on Willingdon Island offers a prime opportunity to expand into new ventures. Thinking outside the box is essential to maximise the port's asset utilisation by leveraging the surplus land and infrastructure for future innovation. Diversification can potentially attract international partnerships and investments while also future-proofing the port against technological disruptions. The port's vision for this diversification should focus on utilising its strengths to drive employment-generation, long-term economic growth, competitiveness, and environmental sustainability.

Four key areas suggested for diversification are: (1) Free Trade Warehousing (FTW) (2) Cruise and leisure tourism with home-porting facilities (3) Bunkering (including LNG bunkering), and (4) Maritime research and academic collaboration. Of course, there could be many more avenues.

Free Trade Warehousing

Free Trade Warehousing Zones (FTWZs) and Multi-Modal Logistics Parks, which offer plug-and-play facilities for export-import (EXIM) cargo consolidation, present many opportunities for Cochin Port. Kerala's consumer-centric economy, along with its growing capability in producing high-quality consumer goods and agricultural products, can be effectively leveraged to create a global export hub, serving markets across the world. In addition to facilitating value-added activities such as processing, repackaging, labelling, quality inspection, and light assembly, these zones enhance supply chain efficiency and global trade competitiveness. Successful FTWs, like Jebel Ali, have transformed themselves into thriving business zones of global trade, generating thousands of employment opportunities.

Cochin Port, with its long-established cargo-handling expertise and a modern container terminal under its jurisdiction, is well-positioned for the development of additional FTWZs. While the DP

World-IGTPL may develop their FTWZ, the port authority should also consider developing its own, as the surplus land available on Willingdon Island provides a strategic opportunity. This would potentially attract global manufacturing and distribution companies, and boost employment. It has the potential to create a streamlined, efficient trade ecosystem, enabling businesses to operate cost-effectively and expand their reach in global markets. Furthermore, ancillary industries supporting warehousing and logistics would thrive, creating a ripple effect of economic benefits across the region.

Cruise Tourism and Home-Porting

Cochin Port has emerged as a premier cruise destination, hosting the highest number of cruise ships among Indian ports. Its strategic strength lies in its proximity to iconic tourist spots, such as Fort Kochi, Trichur, Munnar, Thekkady, Kumarakom, and the backwaters of Alappuzha, offering visitors a rich blend of nature, history, wildlife, cuisine, and culture. To truly optimise its potential, Cochin Port must invest in developing a world-class cruise shipping ecosystem that caters to both domestic and international markets.

Currently, Cochin's cruise business mainly involves hosting international visiting cruise ships. While this provides a strong foundation, the next step is to attract home-porting[1] facilities for cruise shipping companies, allowing ships to start and terminate their journeys at Cochin. This shift would improve passenger engagement, encourage longer stays, and significantly boost the local economy. Such a step would help meet the growing domestic demand for cruise tourism. Coastal cruise circuits, offering

1. Home-porting is the practice of designating a particular port as the starting and ending point of a cruise itinerary. Passengers typically board and disembark at this port, which becomes the vessel's operational base for a season or a series of voyages. Home-ports play a crucial role as key hubs for provisioning, crew changes, bunkering, maintenance, and generate significant local economic benefits through tourism, hospitality, and port services.

cruise services from Cochin to other Indian destinations like Lakshadweep, the Andamans, Chennai, Goa, and Mumbai as well as neighbouring countries like Sri Lanka, Maldives, and Mauritius, present a lucrative business for new entrepreneurs.

Home-porting will require the establishment of modern cruise terminals equipped with world-class facilities that provide seamless experiences for passengers. Expanding the port's capacity to accommodate larger and more frequent cruise traffic is a must. Establishing such infrastructure should precede the demand curve, as the presence of modern facilities is likely to attract business opportunities, rather than waiting for assured growth and returns to justify the investment. Current plans to improve connectivity through seaplane tourism could further complement cruise operations, linking Kerala's various tourist destinations.

Policy reforms are critical to realising this vision. However, successive government policies have often been inconsistent, thereby stalling progress on initiatives like seaplane tourism. Both state and Central governments need to work together to liberalise regulations, provide incentives, and ensure a stable investment climate for private players. Cochin Port should also actively engage with global cruise liners and tourism operators to position itself as a competitive and sustainable home-porting destination while also integrating Kerala's eco-tourism and wellness tourism sectors to offer rich travel experiences.

Bunkering Potential at Cochin Port

Maritime bunkering is the process of refuelling of ships with fuels such as marine diesel, heavy fuel oil, and LNG. In addition to fuel, ships also procure essential supplies like fresh water, food, lubricants, and spare parts through a service known as ship chandelling. Bunkering can take place either in-port or at sea via bunker barges, which help reduce port delays, optimise voyage time, and ensure continuous operations for cargo ships, tankers, and naval vessels.

Cochin Port is a major energy hub in the region, handling a wide range of products such as crude, multiple petroleum products, and LNG. Its strategic location along major international shipping routes provides an excellent advantage, allowing vessels to procure bunkers en route. This eliminates the need for ships to carry heavy bunker loads during long voyages, allowing for better capacity utilisation and increased cargo loads. By expanding its bunkering infrastructure, Cochin Port can capitalise on its location to become a preferred refuelling destination for vessels operating in the region. With its proximity and partnerships with the BPCL Kochi Refinery and the Cochin LNG Terminal, Cochin Port is well-situated for the sourcing, storage, and delivery of bunkers. Economically, a bunkering terminal could generate substantial revenue streams for Cochin Port, attracting increased vessel traffic and stimulating auxiliary enterprises such as fuel storage, blending, and distribution.

In addition, LNG bunkering offers a transformative opportunity for Cochin Port to align with global maritime emission standards while meeting the rising demand for environmentally sustainable fuels. As the shipping industry increasingly transitions to low-sulphur and cleaner fuels to comply with international regulations, Cochin Port has the potential to establish itself as a leader in green bunkering.

On its part, the Government of India must take proactive steps to reduce taxes on marine bunkering fuels as a strategic move to improve the country's competitiveness in the global maritime bunkering market. High bunker prices in India, driven largely by high taxes, discourage international vessels from refuelling at Indian ports. Instead, they opt for more cost-effective alternatives in neighbouring Middle Eastern and Asian countries. This results in a significant loss of opportunities and revenue for Indian ports, undermining their ability to compete.

A competitive pricing strategy could be a win-win, making Indian ports more attractive to international shipping companies. While reducing taxes may initially result in a lower tax collection per unit of fuel, the increased volume of transactions could compensate for this shortfall, if not exceed it. The decision should carefully balance economic benefits with the fiscal implications for state and Central revenues. This approach would likely lead to increased vessel traffic, higher fuel sales, and ancillary benefits such as larger revenue from port charges, pilotage, and other port-related services. Together with bunkering, ships procure other necessities like food, drinking water and other consumables, which could have a ripple effect by stimulating local economies and generating employment.

The proposal to establish a bunkering terminal at Cochin has been in the pipeline for a long time but has yet to come to fruition. For Cochin to succeed in the bunkering business, it is essential to not only offer competitive fuel pricing but also streamline procedures and eliminate regulatory complexities that currently impede efficient bunker operations.

Maritime Research and Academic Collaboration

Cochin Port is uniquely positioned to establish a world-class centre of excellence in advanced technical and policy research in partnership with leading academic and scientific institutions. Such a centre should integrate its resources with institutions such as Indian Maritime University (IMU), the Cochin Shipyard, the Indian Navy, and the Coast Guard, IIM-Kozhikode, the Indian Space Research Organisation (ISRO), Cochin University of Science and Technology (CUSAT), and IIT Madras. The centre would specialise in cutting-edge research and innovative solutions in areas such as port engineering, dredging and sediment management, maritime navigation, green shipping, fisheries, energy security, container logistics, shipbuilding technologies as well as policy formulation, striving to keep India in the forefront of global maritime science and technological advancements. The idea is to create a pipeline of skilled professionals, ready to meet the industry's evolving requirements.

Opportunities are also available at the foundational and undergraduate levels, provided by the IMU. India is one of the leading suppliers of seafarers to the global merchant fleet, with over 250,000 Indian seafarers making up 9.35 per cent of the world's seafaring workforce. High-quality maritime education is crucial for maintaining competitiveness in the global shipping industry, ensuring that Indian officers and ratings are well-trained, adaptable, and capable of meeting the evolving demands of the industry, especially with the increasing automation and technological advancements in shipping. Maritime education programmes offered by institutions like the IMU and various private maritime academies equip cadets and officers with the necessary skills and qualifications to work on international vessels.

The Cochin Port campus of the IMU, which has been operational since 2009, requires expansion and further support from the authorities. Investing in maritime education will not only enhance the employability of Indian seafarers on a global scale but also contribute to the growth of India's shipping industry. Expanding opportunities in merchant shipping are especially important, given the significant remittances earned by Indian seafarers.

Beyond the existing institutions that offer training programmes in seafaring, the proposal here is to establish a global centre of maritime excellence. The focus should be on advanced studies and research in key areas such as environmental sustainability, cutting-edge science, technology, law and policy research.

Willingdon Island is Turning 100

Cochin's iconic Willingdon Island, the man-made port island created in the 1920s using dredged soil, will soon complete 100 years of its existence. Even as we prepare to commemorate and celebrate this historic milestone, there is a legitimate apprehension that this once magnificent island has faded from its splendour and glory and now stands as a mere shadow of its former self. In its prime, Willingdon Island was a thriving hub of trade and commerce. It once had a bustling workforce and housed hundreds of ancillary businesses and several hotels. It served as a vital transportation centre, accommodating both the Cochin airport and the Cochin Harbour Railway terminus, contributing significantly to the growth and development of the city and the region as a whole. However, with the development of modern port infrastructure in Vallarpadam and Puthuvypeen, alongside the relocation of major port activities, Willingdon Island has been experiencing a significant decline in activity and commerce.

Over the past decade, Cochin Port's cargo throughput has tripled, yet its cargo profile today consists of crude oil, petroleum products, LNG, and containers. As global trade increasingly shifts towards containerisation, the bulk-handling of cargo and the number of cargo ships calling at the port have declined. With the relocation of the modern terminal infrastructure to Vallarpadam and Puthuvypeen Islands, situated on the north of the navigation channels, attention and activity have naturally shifted away from Willingdon Island. The introduction of the e-port ERP system, along with consequent digitisation and automation, has further reduced the need for port's administrative and operational manpower. As a result, businesses that once had offices in the island have shifted elsewhere, and families no longer live there, leaving behind a sense of desolation.

Willingdon Island today yearns for rejuvenation. It is important to reclaim its fading glory and breathe new life into this strategically located and beautiful island, which holds immense commercial and tourism potential. The substantial land spaces, which have now been freed up, offer big opportunities for tourism, commercial development, free trade, and warehousing zones. To fully unlock Willingdon Island's potential, the Shipping Ministry must reassess the overly stringent land policies that have hindered the port's efforts to optimise the island's land use. A bold, forward-looking vision is essential. The Port Authority could reimagine the island as a vibrant hub for processing industries, port-related enterprises, tourism infrastructure and entertainment zones.

There are two global models that could potentially inspire and guide us while drawing up a vision for the future of this island—Dubai's Jebel Ali and Singapore's Sentosa Island. Ideally, the redevelopment vision for Willingdon Island should aim at creating a multidimensional hub, with both business and tourism elements, combining a Jebel Ali-like processing zone and a Sentosa-like tourism and entertainment destination. By leveraging its strategic location, modern port facilities, and the existing infrastructure, Willingdon Island can indeed become a thriving business zone for processing centres, logistics, manufacturing, storage, assembly, packaging, export-import trade, and services. This would attract businesses from around the world, capitalising on the island's potential for seamless domestic and international trade. An extension of the existing PBSEZ, or establishment of a new one, will make it attractive to investors.

Simultaneously, Willingdon Island's scenic beauty and waterfront location need to be redesigned for its tourism and entertainment potential. It would be crucial to develop a long-term vision for the island, involving both the Union Ministry of Tourism and Kerala's Tourism Department while also engaging the local citizenry in the conversation. Thus, one part of the island can be transformed into a vibrant public space, offering a variety of attractions for visitors to enjoy, such as recreational areas, parks, walkways, cultural centres, and food parks. Visitors can have a memorable experience with a wide range of activities, including entertainment, culture, cuisine, and shopping opportunities. Much like Singapore's Sentosa Island, Willingdon Island can become an attractive destination in itself for both international and domestic tourists as well as the local population.

Willingdon Island holds immense potential to re-emerge as a thriving hub of commerce and tourism in Cochin. Cochin Port has a unique opportunity to revitalise this historic space, restoring its commercial significance while also reimagining parts of the island as dynamic zones for tourism, leisure and cultural experiences. With thoughtful planning, the island can become a thriving destination for both the local communities and visitors.

8

REFLECTIONS FROM WILLINGDON ISLAND

The Futures of Cochin Port and its Hinterland are Intertwined

Cochin Port today stands as a testament to human enterprise, resilience, and transformation. However, its future growth remains inextricably intertwined with the broader economic development of its hinterland, Kerala. It would, therefore, be useful to reflect on some facets of the state's growth story in this final chapter. In its own modest yet impactful way, the port has shown that it is possible to resolve labour issues, improve efficiency, streamline operations, and execute large-scale infrastructure projects, when employees, political leaders, trade unions, business partners, and customers come together with a shared vision and purpose. Such success stories are likely found throughout Kerala, pointing to the potential for a wider campaign that celebrates these achievements, sheds negativity, and cultivates a positive, productive work culture.

At this juncture, both Cochin Port and Kerala share an extraordinary opportunity. In this journey, Kerala's democratic institutions and progressive social infrastructure provide an exceptional starting point. With its social achievements like total literacy, gender equality, a well-educated workforce, high life expectancy, and robust primary healthcare, the state has set benchmarks that rival some of the most developed regions of the world. These accomplishments should not only be celebrated but also leveraged as the foundation for Kerala's next great leap.

What is Holding Kerala Back?

This is a profound and existential question that has perplexed many political leaders, administrators, and development economists for years. Kerala's development path has been marked by progressive social policies, political awareness, and an emphasis on human development. Land reforms, universal education, and robust public healthcare laid the foundation for a literate, healthy, and politically conscious society. These achievements were driven by a vibrant political culture, strong civil society engagement, and active trade unionism.

However, as brought out in earlier chapters, the so-called "Kerala Model" of development carries with it certain inherent contradictions. While the state has made outstanding progress in social indicators, its economic growth has stagnated, particularly in industrialisation, infrastructure development, and employment generation. A highly educated yet underemployed workforce, combined with a complex labour environment, has posed persistent challenges. These contradictions between social progress and economic underperformance require deeper reflection and open, democratic dialogue. Against this backdrop, we must ask: What is holding Kerala back?

Some Debate Questions from Willingdon Island

As a lay observer, I would like to share a few thoughts, some of which may be seen as audacious and provocative, and may not be well-received by everyone. The intention here is not to make lofty declarations, or propose definitive solutions, but to offer points for discussion, drawn from personal observations during a particularly tumultuous period at Cochin Port. These reflections are shared with a full understanding of the complexities involved and the risks of oversimplification. The intention is to highlight issues that merit public attention and spark a constructive debate, which may further refine these ideas and their practicality.

Here, I outline a few compelling observations from Willingdon Island, which are presented as 11 sets of questions for debate, inviting participation from political leaders, policymakers, academics, industrialists, businesspersons, and citizen stakeholders. Many of these issues are, perhaps, cross-cutting, interconnected and overlapping. I am aware that there may be differing perspectives, in keeping with Kerala's democratic traditions of discourse, debate, and dissent. Addressing these challenges will involve reconciling contested perspectives and balancing competing interests such as labour rights and business imperatives. I present each of these issues from a Cochin Port perspective, with some stories or statements to illustrate the problem and pose questions for the debate. My hope is that such discussions will also create space for fresh, innovative ideas to emerge.

1. The Silent Crisis of Plastic and Solid Waste Pollution

In the quiet, early hours of the night, when most of the city sleeps and road traffic is sparse, a pick-up van slows down at a bridge over one of the waterbodies. Under the cover of darkness, some people swiftly dismount, unload several sacks filled with waste and hurl them into the backwaters below. Within moments they slip back into the van and drive away.

One of the most distressing and reprehensible experiences that I encountered in Cochin was the sight of solid waste being jettisoned into backwater bodies from bridges and roadsides. The culprits include not only hotels and abattoirs but also households. Once dusk sets in, loads of waste from vehicles are frequently thrown into the backwaters, sometimes even by people arriving in luxury vehicles. Persistent efforts to tackle this issue even on Willingdon Island and its neighbourhood yielded limited success, despite working with the Cochin corporation authorities and strategic placement of personnel by the port administration.

In fact, the menace is not limited to Cochin but is prevalent throughout Kerala, a state that claims to have educated and enlightened citizens. This indiscriminate dumping of solid and plastic waste has been contributing to the degradation of the waterbodies. Roadsides, too, are littered with lumps of waste in many parts of the state. This raises uncomfortable questions about how Kerala, as a state, society and a people, deal with and manage plastic and municipal waste.

Except for sporadic initiatives in some localities, both the government and the people of Kerala have been ignoring the problem of pollution and degradation of their environment for far too long. In no civilised country in the world, would one find such wanton degradation of waterbodies as is experienced here. The seriousness of this problem cannot be overstated. Kerala's extensive network of backwaters and rivers is not only a vital natural resource but also a major attraction for tourists. The continued pollution of these waterbodies threatens to damage the state's environment irreparably, jeopardising both its ecological balance and its tourism industry. Tourists are increasingly aware of environmental issues, and the sight of polluted rivers or lakes filled with floating waste greatly tarnishes Kerala's image as a pristine destination. Moreover, this pollution poses severe health risks to local communities, affecting the quality of water and contributing to the spread of disease.

Many people believe that it is the job of the government to keep their surroundings clean while happily continuing to litter. A cultural shift towards environmental responsibility is needed, where every citizen takes responsibility for their waste. It is also crucial to keep a vigilant eye on untreated sewage from industries and housing complexes being discharged directly into rivers or backwaters. There is an urgent need for a statewide awareness campaign in schools and communities at village and ward levels to promote responsible waste disposal habits. It is high time that schools, colleges, the media, and even the Legislative Assembly talked about this problem, which poses a serious threat to the quality of life in Kerala. It is necessary to empower citizens to report illegal dumping, supporting a community policing model to hold offenders accountable. Achieving this vision demands bold leadership and resolute community-level action, moving beyond symbolic gestures and photo opportunities. The state needs to rise to the challenge, galvanise its people, and work towards restoring its pristine environment. Everything else can wait.

Not entirely on a lighter note, I have some unsolicited advice for Kerala's highly energetic political parties and trade unions. Instead of relying solely on *satyagraha*s, why not resort to some protest *swachagraha*[1] to draw official attention while also tackling the state's littering emergency? The irrepressible urge for flash strikes could manifest as sudden eruptions of protest clean-ups in the surrounding areas. For party workers with a penchant for political violence, whenever they feel an uncontrollable urge to take the law into their own hands, they could grab a broom and do a demonstrative sweep show.

Likewise, politicians who seek votes by dividing society along religious, caste, or identity lines might rebrand their approach by calling for a complete division or separation of solid waste. As they carry vibrant banners and placards during demonstrations and rallies, why not also carry colour-coded waste containers, turning

1. Inspired by Mahatma Gandhi's concept of *satyagraha*, *swachagraha* means "the quest for cleanliness." It emphasises voluntary action to promote hygiene, sanitation, and responsible civic behaviour, encouraging individuals and communities to commit to a cleaner environment.

every rally into a message for responsible waste segregation? Now, let us begin a debate:

- Should the fight against solid waste in Kerala's public spaces, rivers, and backwaters take precedence over all other priorities?
- What innovative strategies can help decentralise and democratise waste management?
- How do we build a culture where waste management is seen as a collective civic responsibility rather than just a government function?
- What is the role of educational institutions, from primary school upwards, in inculcating environmental responsibility?

2. Stop *Nokku Kooli*

At a waterfront worksite where a harbour deck is under construction, a convoy of concrete-mixer trucks arrives in a neat procession and begin discharging concrete through the chute of their automated turbine-drum systems. Out of nowhere, a motley group of self-proclaimed union workers appears on the scene and brings all activities to a halt. They assert that the use of automated mixers is displacing the jobs of at least eight workers per truck, and if the machinery was to continue its work, the contractor would be required to compensate the workers who have "lost" their jobs, by paying the equivalent of eight workers' wages for every mixer truck employed. What follows is a tense round of fervent negotiations, with a palpable sense of unease hanging in the air. After protracted discussions, a compromise is finally struck. As against the demanded eight wages, the contractor agrees to pay an amount equivalent to the wages of two or three workers for each truck employed. With the financial dispute resolved, the concrete mixers resume their churning, some money changes hands in the name of workers' original rights and the union leaders quietly walk away.

Welcome to the land of *Nokku kooli*. The practice, of course, was not confined to Cochin Port alone. Ingenious and widespread, it has taken root throughout Kerala, where people are compelled to pay for loading, unloading, and supervision services, even if they haven't hired anyone for the job. The ideological claim behind *Nokku kooli* is that workers have an "inherent right to work" and be compensated for work, whether they actually performed it or not. And for the uninitiated, *Nokku kooli* is a generic name, with numerous species and subspecies known under different popular names, depending on the region or the context. In Cochin Port, we encountered several rampant manifestations and variations of *Nokku kooli,* each known by its own unique pet name. Chapter 2 narrates some stories of how Cochin Port confronted and decisively stopped this illegal practice.

Outside the port, the scourge continues to flourish throughout the state to this day. What is shocking is the pervasive acceptance of this illegal practice, which has been conceptualised, encouraged, or fanned by the Left parties and perpetrated in an atmosphere of political ambivalence for which every political party of Kerala should bear moral responsibility. Strong pronouncements by the Kerala High Court declaring the practice illegal have not helped. Our political parties have been reluctant and risk-averse in addressing the issue of *Nokku kooli* head-on, possibly driven by the fear of voter backlash. Apart from occasional ideological proclamations, no political leader of standing has shown the courage to confront this unlawful and regressive practice. This aversion to confront reality has stymied progress and perpetuated existing challenges, and serious labour reform still remains an elusive, unrealised vision. In the guise of protecting workers' rights to work, this practice often deteriorates into blatant harassment and even violence in some cases. Ordinary citizens and entrepreneurs usually lack the gumption to challenge this practice. And the people of Kerala have no option but to suffer in silence.

The Kerala Headload Workers Welfare Act, 1978, which aimed to safeguard marginalised headload workers, has ironically been cited as enabling *Nokku kooli*. This has led to growing calls for an amendment or re-imagination of the law to prevent its misuse. Excessive union interference, lack of transparency, and outdated practices in work allocation have been contributing to highhanded behaviour, inefficiencies, and rising employer costs. The law has been seen as excessively rigid, hindering its adaptation to the evolving industry needs.

The time has come to develop an efficient, fair labour-booking system that balances workers' welfare and business needs. Integrating modern information technology and mobile apps could be a transformative solution. A digital platform could be developed to streamline worker registration, categorise them by skills and availability, and provide transparent work allocation. A mobile app with GPS-enabled features would allow employers to book workers efficiently, while workers could accept tasks digitally, ensuring fairness.

The time has come for the government to put a decisive end to the practice of *Nokku kooli*. Strict penalties must be enforced against those who engage in it, along with robust grievance-redressal mechanisms, and the implementation of fair, standardised wages. Policymakers can leverage data from the platform to make informed decisions. The need of the hour is to decisively eliminate coercive practices and encourage a win-win environment for workers and employers.

Now, let us ask ourselves:

- Should *Nokku kooli* be abolished or should Kerala learn to live with this festering disease? How can political parties work together to tackle it while ensuring fair labour practices?
- How can trade unions be persuaded to move on from fringe activities like *Nokku kooli*, making them partners in a positive, enabling work culture? What are the possible strategies to protect the interests of workers and empower them?

- What role can citizens play in effectively combating *Nokku kooli* and supporting ethical labour practices? How can technology and mobile apps help to connect workers and employers?

3. Political Responsibility and Responsible Trade Unionism

A reputed garment-manufacturing company, once seen as a symbol of Kerala's industrial potential, reportedly faced repeated disruptions, including multiple intrusive inspections by government departments in a single month. It was also alleged that coercive tactics by trade unions pressurised the company with unreasonable demands. Frustrated by these challenges, the company decided to relocate its Rs *3,000-crore expansion project to another state, citing a more business-friendly environment. This was one of the companies whose raw materials and finished products passed through Cochin Port, giving the port a direct stake in its growth and success. The episode sparked widespread debates on balancing workers' rights with a conducive business environment to generate employment.*

The question of whether perceptions of hyperactive trade unionism and frequent strikes have stunted Kerala's economic growth has been the subject of extensive research and debate. Social scientists have studied this issue in great detail. Kerala has often been perceived, rightly or wrongly, as a state characterised by hardline trade unions and frequent industrial unrest. These perceptions, although heavily contested, have had profound consequences for the state's ability to attract investment. From my own experience at Willingdon Island, I have witnessed the disruptive impact of repeated strikes at Cochin Port, which has resulted in significant losses of productivity, migration of business to other ports in the country and outside, incalculable financial losses, and a deterioration of customer goodwill, as narrated in the previous pages.

While trade unions have historically played a vital role in protecting workers' rights, the culture of frequent strikes has often spiralled into unnecessary workplace conflicts. The compounded impact of labour disruptions over the years has led to Kerala's persisting reputation as an industry-unfriendly state. Despite successive governments implementing many progressive policies to attract investment and improve labour rights, the negative perception persists.

Kerala has missed many opportunities due to such longstanding negative perceptions of its labour and industrial climate. The fact remains that numerous industries, both public and private, have either shut down or fallen into severe distress, partly due to militant trade unionism and partly due to multiple other factors. Unfortunately, labour militancy has often been singled out and blamed as the primary cause in most of these cases, severely tarnishing the state's reputation.

Some of these negative perceptions may well be unjustified or even unfair. But how do you tackle them? That is where some collective reflection is required. Unfortunately, outright denial is the prevailing flavour. Honest introspection and open discussions on these issues remain politically charged and fiercely resisted. There remains a persistent reluctance among political parties and leaders to confront some of the harsh realities concerning the labour situation.

Labour unrest is not unique to Kerala. Many regions in India and abroad have successfully addressed these problems by adopting innovative models that promote labour engagement and industrial harmony. Kerala must draw inspiration from such examples to overcome these historical challenges. Fortunately, there are encouraging signs. Recent reports indicate a steady improvement, with fewer disruptions and a noticeable decline in the number of lost workdays. However, the problem is far from over, with sporadic disturbances continuing to haunt different parts of the state. The financial and opportunity costs of such disruptions continue to remain substantial.

A collective sense of political responsibility and proactive consensus among all political parties are essential to dispel the negative perceptions that have impeded Kerala's industrial progress. Trade unions, in turn, must choose responsible unionism, limiting strikes to last-resort situations. They should educate members about the sapping economic effects of unjustified strikes and encourage constructive alternatives like mediation and arbitration. Unions must also confront and end harmful practices like flash strikes, which tarnish their credibility, disrupt economic growth, and hamper investment.

Kerala's path forward lies in shedding the negative image that has held it back for far too long. The state's political leadership and trade unions must acknowledge the reality of such perceptions rather than live in denial. The time has come to move beyond the archaic doctrines of perpetual conflict between capital and labour. Should we allow the 19th-century slogans to dictate the realities of a 21st-century labour landscape? Kerala's political and trade union leaders, the governments in power, civil servants as well as the civil society as a whole must do everything possible to take a unified stance in addressing negative perceptions through bold and innovative reforms.

True justice for workers will come when the protagonists of workers' rights are able to secure sufficient opportunities for the working population to find employment. Is it realistic to expect political parties in Kerala to hold their leaders and workers accountable for promoting labour peace and ensuring that they actively work towards resolving conflicts? In an atmosphere of political one-upmanship, this may sound idealistic or utopian, but many societies have demonstrated that such an approach is possible.

At the same time, without honest and decisive action, Kerala risks undermining its social achievements and losing its competitive edge. Political parties must demonstrate the courage and foresight to work together towards this common goal. Kerala stands at a critical juncture, where the potential for progress is immense. To tackle these challenges effectively, Kerala must initiate a statewide, inclusive dialogue to build a consensus among political parties, trade unions, and citizens. Let us confront these issues honestly and seek out practical and workable ideas through open and constructive debates:

- Is Kerala's reputation as a "labour problem state" justified? What steps should political parties, trade unions, and civil society take to change this perception?
- Will the state's trade unions strive to reduce the indiscriminate weaponisation of strikes and unlawful labour practices?

4. Diversify or Stagnate

The remarkable success of Technopark in Thiruvananthapuram is a shining example of Kerala's immense potential in the knowledge economy. It was made possible through the visionary efforts of two successive chief ministers, and the teamwork of their ministers, dedicated civil servants, and technocrats. It is a rare success story for a state government-run initiative of its kind and scale anywhere in India. The Thiruvananthapuram Technopark project was envisioned under the leadership of Chief Minister E.K. Nayanar, who laid its foundation stone in 1990, recognising the transformative potential of the IT industry to diversify Kerala's economy. The construction and commissioning of the project were subsequently overseen and accomplished by an equally visionary chief minister, K. Karunakaran, and his team. In November 1995, Technopark was formally dedicated to the nation by Prime Minister P.V. Narasimha Rao. A major milestone in India's IT revolution, at the time of its inception, Technopark was India's largest IT park, and continues to be so. By the end of 2024, it was home to over 490 IT companies, including some of the top national and global leaders in Information Technology and IT Enabled Services (ITES). Today, it employs more than

75,000 professionals, symbolising Kerala's remarkable stride into a knowledge-driven economy.

While Kerala's entry into the IT sector marked a big step in its economic diversification, the time has now come for the state to proactively push the boundaries into cutting-edge IT research and innovation. With AI poised to drastically shrink job opportunities in the IT sector, Kerala cannot afford complacency while major disruptions loom on the horizon. To remain competitive, the state must invest in building a strong digital infrastructure, including high-speed internet connectivity, state-of-the-art research hubs, cutting-edge data centres, and uninterrupted and high-quality power supply. Equally important is the development of a long-term workforce strategy to enhance the employability of fresh graduates and foster strong industry-academia collaboration.

One major constraint to IT expansion has been the limited availability of large land parcels in major cities. However, the ongoing national highway expansion, which will significantly improve north-south connectivity, creates an opportunity for strategic planning of new IT enterprises not only in established urban centres such as Thiruvananthapuram, Kochi, Kozhikode, and Kannur but also in surrounding suburbs and adjacent districts. Such a decentralised approach can help distribute the benefits of IT growth more evenly across the state.

Kerala's limited economic diversification makes it susceptible to external shocks, creating a fragile foundation that may weaken its resilience and hinder its growth. This model will not be able to sustain the state's development aspirations unless it is supported by a broader and more resilient industrial and commercial base. Kerala needs to diversify its economy to move beyond its dependence on remittances, tourism and IT services. While these sectors have contributed significantly to the state's growth, there is a growing realisation that a resilient future cannot be built on tourism and IT alone. The state needs to expand its industrial footprint into new sectors that offer high value without compromising its delicate environment. Economic diversification is crucial not only for creating sustainable jobs and attracting investment but also for retaining Kerala's educated and skilled workforce. To achieve this, the state must draw up an ambitious, forward-looking strategy that leverages its natural advantages, such as its extensive coastline, high literacy rates, and strong social infrastructure, while remaining mindful of its environmental vulnerabilities.

Beyond IT and tourism, Kerala holds immense potential to expand into a range of new sectors that align with its long-term development goals. Emerging areas include LNG-based downstream industries, integrated logistics hubs, container freight stations and warehousing parks as well as high-value agri-tech and value-added food processing and development of the blue economy. Cochin Port is well-positioned to serve as a vital enabler in anchoring or catalysing some of these sectors. The next sections explore how these opportunities can be effectively harnessed for Kerala's inclusive and sustainable growth as well as its economic transformation.

Achieving this transformation will require attracting substantial investments and adopting a much grander vision, and a strategic shift towards politically bold policy initiatives. What is needed is a strong and clear message that Kerala is a profitable and secure destination for investment, backed by visible efforts to build a conducive and enabling environment. To break free from its economic stagnation, Kerala must engage in honest introspection to identify the reasons behind investors' general reluctance to come to the state. Ignoring this reality does not bode well for the state, so let us debate on this critical question:

- What are the opportunities and challenges for the diversification of Kerala's economy?

5. Realising the Full Potential of the Cochin LNG Terminal

A tale of two LNG terminals: One evening back in 2010, I stood atop one of the towering LNG storage tanks at the Dahej Terminal in Gujarat and marvelled at the sprawling and stunning panorama of industrial complexes that had sprung up in the region, stretching out as far as the eye could see. I was visiting Dahej on an invitation from the Petronet LNG Ltd (PLL) Managing Director P. Dasgupta, who explained that the array of downstream industries that had sprung up went beyond petrochemicals, pharmaceuticals, chemicals, and ancillary units apart from a diverse mix of manufacturing industries, taking advantage of the stable supply of cost-effective and clean energy. Bharuch had emerged as a land of opportunities, attracting a multitude of business conglomerates from across the world. Dahej had already become an industrial powerhouse, having been designated as a Petrochemicals and Petroleum Investment Region (PCPIR), with a thriving multiproduct Special Economic Zone (SEZ), which was ranked among the world's top 25 global SEZs. LNG had catalysed the region's industrial and economic growth, drawing significant global investments and had generated employment for tens of thousands of people. Within some six years of the commissioning of the Dahej LNG Terminal, the once-sleepy towns of Dahej and Bharuch region had undergone an amazing transformation. In contrast, the Cochin LNG terminal, commissioned in 2013, has been struggling, unable to replicate Dahej's success. Despite its potential to supply clean and affordable energy for industries, power generation, and city gas distribution, its utilisation remains underwhelming.

The two LNG terminals that India developed in the early part of this millennium, had begun their journeys together. The Government of India had conceptualised them together, but they had vastly different trajectories, much like the storyline of a Bollywood movie about twin brothers—one, through intelligent foresight and strategic effort, quickly rises to become a multimillionaire while the other, due to his lackadaisical approach, remains stagnant, never moving beyond where he started.

The transformative potential of LNG in shaping the industrial and economic landscape of the southern states of Kerala, Tamil Nadu, and Karnataka, is huge. Beyond providing clean energy for both MSMEs and heavy industries, LNG could have critical applications in industrial refrigeration, cold storage, and food processing, the key sectors for agriculture and fisheries. Extending pipelines to southern Kerala as well as Karnataka and Tamil Nadu could unlock significant growth through industrial applications and city gas distribution networks, potentially boosting the regional economy. However, Kerala's apparent lack of appetite for consuming LNG has been surprising. This limited industry demand raises important questions about underlying factors, such as awareness, pricing, or infrastructure gaps. An analysis and introspection into this lack of industry response are essential to identify the barriers and devise strategies to promote the wider adoption of LNG.

A commonly cited reason for the suboptimal consumption of LNG in Kerala is the challenge of laying pipelines across the state, primarily due to difficulties in land acquisition. With extensive widening of national highways underway across Kerala, integrating gas pipelines into these highway projects presents an opportunity to expand LNG's reach. The technical standards and specifications for natural gas pipelines under the Petroleum and Natural Gas Regulatory Board (PNGRB) regulations permit gas pipelines along roadsides, subject to safety standards. Compliance with international standards is required. Coordination with road authorities and obtaining necessary permissions are mandatory. This may be the right time to lay the pipelines along the NH alignments. A concerted effort on the part of the state and Central governments, the PLL, the GAIL, the NHAI, and the Cochin Port Authority to overcome challenges can unlock the Cochin LNG terminal's potential, driving industrial growth and sustainable development in Kerala and beyond.

It is to be noted that the Cochin LNG terminal, the regasification plant, and the pipelines have already invested over $1 billion in the project, and the country cannot afford to allow such a huge national asset to remain underutilised. A public debate is called for:

- Can the Cochin LNG terminal drive the industrial growth of Kerala, Tamil Nadu, and Karnataka, akin to the transformation seen in Dahej? What policy interventions from the state and Central governments are needed to unlock its full potential?
- What strategic steps should be taken to expand city gas distribution networks across Kerala and neighbouring states?
- How can the stakeholders collaborate to nudge the industrial houses and the MSME sector to maximise LNG utilisation for industrial and domestic purposes?

6. A Roadmap for Leveraging Kerala's Blue Economy

Traditionally, human activity has centred around the exploitation of land-based resources. Only in recent times has there been a growing awareness that the ocean too holds immense potential as a rich storehouse of resources. Alongside this realisation, however, comes an equally urgent awakening that our seas are under serious threat from human actions, particularly from plastic pollution and marine litter, which are degrading ocean health at an alarming rate.

The "blue economy"[2] refers to the sustainable use of ocean and coastal resources to promote economic growth, improve

2. The term "Blue Economy" was first popularised by Gunter Pauli in his 2010 book *The Blue Economy: 10 Years, 100 Innovations, 100 Million Jobs*. Pauli, a Belgian entrepreneur and sustainability advocate,

livelihoods, and protect the marine ecosystems. It emphasises the need to balance development with conservation, ensuring that activities like fishing, shipping, tourism, and other means of exploitation of marine resources are conducted without compromising the health of the oceans. As a vehicle for inclusive and sustainable development, the blue economy promotes innovation and responsible resource management, enabling coastal communities and nations to benefit from the ocean's resources while preserving it for future generations. Many countries are increasingly exploiting ocean resources by adopting blue economy principles that emphasise sustainable and inclusive development.

Norway is among the global leaders in the blue economy. With one of the world's most advanced and productive aquaculture sectors, particularly in salmon farming, Norway has turned marine resources into major export earners. The country invests heavily in marine research, innovation, and ocean monitoring. Its integrated ocean management model balances economic use with conservation, making it a benchmark in blue economy practices.

Kerala, like other coastal Indian states, holds immense potential to harness its rich marine wealth. With a 590-kilometre coastline and abundant marine biodiversity, the opportunities are vast. While certain sectors have begun tapping into this potential, there remains a compelling need for a more focused and coordinated strategy to fully realise the opportunities offered by Kerala's ocean resources while ensuring their sustainable and inclusive development.

A comprehensive strategy for the blue economy will have several elements, including (1) Sustainable fisheries and marine biodiversity conservation; (2) Coastal and blue water tourism; (3) Ports, shipping, and integrated maritime transport systems; (4) Blue

---

introduced the term to describe a model of economic development that uses locally available resources in innovative, sustainable ways—drawing inspiration from nature to create zero-waste systems. However, the term gained broader global recognition in 2012 during the Rio+20 United Nations Conference on Sustainable Development, where it was adopted.

biotechnology (5) Research, innovation, and incubation of blue economy start-ups; and (6) Strengthening coastal resilience against climate risks and environmental degradation.

Most importantly, the strategy must place the livelihoods, welfare, and inclusion of coastal communities at its core. Ensuring that economic growth is both inclusive and environmentally sustainable will be vital for the long-term success of Kerala's blue economy.

Sustainable Fishing and Aquaculture

The first and foremost pillar of the blue economy strategy will be the revitalisation of the fisheries sector. Emphasis should be placed on adopting sustainable harvesting practices through scientific stock assessments, regulated fishing zones, and strict enforcement to prevent overfishing. Investing in aquaculture, especially with native species, offers tremendous promise, thereby easing pressure on marine ecosystems. Advanced technologies, such as ISRO's remote sensing tools, can revolutionise the sector by providing real-time data on fish shoals, sea temperatures, and water quality, enabling more efficient and eco-friendly fishing. Protecting coastal livelihoods, training of fishermen as well as strengthening and modernising the state's fisheries harbours should be part of such a strategy.

Aquaculture and seaweed farming are other profitable blue economy initiatives that offer significant opportunities for sustainable development. Seaweed cultivation is climate-resilient, providing nutrient-rich food and animal feed while mitigating climate change by absorbing CO_2 and improving water quality. Integrating seaweed with mollusc and fish farming enhances productivity.

Blue Water and Coastal Tourism

Blessed with a stunning coastline and serene backwaters, Kerala has tremendous potential to move beyond conventional beach tourism.

By promoting ecotourism, yachting, scuba diving, sea kayaking, and coastal heritage cruises, the state can tap into diverse niche tourism markets. Cruise circuits connecting other Indian ports like Mumbai, Goa, and Lakshadweep, with international destinations like Colombo, Maldives, Mauritius, and Singapore can further enhance Kerala's appeal.

Reimagine the String of Kerala Ports

Apart from the major port of Cochin, Kerala has 16 non-major ports lining its coast. Some of them are non-functional at present. Reimagining this string of seaports and upgradation of their infrastructure can provide a unique opportunity to transform these underutilised assets into vibrant multimodal logistics hubs and coastal tourism gateways. Many of these ports can be upgraded in phases, with improved berths, warehousing, cold chains, and better road-rail connectivity. Integration with inland waterways and coastal shipping will further enhance freight efficiency. Passenger terminals may be needed to support cruise tourism and regional travel. Leisure cruises linking heritage ports and scenic backwaters have the potential to generate new tourism circuits. Kerala should also explore direct passenger shipping services to Gulf destinations, offering an affordable and comfortable alternative for expatriates and tourists alike.

A Blue Economy Incubation and Startup Hub

Establishing a Blue Economy Incubation and Startup Hub is an exciting opportunity that Kerala should actively pursue. Cochin Port, with its strategic location and maritime heritage, is well-positioned to anchor such an initiative in partnership with the state government. The proposal envisions a dedicated marine innovation and incubation hub that supports startups and applied research across various blue economy sectors.

These hubs would serve as collaborative zones, integrating startups, academic institutions, industry players, and R&D facilities. Common components would include structured incubation programmes, partnerships with academia and industry, and different forms of public-private funding. Key offerings such as mentorship, incubation support, and access to oceanographic data would make the hub particularly attractive to innovators and entrepreneurs. The project could adopt a PPP model, with Cochin Port providing land and infrastructure, while funding is sourced from Central and state government schemes, CSR initiatives, and private investors.

The hub can, for example, include sectors like sustainable livelihoods (fisheries, aquaculture, marine tourism), marine-based food production (including seaweed and sustainable aquaculture), climate resilience (prevention of coastal erosion, carbon sequestration through mangroves and ocean ecosystems), and innovations in marine biotechnology, oceanography, underwater robotics, and ocean data analytics. Potential startups may explore areas like seaweed processing for food and biofuels, marine weather analytics, smart aquaculture systems, eco-friendly coastal/marine tourism platforms, marine biodiversity monitoring, and ocean plastic retrieval and recycling technologies.

To ensure academic rigour and technical depth, the proposed incubation zone should partner with institutions such as Cochin University of Science and Technology (CUSAT), University of Kerala, and multiple scientific organisations under the Ministry of Science and Technology like the Indian National Centre for Ocean Information Services (INCOIS), NIO (National Institute of Oceanography), Indian Institutes of Technology and Central Marine Fisheries Research Institute (CMFRI) and other institutions of excellence.

Coastal Resilience

Coastal resilience refers to the ability of coastal communities and ecosystems to prepare for, respond to, and recover from natural hazards such as storms, coastal erosion, sea-level rise, and climate change. It involves strengthening infrastructure, protecting natural buffers like mangroves and coral reefs, and planning sustainable land use. Building coastal resilience also includes empowering local communities through education, early warning systems, and adaptive livelihood options. As climate-related risks intensify, investing in coastal resilience is crucial to safeguarding lives, livelihoods, and biodiversity. A resilient coastline ensures long-term economic stability, environmental protection, and social well-being for current and future generations.

Governance and Policy Framework

The Kerala government must craft a bold blue economy policy framework and set up a professionally managed and empowered implementing organisation. Robust governance mechanisms, community participation, and adherence to environmental safeguards should be at the foundation of all initiatives. The questions to debate are:

- Should India adopt a decentralised, state-led approach to developing its blue economy, or rely primarily on national maritime policies?
- What strategic choices must Kerala make to harness the potential of its blue economy, for the optimal exploitation of its marine resources without jeopardising its environment?

7. Shipbuilding: India's Strategic Imperative

The remarkable journey of Cochin Shipyard Limited (CSL), India's foremost shipbuilding enterprise, has been an inspiring success story. Since its inception in 1972, the CSL has steadily grown, showcasing its engineering and strategic capabilities through milestones like the construction of India's first Indigenous Aircraft Carrier, INS Vikrant. The CSL has also made its mark globally by exporting high-quality vessels to countries such as Norway, Germany, the UAE, and the USA.

Yet, shipbuilding has remained a hugely under-recognised sector in India, even as other nations are forging ahead. China, for instance, has emerged as the global leader in shipbuilding, overtaking traditional maritime powers like Greece, South Korea and Japan. China's astounding success has been the result of a coordinated strategy driven by long-term state planning, policy, and massive investments. Interestingly, China integrated its naval and civilian shipbuilding programmes under the policy of military-civil fusion (MCF), allowing shared infrastructure, and identifying shipbuilding as a core strategic sector. Simultaneously, it also developed a robust maritime ecosystem, including world-class ports, logistics networks, and training institutes while scaling up workforce capabilities to support its rapid maritime industrialisation.

In contrast, India has lagged far behind. Its share of global shipbuilding remains minimal, with domestic shipyards being fragmented, under-capitalised, and lacking access to world-class infrastructure. According to statistics available in the public domain, during the year 2024, Chinese shipbuilding industry accounted for approximately 71 per cent of global shipbuilding orders, whereas during the corresponding period, India's share in the global shipbuilding market remained between 0.06 and 1 per cent. Needless to say, there is need for a bold and forward-looking national strategy, backed by clear policy goals and financial incentives. The country should identify strategic coastal locations for the development of shipbuilding clusters with modern dry docks, facilitating their development through public-private partnerships. It is time for India to integrate shipbuilding into its larger national development strategy.

India's "Maritime India Vision 2030" aims to position the country among the top 10 shipbuilding nations by 2030, while the "Maritime Amrit Kaal Vision 2047" aims to elevate India into the top 5 shipbuilding countries. Where are we today? Interestingly, the 368th Report of the Parliamentary Committee attached to the Shipping Ministry, tabled on 8 February 2024, identifies several factors behind the stagnation of India's shipbuilding sector, including high financing costs, expensive inputs such as steel, and even "high labour costs". If India is to drastically upgrade its shipbuilding capacity and catch up with the leading shipbuilding nations, it must urgently adopt a bold and pragmatic national policy that fosters an enabling ecosystem and attracts large-scale investments. A national shipbuilding policy framework that offers fiscal incentives, regulatory clarity, infusion of modern technology and targeted investment in research and development is essential to transform shipbuilding into a powerful engine of employment and coastal economic growth.

The shipbuilding sector needs to be comprehensively designated as "infrastructure". With the global shift toward green shipbuilding, India must also invest in sustainable and futuristic shipbuilding technologies. Shipbuilding capacity is also integral to our national security, as it strengthens the country's ability to build, maintain, and deploy naval and coast guard fleets as required. It also enhances economic resilience by creating high-value jobs, adds to our export capabilities, and supports a strong maritime logistics and manufacturing ecosystem.

Kerala, with its long coastline, has the potential to become a major shipbuilding state through a decentralised strategy. The state should identify suitable locations, which can include existing ports like Beypore, Azheekal, Kollam and Vizhinjam. Some of these facilities can be anchored by Cochin Shipyard and supported by public-private partnerships. Shipbuilding, if strategically developed, has the potential to drive Kerala's industrial growth, boost export earnings, generate large-scale employment, and make a significant contribution to India's national security.

Environmental safeguards must be integral to such a strategy, with inbuilt precautions. These should include strict adherence to Coastal Regulation Zone (CRZ) norms, adoption of zero-discharge policies, and stringent environmental impact assessments (EIA). All concerns involving the treatment of effluents and solid waste should be addressed through certified green technologies and zero tolerance enforcement. Now let us debate:

- What bold policy measures should India adopt to transform its shipbuilding sector into a globally competitive industry?
- How can Kerala have a slice of India's shipbuilding ambitions by establishing a string of shipyards along its coastline?
- Will the push for large-scale shipbuilding risk long-term coastal and marine degradation? How can the shipbuilding industry be integrated with strong environmental responsibility?

8. Limited Land, Unlimited Demands

When the Cochin LNG terminal and regasification plant was under construction, the PLL requested the Port to allocate a suitable parcel of land to set up a power-generation plant that would utilise LNG as fuel and harness the cold energy unleashed during the regasification process. Although there was a 40-hectare plot of land nearby, a dispute between the Kerala government and Cochin Port about its ownership prevented its allocation for this purpose. Later, the state government decided to earmark this land for non-commercial purposes. The proposal thus, died in due course.

The cold energy released during LNG regasification has several industrial applications, including cryogenic air separation, data centre cooling, frozen food storage, and power generation. In Cochin, where seafood exports play a major role in the local economy, harnessing this cold energy for industrial refrigeration and cold storage could be a game changer. It would cut operational costs and reduce carbon emissions—paving the way for the efficient development of sustainable industrial clusters around the LNG terminal. However, the lack of suitably located land parcels in the immediate vicinity of the terminal has been a major constraint to realising this potential.

A similar challenge was faced during the development of the Vallarpadam ICTT, where there was a heavy demand for land to establish Container Freight Stations (CFS). While some CFS facilities have been developed nearby, their numbers remain inadequate, and the plots available are often too small and economically unviable. Even the two PBSEZs, established under Cochin Port, lack land areas to accommodate large-scale enterprises.

One of the commonly cited hurdles in setting up new enterprises in Kerala is the non-availability of free or surplus land. Kerala has seen several instances where industrialisation proposals were abandoned due to challenges in land acquisition and related issues. The state's narrow land area, flanked by the Western Ghats and the Arabian Sea, along with its hilly terrain and dense population, limits the availability of flat, usable land. The presence of extensive waterbodies like backwaters, river systems, and wetlands further reduce the land availability for industrial and commercial use. Moreover, Kerala's habitations are spread over sprawling areas, resulting in inefficient and suboptimal land utilisation. Much of the land is used for housing, agriculture, and infrastructure while more than 55 per cent of the state remains under forest cover or is designated as ecologically sensitive, restricting industrial use. Fragmented landownership complicates the acquisition of contiguous plots for large enterprises.

Across Kerala, several promising industrial projects and substantial investment proposals have either been abandoned or significantly downsized due to persistent challenges in acquiring suitable land. Very often, Kerala's ability to dream is constrained by the plot sizes available!

It must, however, be noted that the issue of land scarcity is not unique to Kerala. Many countries face similar constraints, but have overcome them through innovative solutions and efficient land management practices. Kerala can benefit by studying and adopting national and international good practices to address this critical challenge effectively. For example, Japan maintains approximately 70 per cent of its land area under forest cover for environmental conservation and disaster prevention. As a result, the remaining 30 per cent of the land must accommodate urban and rural development, infrastructure, agriculture, and industry. This limited availability of habitable land, combined with the high population density in urban areas, creates intense competition for space, increasing land prices and putting significant pressure on available land resources. Japan efficiently uses its limited land through vertical development and high-density housing. In fact, multistoryed residential buildings maximise the use of available space while still maintaining high-quality living conditions.

There are many Indian success stories as well. Land pooling has been effectively implemented in several places in India to facilitate urban development, infrastructure projects, and industrial expansion. One notable example is the Gujarat International Finance Tec-City (GIFT City), where farmers voluntarily contributed their land in exchange for a share of the developed land, which increased in value due to its enhanced infrastructure. Similarly, Amaravati, the capital of Andhra Pradesh, adopted land pooling on a large scale, involving over 25,000 farmers and making available more than 33,000 acres of agricultural land for urban development, with landowners receiving developed plots and other incentives.

While Kerala needs to develop its own model of land usage and urban planning to suit its unique cultural milieu, it should learn elements from these practices from within India and abroad and develop innovative strategies for village and urban planning. Land pooling can monetise land resources both in urban and rural areas, including in backward villages, as well as enhance the inhabitants' quality of life. Consolidating small, fragmented land parcels into larger, cohesive development areas through land pooling can enable efficient and organised land use. This should attract investments for infrastructure and commercial projects like IT parks, hospitals, universities as well as residential, industrial and shopping complexes, common community spaces, green areas, and cultural centres.

The land pooling concept is not new to Kerala. However, some ambitious proposals for this have not taken off, owing to local resistance. An important lesson is that these schemes should not be approached with the colonial-era land acquisition mindset. Open communication and extensive consultations with landowners is essential, with regular awareness campaigns to highlight the benefits, such as enhanced land value, modern infrastructure, and improved connectivity. Offering fair compensations, including monetary incentives or a share in the developed land, can help address financial concerns. Establishing a dedicated land pooling regulatory authority could be a way forward. It is important to address the social, economic, and procedural concerns to mitigate resistance to land pooling that is commonly encountered here.

Let me throw another idea that will likely be vehemently opposed in Kerala. Many countries like China, the Netherlands, Japan, the UAE, and Singapore have extensively created artificial islands through land reclamation, sand dredging, and infill techniques to develop military bases, airports, and civilian infrastructure. Singapore, in particular, has systematically expanded its territory, following advanced engineering to stabilise the seabed. In doing so, they carry out thorough environmental impact assessments to mitigate coastal erosion and marine biodiversity loss. Of course, reclamation activities by China have led to geopolitical tensions in contested waters.

For India too, creating precious land and artificial islands for commercial, recreational, and strategic purposes presents exciting opportunities. This would require comprehensive impact assessments and strong environmental safeguards to protect marine ecosystems and addressing concerns of coastal erosion. Today, sustainable materials and eco-friendly dredging technology are available to reduce damage. Establishing artificial reefs and mangrove buffers will help prevent erosion while strict pollution control and efficient waste management should be built into the plan for sustainability. The questions for debate are:

- Can land pooling models and vertical development address Kerala's land scarcity challenges effectively?
- What strategies can Kerala adopt to overcome resistance to

land pooling and acquisition for large-scale projects? How can affected communities be made active stakeholders and willing partners in such development initiatives?

- Is it time for India to explore the creation of precious land in selected coastal areas and artificial islands for commercial, recreational, and strategic purposes?

9. Taking Kerala's Blue Tourism to the Next Level

Queen Mary 2 is one of the world's most celebrated and among the largest of luxury cruises that call at Cochin Port regularly. Carrying nearly 3,000 passengers and about 2,000 crew members, it is a veritable floating city on a global voyage. During one of Queen Mary 2's calls to Cochin, the company had graciously invited my wife and me to join the ship's captain for dinner with a select group of passengers. It was a relaxed evening, filled with lively interactions, and I encouraged the passengers to share their impressions of Cochin.

The initial responses were overwhelmingly positive, with guests raving about the city's pristine natural beauty, delicious cuisine, and warm hospitality. However, the tone shifted when one passenger shared some critical observations, followed by a few others. The lack of cleanliness in public spaces was a recurring theme, with specific mentions of floating plastic bottles in waterbodies and garbage dumps on roadsides. One observation was about the tendency of some vendors, including taxi drivers, to jostle around tourists, offering their services and some persistent hawkers aggressively soliciting business. Others expressed their concern about the shortage of clean toilets in tourist areas. But most guests expressed their admiration for Cochin's charm and warmth, with many vowing to return for a longer visit.

As an enabler and service provider, Cochin Port has been a keen stakeholder in Kerala's tourism development. Here, I must mention that the port received the National Tourism Promotion Award in the year 2009.

Kerala's abundant natural beauty and rich cultural heritage have positioned it as one of the most sought-after, prime destinations for tourism and hospitality. However, despite the state's success in establishing a strong Kerala brand, the fundamental tourism infrastructure within the state remains largely unremarkable. Despite its rich cultural heritage and natural beauty, Kerala has struggled to position itself as a top tourist destination on the world stage due to fundamental shortcomings in maintaining a clean environment and providing adequate facilities.

Kerala tourism has achieved global recognition through the visionary and persistent efforts of its officials, elected representatives as well as some private sector players, who successfully branded it as "God's Own Country". The state's emphasis on sustainable tourism, eco-friendly initiatives, and community participation has set a benchmark for other destinations in India. However, to elevate Kerala to the level of the world's top tourist destinations, further efforts are required in delivering consistent, high-quality services, and accelerating infrastructure development.

The state requires substantial investments in an imaginative tourism infrastructure that caters to both domestic and international travellers, meeting the needs of both the affluent and middle class travellers. Employing a sufficient number of trained personnel dedicated to maintaining hygiene standards at tourist sites will ensure a pleasant experience for visitors. Kerala must develop a unified Blue Tourism strategy that integrates its coastline, backwaters, and rich marine heritage into a sustainable model. This should involve promoting environment-friendly maritime, cruise, and ecotourism; modernising infrastructure; and enhancing community-based livelihoods. The strategy must also ensure stringent environmental safeguards, in alignment with Kerala's broader Blue Economy objectives. With some bold, imaginative and determined initiatives, Kerala can raise its reputation as a top-tier domestic and global tourist destination. The questions that need to be debated are:

- What innovative approaches can Kerala adopt to balance its rich cultural and natural heritage with the demands of modern, sustainable tourism?
- How can Kerala address critical challenges like cleanliness, waste management, and tourist safety to compete with top global destinations?
- What role must local communities, local businesses, and service providers like taxi drivers and hospitality operators play in driving Kerala's tourism growth?
- What lessons can Kerala learn from other successful global tourism destinations to elevate its offerings and services?

10. The Power of Consensus

Cochin has successfully executed several major infrastructure projects, including the Cochin International Airport (CIAL), the Goshree Bridges, the Vallarpadam ICTT, the Cochin LNG terminal, and the Kochi Metro—achievements made possible by a robust political consensus. These milestones highlight how consensus and collaboration can ease land acquisition, streamline approvals, and ensure timely completion, demonstrating the power of collective political will. However, these success stories of political cooperation that helped in overcoming challenges and in transforming ambitious visions into realities have not received adequate visibility while negative perceptions about the business climate do linger.

These examples illustrate why it is important to develop and consolidate a culture of collaboration across political parties to create a stable and reasonably predictable political environment for developmental work. Unfortunately, consensus is often the exception while contestation and discord are the general rule. There are also many stories to show how a lack of political consensus effectively scuttled many ambitious development projects. It has often been observed that large, visionary projects proposed by one party are opposed tooth and nail by their political opponents, deploying spirited protests, rallies, and sometimes even physical obstruction. This shows not only a lack of constructive cooperation by the Opposition but also a lack of willingness on the part of the ruling party to consult and engage major stakeholders before declaring potentially controversial projects. Consequently, one party proposes and the other party disposes, resulting in missed opportunities for the state. There is also a broader reluctance to share credit for initiatives across party lines. The jury is still out over who should take credit for the Vizhinjam project!

Take, for example, the proposed "SilverLine" high-speed rail corridor, aiming to connect the northern and southern ends of the state, promising to reduce travel time significantly while helping to decongest the roads. Without passing value judgements about the merits and demerits of the proposal, it can be said that the manner in which this project proposal was handled by the ruling party and the Opposition reflected the fraught nature of the political discourse in the state. On the one hand, the opposition's massive protests against the project demonstrated a tendency to summarily dismiss ambitious initiatives for political gain, undermining the very idea of constructive dialogue. On the other hand, the ruling coalition's failure to build a consensus and involve all stakeholders was indicative of a lack of political foresight. Large-scale projects with the potential to reshape the state's economy require broad-based support and political consensus. Instead of presenting the SilverLine project as a shared vision for Kerala's future, it became a crass partisan show, emblematic of the state's adversarial political culture.

Debate, dissent, and persuasion are the lifeblood of a vibrant democracy. While consensus building in such an environment may be challenging, it is certainly not impossible. It requires a broader political vision and statesman-like leadership to raise the standard of discourse and include all voices. However, in an atmosphere fraught with political disagreements, a consensus would be difficult to achieve. Let us ask ourselves:

- Is it possible for Kerala to balance political differences while promoting constructive dialogue for the larger public good?
- To what extent is it possible to build a political consensus to achieve a stable and predictable policy environment, and how can Kerala ensure this consensus without compromising democratic debate and the right to dissent?

11. Rebranding Kerala and its Political Discourse

What is holding Kerala back from realising its potential? In friendly conversations, I keep asking this question to many people from different walks of life, and often get hilarious responses.

"Just watch Malayalam television; you will get the answer," said a school teacher.

Kerala's vibrant print and electronic media is largely independent though there are some 'honourable exceptions'. They project diverse viewpoints and play a vital role in holding those in power accountable. Through open dialogue, citizens challenge ideas and address societal issues. Debate, discussions, and discourse form the core of democracy. They promote public awareness, help expose corruption, inefficiency, and misuse of authority, and above all, amplify citizens' voices. They highlight social problems, prompting public scrutiny of policies and encouraging corrective action. Similarly, public protests and the expression of dissent do empower citizens to voice concerns, challenge injustices, and demand accountability. Dissent is crucial to protect minority views, and most importantly, prevent authoritarianism.

While the people of the state are often criticised for their penchant for activism and dissent, this deeply rooted culture reflects a society that refuses to remain silent in the face of injustice. Whether fighting for labour rights, environmental conservation, gender equality, or social justice, Malayalees have shown an extraordinary ability to mobilise, organise, and demand change. Their active democratic participation ensures that those in power remain responsive to public concerns.

Though debate and dissent are central to democracy, many also believe that the state suffers from an excessive addiction to daily rallies, processions, protests, demonstrations, blockades, gheraos, *hartal*s, and work stoppages that come in different names, shapes and sizes. The political discourse can, at times, border on the hilarious, or even the absurd. While some level of political sparring is inevitable in a democracy, citizens expect political dialogue to be more of a constructive exchange of ideas over real issues and long-term policy vision rather than being reduced to populist rhetoric.

Much of the activities that political parties engage in are not necessary or justifiable, wasting a lot of the people's time. While in a democracy it is crucial for political leaders to engage with the people, the current focus of parties revolves around self-promotion, hurling baseless accusations at each other, and basely criticising their opponents rather than being guided by issues of ideology, or what should be done to improve governance, or raise standard of living. Many political parties are blind to the inconvenience and disruption that their indiscriminate rallies cause to people's lives. The Kerala High Court has repeatedly asked the state government to put an end to the practice of political parties holding rallies and meetings on public roads and highways, citing the risks they pose to public safety, as well as the disruption of traffic, and the widespread inconvenience caused to commuters.

Even some ministers dedicate excessive time to political display work, leading to a misallocation of their time, attention and resources, and diverting from essential governance and developmental work. Of course, in electoral politics it is only natural that political activity aims to garner public support and sympathy. However, when winning the next election is the largest goal in life for parties, such excessive political display becomes burdensome for the common people. It would be wise for political parties addicted to "a rally a day" to rebrand and re-imagine the nature of their political engagement, spending more time on outreach and consultation programmes, understanding people's problems and articulating their developmental vision, rather than indulging in aggressive or vicious forms of hostile rhetoric.

Over the years, Kerala's political parties have developed a culture of blindly and indiscriminately opposing any proposal by their political opponents. Only very few political leaders have shown the sagacity and courage to speak objectively and independently. Kerala's politically conscious and active citizens expect an elevation in the standard of the political discourse.

It is disheartening that with a scarcity of statesman-like role models—save for a few inspiring figures—even student politics fails to reflect high standards, ideals, or vision. The country needs to transform its younger political aspirants into future statesmen, grounded in democratic and constitutional values, ethics, and the responsibilities of leadership. It is important to nurture a new generation of leaders who prefer values over immediate political gains, upholding the true spirit of statesmanship.

A transformative rebranding of Kerala is possible through a re-imagination of its political discourse in a subtle, yet impactful way. Such a transformation would indeed be a positive celebration of its democratic traditions of active political participation, spirited public debates, asking questions, demanding answers, and holding power accountable. The discourse must channel political energy into addressing people's issues, protecting constitutional rights, raising environmental awareness, combating societal ills like drug trafficking and usage, social security of the underprivileged, fostering economic growth, and shaping a sustainable future. This will involve moving beyond the rhetoric of acrimony and empty polemics, towards a culture where bold ideas meet constructive debates. Elections should be contested not based on the politics of religion, caste and one-upmanship, but on real issues like health, education, infrastructure, and human development.

It may sound ambitious to expect Kerala's political parties to unite in rebranding the state, giving up their old ways of populist rhetoric and acrimony. But it is not a naïve idea. Nor is it utopian. This is a land where innovative ideas have taken root, leading to big social reforms and political changes in the past. Indeed, Kerala's enlightened citizens can decisively drive such a transformation. Let us ask ourselves:

- Is it realistic to expect Kerala's political parties to work together for a transformative rebranding of the state's political and developmental narrative?
- Will Kerala's new generation of student and youth leaders strive for a new brand of politics, grounded on constitutional values, statesmanship, ethical governance, and a long-term developmental vision for the state and country?
- How can citizens force such a transformation?

The Last Word

Kerala's paradoxes make life here dynamic, vibrant, and exciting, offering a remarkable blend of tradition and modernity. The people here are deeply involved in the democratic process and in political participation. Debate, discourse, art, literature, community life, religious events, and cultural festivals create a lively and participatory society, making life in Kerala both stimulating and deeply fulfilling. This intense civic engagement is also fuelled by a diverse and dynamic newspaper industry, which has played a historic role in shaping the social and political discourse. The robust tradition of journalism, both print and electronic, has immensely contributed to a highly informed and democratically active population, enabling deeper civic awareness and participation.

As for Cochin Port, its resurgence is more than just an idea, it is a tangible reality. This revival has been an ongoing process, powered by centuries of adaptation, innovation and re-invention. Since ancient times, the port—and the city that grew around it—has witnessed several transformations, adapting to the ever shifting sociopolitical and economic milieu, and continually evolving into the modern port city that it is today. The mingling of people from diverse corners of the world has undeniably enriched its cosmopolitan character. Over centuries, this vibrant port city became a melting pot where traders, explorers, and settlers from various cultures converged and mingled with the natives. This cross-cultural interaction gave rise to a unique fusion of customs, cuisines, architecture, artistic expressions, and way of life. Cochin's cosmopolitan character not only nurtured tolerance and diversity but also ignited the creative synergy that produced a rich and eclectic heritage. Cochin's infrastructure development and modernity blend organically with its multiculturalism, tolerance, and spirit of coexistence. It is a true story of resurgence.

The interwoven nature of Cochin Port's future and the development of its hinterland is obvious. Kerala has long been admired for its values of openness, tolerance, equality, and inclusivity, which shaped its unique development model. However, for Kerala to achieve broad-based prosperity for its entire people, it must go beyond tradition. This will require the collective will and concerted efforts of policymakers, political leaders, civil society, and, above all, the youth of the state.

While democratic debate and dissent are crucial, Kerala also requires a shared understanding across party lines on important development priorities. Establishing a baseline of consensus is essential for driving innovation, attracting investment, and pushing forward with clarity and purpose. With these conditions in place, Kerala can position itself to emerge as one of India's most prosperous states, aspiring to even higher standards of human development and quality of life for its citizens.

The central message of this book is that it is both possible and necessary to keep polemics and political obscurantism out of economic activity and development. Equally important is to insulate the state's educational institutions from toxic, divisive, and acrimonious political influences, focusing instead on high-quality academics and impactful research. Similarly, while fundamental labour rights—such as the right to fair wages and just equitable working conditions—are sacrosanct and inviolable, it is equally imperative to prevent individuals from exploiting these rights for personal agendas and political brinkmanship. Such exploitation ultimately undermines labour rights while also jeopardising the very survival of enterprises.

Kerala's story is one of immense promise, waiting to be realised. There are two paths forward: one is the easier, more popular route of doing nothing or continuing with a "business as usual" mentality. The other is a more difficult, bold, and transformative journey. This path requires political parties, policymakers, the youth as well as the people of the state to rise together, dare to dream big and launch a massive but decentralised movement for positive change. To embark on such a visionary path, the first democratic duty of the people is to elect and empower an increasing number of idealistic, forward-thinking political leaders to lead this path—a dynamic bank of young changemakers, ready to guide the state and the nation into the future.

Such a collective movement can indeed achieve a transformation that inspires not just its citizens but also those of other Indian states and the world. The time is now. The opportunity is here. The future belongs to those who dare to shape it.

INDEX